Series Editor: George S. Everly, Jr.

Innovations in Disaster and Trauma Psychology,

Volume One:

APPLICATIONS IN EMERGENCY SERVICES AND DISASTER RESPONSE

Innovations in Disaster and Trauma Psychology,

Volume One:

APPLICATIONS IN EMERGENCY SERVICES AND DISASTER RESPONSE

Edited by:
George S. Everly, Jr., Ph.D., F.A.P.M.
International Critical Incident Stress Foundation, Inc.;
Union Memorial Hospital, Baltimore;
and
Loyola College in Maryland

Chevron Publishing Corporation
5018 Dorsey Hall Drive
Suite 104
Ellicott City, Maryland 21042

Editorial / Production Supervision and Interior Design:
Douglas L. Lamb

Cover photograph donated by Jeffrey T. Mitchell

Ellicott City, Maryland 21042
(410) 740 - 0065

Printed in the United States of America

ISBM 1-883581-04-6

DEDICATIONS

To Elmer and Alma Schabdach, for their support and kindness; and,

To the men and women of all the emergency and disaster response professions for whom uncommon courage is common, and for whom heroism is routine.

G.S.E.

CONTRIBUTORS

Atle Dyregrov, Ph.D., Senter for Krisepsykologi
Bergen, Norway

George S. Everly, Jr., Ph.D., Union Memorial Hospital
Baltimore, Maryland

John Havenhill, Fire Department, City of Emeryville
Emeryville, California

Jeffrey T. Mitchell, Ph.D., Department of Emergency Health Services, Universiy of Maryland Baltimore County
Catonsville, Maryland

Diane Myers, RN, MSN, Disaster Consultant
Monterey, California

Colonel Richard L. Jaehne, United States Marine Corps
Washington, D.C.

Robyn Robinson, Ph.D., F.A.Ps.S., Trauma Support Consultants
North Carlton, Australia

Francine Shapiro, Ph.D., Mental Research Institute
Palo Alto, California

Guy Schiller, MA, CAC, Family Counseling Services
Cheshire, Connecticut

Roger Solomon, Ph.D., On Site Academy
Gardner, Massachusetts

Robert van Goethem, Disaster Services, Alberta Public Safety Services, Edmonton, Alberta, Canada

PREFACE

This volume is designed to be a presentation of innovations in the field of disaster and trauma psychology as they may be applied to emergency service personnel, disaster and humanitarian aid workers, as well as, public safety personnel of all varieties. Although it may be difficult to imagine, the recognition that these various occupational groups are at high risk for disabling traumatic stress syndromes, as well as, occupational "burnout" is a relatively new phenomenon. Prior to the 1980's, organized concern for the psychological well-being of emergency personnel was virtually unknown. Fortunately, we've come a long way since then in terms of recognizing the increased risk of emergency - related work, as well as, the value of traumatic stress prevention / mitigation programs for emergency personnel. In an account of ongoing research with firefighters, Canadian researcher Wayne Corneil found the prevalence rate of diagnosable post-traumatic stress disorder (PTSD) was 16.5% compared to a 3% prevalence rate for the general population (DeAngelis, 1995). It is further reported that firefighters from the study faced, on average, 4 traumas per year. This is important to note in that the research reportedly found that firefighters' risk of developing PTSD was 150 times greater if he/she was exposed to a traumatic event as opposed to not having been exposed to such an event. Further, the risk of PTSD was 129 times greater if adverse organizational factors, such as heavy workloads were present. On the other hand, fire personnel who had family, peer, or supervisory support were 40% less likely to develop such psychological problems according to the report (DeAngelis, 1995).

Indeed, emergency services stress as a subset of the field of disaster and trauma psychology has finally come of age. It is the purpose of this volume to assist in its continued maturation through a presentation of innovations in phenomenology, program development, and specific intervention protocols.

This volume is offered as a tribute to some of the few remaining "heros" of our time ... the men and women of the emergency professions.

George S. Everly, Jr., Ph.D., F.A.P.M.
February, 14, 1995

REFERENCES

De Angelis, T. (1995). Firefighters PTSD at dangerous levels. A*PA Monitor*, 26, 36 - 37.

CONTENTS

PART II

CHAPTER 10

Roger Solomon

CHAPTER 11

Diane Myers

"The only true gift is a portion of thy self."

- Ralph Waldo Emerson

PART I

TRAUMATIC STRESS: ITS NATURE AND IMPACT

PART I

TRAUMATIC STRESS: ITS NATURE AND IMPACT

This volume is dedicated to a presentation of innovations in the field of disaster and trauma psychology as they are applicable to emergency services personnel, disaster and humanitarian aid workers, as well as public safety personnel. No such presentation would be complete without first providing a phenomenological foundation upon which to base the more operational, or applied, sections of this volume. This, then, is the goal of Part I.

Within Part I, we shall find six chapters which attempt to provide the reader with a basic understanding of traumatic stress and its impact upon the emergency services and disaster personnel who are too often "forgotten victims."

In Chapter One, we begin by introducing the concept of post-traumatic stress; but more importantly later in the chapter, we examine and speculate upon the psychological hazards of emergency and disaster response functions themselves. Finally, brief mention is made of the notion of providing psychological support services to the emergency-related professions.

Chapter Two begins by broadening the reader's perspective by examining the boundaries of the new field of psychotraumatology. Once that perspective has been added, the chapter takes a closer phenomenological view of post-traumatic stress. A two-factor constituency is revealed and analyzed. By conducting such detailed components' analysis of post-traumatic stress, it is hoped that all types of psychological support services may be better directed.

Chapter Three brings the reader closer to one of the most difficult problems an adult will ever face ... death or injury to a child. Yet emergency workers face this tragedy on a recurrent basis. What are the effects of such repeated exposure to child-related crises, and why?

Rounding out the effects of crisis and trauma upon emergency personnel, Chapter Four takes a look at the family. Can the family of an emergency worker be the victim of traumatic stress? In this chapter, provocative speculative is offered into the biological and psychological roots of trauma-related familial discord.

Chapters One through Four offer descriptions and discussions that are postured more from an academic foundation. No textbook on trauma psychology would be complete without a personal viewpoint, however.

Chapter five represents what may be one of the most penetrating yet concise personal accounts of traumatic stress available in any volume such as this. Although it relates accounts that are military in nature, the descriptions are relevant to any emergency, disaster, humanitarian aid, or public safety professional.

Finally, Chapter Six, is the shortest chapter in this volume, yet its power is significant. The author allows the reader to see the world of high risk occupations from the author's eyes in the form of a brief poem and may provide some insight into the motivation behind the pursuit of emergency and disaster related careers.

Chapter 1

TRAUMATIC STRESS AS A CONSEQUENCE OF EMERGENCY AND DISASTER RESPONSE

GEORGE S. EVERLY, JR.

"The most acceptable service to God is doing good to man."
- Benjamin Franklin

Exposures to markedly distressing events "outside the range of usual human experience" (APA, 1987), or exposures to traumatic events which engender "intense fear, helplessness, or horror" (APA, 1994) are now generally accepted as being capable of causing reactions of such proportions as to be considered pathognomonic. And, indeed, the psychiatric diagnosis of post-traumatic stress disorder (PTSD) has commonly been applied to those primary victims most directly affected by crisis, disasters, disabling events, or life threatening situations (see Everly and Lating, 1995). But what of the secondary victims of crisis and disaster? Secondary victims may be thought of as "those individuals who are in some way observers of the immediate traumatic effects that have been wrought upon the primary victims" (Mitchell and Everly, 1993, p.2). Examples of potential secondary victims would be emergency response personnel, disaster workers, and other public safety personnel. The secondary victims may be thought of as the "vicarious victims of trauma" and they shall be the focus of this volume.

George S. Everly, Jr. • International Critical Incident Stress Foundation, Ellicott City, Maryland.
In G.S. Everly, Jr. Innovations in Disaster and Trauma Psychology, Volume One: Applications in Emergency Services and Disaster Response. Baltimore: Chevron Publishing Corp, 1995.

PSYCHOTRAUMATOLOGY: THE BROADER PERSPECTIVE

As "traumatology" refers to the study of wounds and serious injuries, the term "psychotraumatology" refers to the study of psychological trauma. More specifically, the term "psychotraumatology" may be defined as "the study of the processes and factors that lie a) antecedent to, b) concomitant with, and c) subsequent to psychological traumatization" (Everly, 1995, p. 4).

The study of psychological trauma is relatively new. Spawned largely by the recognition that soldiers were being psychologically disabled by the experiences of war, the phenomenon of psychological trauma among other populations remains far less understood. The recognition that emergency response, public safety, and disaster personnel are also potentially vulnerable to the disabling effects of post-traumatic stress represents perhaps the newest emergence within this nascent field and is often referred to as the subspecialty of "critical incident stress" (a critical incident may be thought of as a synonym for traumatic event).

The goal of this volume it to help assure that the emergency service, public safety, disaster response personnel and other potential vicarious victims no longer remain the "lost generation" of psychotraumatology.

Let us now take a closer look at the nature of symptoms that may arise as a consequence of psychological trauma.

POST-TRAUMATIC STRESS DISORDER (PTSD)

Since the year 1980, the official nosological compendium of psychiatric disorders has recognized that exposure to extraordinarily adverse (traumatic) situations could psychologically traumatize an otherwise normal, healthy human being (APA, 1980, 1987, 1994).

The American Psychiatric Association recognizes two primary psychiatric disorders that may arise in response to exposure to a traumatic stressor: 1) post-traumatic stress disorder (PTSD), and 2) acute stress disorder.

The key features of PTSD are as follows:

A. Exposure to a traumatic event wherein the person experiences a situation involving actual or threatened death or serious injury as well as the spawning of intense fear, horror or helplessness.

B. Recurrent reexperiencing of the traumatic event in ways such as flashbacks, dreams, and persistent intrusive recollections of the event.

C. Avoidance of factors associated with the trauma and a numbing of general responsiveness.

D. Persistent symptoms of arousal, stress, or anxiety.

E. A duration of symptom clusters B, C, D for more than one month.

F. The symptoms must cause significant distress or impairment

(APA, 1994).

Acute stress disorder, on the other hand, may be viewed as a less chronic variant of PTSD. Acute stress disorder may last from 2 to 30 days, but it possesses the same key phenomenological features as does PTSD (APA, 1994).

PSYCHOLOGICAL HAZARDS OF EMERGENCY AND DISASTER RESPONSE

Having reviewed the aforementioned symptom patterns, it is important to note that much of the emergent interest in emergency service and disaster response personnel as potential "secondary victims" of post trauma syndromes may be traced back to the efforts of two pioneers in the field of psychotraumatology: Jeffrey T. Mitchell (1982, 1983, 1985), in the United States, and Beverly Raphael

(1975, 1977, 1986) in Australia. Their work has done much to focus necessary attention upon the psychological hazards associated with emergency services and disaster response functions.

Let us take a closer look at these hazards.

According to Dunning (1985), "Emergency response agencies have found both immediate and delayed organizational dysfunctional as a result of the physiological and psychological reactions among those assigned to scenes of disaster. While researchers and psychologists who specialize in job stress generally agree that those attracted to emergency work as a group are more emotionally stable than the general population, and are less likely than the ordinary citizen to crack under intense pressure, emergency workers are subject to an increased incidence of diseases of adaptation (Dunning and Silva, 1980). " (p. 126).

Investigators such as Killian, Lifton, Raphael, Mitchell and Jones were among the first who empirically chronicled the development of adverse psychological reactions among emergency service, rescue, public safety, and disaster response personnel as a consequence of their job functions. For example:

In an early anecdotal treatise, Killian (1952) reported that emergency response personnel, who responded to a 1947 Texas oil depot explosion, were observed to develop symptoms of psychological discord similar to those symptoms reported by the primary victims of the disaster.

In his elegant treatise on the atomic cataclysm entitled Death in Life, Survivors of Hiroshima, Robert Lifton documented "psychic numbing" and the emergence of a "death imprint" among rescue workers who responded to the atomic disaster at Hiroshima. Lifton also reported on the development of "survivor guilt" among rescue personnel in response to seeing such unparalleled mass destruction and loss of human life.

Raphael and her co-workers (Raphael, Singh, Bradbury, and Lambert, 1983-1984) investigated a major Australian train disaster.

Their work yielded evidence that 70% of the rescue workers showed symptoms similar to PTSD.

In September of 1978 a Boeing 727 jet aircraft collided with a small propeller plane over the city of San Diego. According to Mitchell (Mitchell and Everly, 1993) the consequences were devastating: all 110 passengers were killed, 16 homes were destroyed by falling debris, 15 civilians were killed on the ground. Over 10,000 body parts were recovered. Over 300 emergency response personnel were dispatched and engaged in this disaster. As an apparent consequence of this ordeal, mental health utilization by emergency response personnel increased by 31% in the wake of this catastrophe (Mitchell and Everly, 1993).

Subsequent to the 1982 crash of Air Florida 90 in Washington, D.C., Mitchell (1982) reported that rescue and public safety personnel were plagued with symptoms of fear, anxiety, guilt, depression, self-doubt, nightmares, flashbacks, and pervasive resentment of media and supervisory personnel.

In a general survey, Mitchell (1985) found that of 360 emergency services workers, 86.9% (313) "stated that they had been emotionally and physically affected by their work at one or more emergency events" (p. 113).

In another important paper, Jones (1985) described the plight of the "secondary victim" in response to the handling and recovery of human remains. Jones detailed the development of symptoms among U.S. Air Force personnel in response to body recovery activities after the infamous "Jonestown massacre". Jones noted that 32% of the recovery personnel developed symptoms of dysphoria in response to handling human remains that had been exposed to the harsh elements of the subtropical jungle.

Other empirical investigations have consistently documented the apparent fact that public safety and emergency services functions as well as rescue work of virtually any kind represents a high risk endeavor. The potential consequences of such work include the development of emotional discord, most typically post-traumatic stress syndromes, which include but are not limited to PTSD. For example:

Corneil (1993) investigated the degree to which traumatic events may be an occupational risk factor for metropolitan firefighters. In his investigation of the prevalence of PTSD among firefighters, he discovered a 16% prevalence rate using conservative psychometric criteria. Interestingly, the prevalence discovered by Corneil is similar to the prevalence of PTSD discovered among American veterans of the Vietnam conflict (Schlenger, et al., 1992).

Thompson and Suzuki (1991) assessed the prevalence of stress among a sample of London ambulance workers. Using the Impact of Events Scale and the 28 item General Health Questionnaire, these researchers found a 17% prevalence of "severe stress". Respondents listed as their most distressing situations accidents involving children, followed by multi-casualty incidents and disasters. Their primary symptoms of post incident stress were intrusive recollections of the event and avoidance symptoms.

An empirical investigation conducted by Ravenscroft (1994) yielded results similar to those of Thompson and Suzuki (1991). Ravenscoft investigated critical incident stress among London ambulance workers sampling 1420 out of 1450 ambulance personnel. Data showed 97% of respondents indicated stress was a significant occupational hazard. Using the Impact of Events Scale, the "current" prevalence of PTSD among London ambulance workers was found to be 15%.

Finally, Robyn Robinson (1994) has focused her research on ambulance workers, as well, but her research has been conducted half a world away from that of Ravenscroft. Robinson investigated symptoms of stress among ambulance workers in Melbourne Australia. Of 1380 ambulance workers, she contacted 823. Her data revealed that roughly 17% of the respondents were "currently" experiencing pervasive and "strong" symptoms of stress originating as a result of prior emergency response situations. The primary symptoms of stress identified were consistent with those of PTSD and consisted of flashbacks, sleep disturbances and concentration problems.

ASSESSING THE PSYCHOLOGICAL RISKS OF EMERGENCY AND DISASTER RESPONSE

In sum, it appears as if the role of helping others, especially as that role is embodied in the emergency service and disaster response functions, is accompanied by an inherent psychological risk. Those who choose to help others in the midst of, or in the wake of, crisis expose themselves to an increased risk of suffering some form of dysphoric reaction such as posttraumatic stress disorder.

Conceptually, we can express the risk of developing a post-traumatic stress syndrome (PTSS) as follows (See Table 1.1):

Risk of PTSS = (# of traumatic events) x (severity/magnitude of traumatic events) x (personal relevance of traumatic events) x (pre-existing factors) - (level of pre-trauma preparation) - (support resources available) - (rapidity of crisis intervention).

TABLE 1.1

MAJOR FACTORS AUGMENTING AND MITIGATING THE RISK OF POST-TRAUMATIC STRESS SYNDROMES

Augmenting Factors	*Mitigating Factors*
1. Number of traumatic events	1. Level of pre-trauma preparation
2. Severity or magnitude of the traumatic events	2. Support resources available
3. Personal relevance of the traumatic events	3. Speed of implementation of support services
4. Pre-existing risk factors	

Statistically, the risk of PTSS among emergency services and disaster response personnel is even harder to estimate. Overall the prevalence of PTSD has been estimated to be about 1% to 3% in the general population (Helzer, et al, 1987). Based upon our previous reviews, it may be estimated that the risk of developing some variant of PTSS among the population of emergency personnel is roughly 15 to 18 times, greater yielding an expected prevalence of 15 to 18%, or more.

PSYCHOLOGICAL SUPPORT SERVICES FOR EMERGENCY AND DISASTER RESPONSE PERSONNEL

Given the risk of psychological injury associated with the emergency response professions, what is being done to respond to such an occupational hazard?

As we noted earlier in this chapter, the work of Mitchell (1982, 1983) and Raphael (1986) serves as two of the foundations for the newly developed interest in the phenomenology and treatment of what has been called "critical incident stress" (Mitchell 1983; Mitchell and Everly, 1993), i.e., the study of traumatic stress among emergency services, disaster response and public safety support personnel.

The interest in the subspecialty within the field of psychotraumatology has been largely sustained not by conceptual publications in scholarly journals, but rather by the pragmatic operationalization of relevant theories, concepts and tactical interventions.

The most noteworthy tactical development in the entire field of "critical incident stress" is the Critical Incident Stress Debriefing (CISD) developed by Jeffrey Mitchell (1983; Mitchell and Everly, 1995) as a means of mitigating post-traumatic stress among emergency services and disaster response personnel.

The specific CISD model developed by Mitchell (described later in this volume) has been implemented throughout the world. The

CISD protocol has given rise to the development of numerous other "debriefing" models which are largely variants of the original "Mitchell model" (Armstrong, O'Callahan, Marmae, 1991; American Red Cross, 1991). So successful has the CISD become that the term "CISD" is now inappropriately used as a generic term referring to virtually any form of post-disaster psychological support technology. This fact has greatly inhibited useful empirical research into the efficacy of CISD and related interventions. Some researchers have naively assumed that all CISD technologies are the same. This is similar to assuming all psychotherapies are the same. Thus, the status of empirical research in the assessment of the CISD and related interventions is void of external validity, a problem that will be rectified as tactical standardization improves (Mitchell and Everly, 1995).

The collective aggregation of post trauma psychological support technologies for emergency personnel is now most appropriately referred to as "critical incident stress management" (CISM). CISM may be thought of as including CISD, defusing (shortened versions of the CISD) one-on-one crisis intervention programs, family support programs, and many other such psychological/behavioral technologies designed to mitigate or prevent posttraumatic stress among emergency services and disaster response personnel (Mitchell and Everly, 1995). Thus, the field has grown far beyond its origins with the CISD and preincident awareness programs.

Therefore, in this volume, we shall review the phenomenology of post-traumatic (critical incident) stress, the development of programs designed to prevent and mitigate post-traumatic stress, and finally innovations in the treatment of post-traumatic stress. What makes this volume unique, however, is that all of this is achieved with the focus upon emergency service, disaster response, and public safety personnel.

SUMMARY

1. While post-traumatic stress has been acknowledged for years among the military, it has only recently been acknowledged as a

potential hazard for emergency services, disaster response, and virtually all public safety personnel.

2. The term "psychotraumatology" refers to the study of psychological trauma.

3. The term "critical incident stress" commonly refers to post-traumatic stress as it applies to emergency services personnel, disaster workers, public safety, and humanitarian aid personnel.

4. Post-traumatic stress disorder (PTSD) and acute stress disorder are the officially recognized psychiatric syndromes commonly associated with the exposure to an adverse stressor event outside the usual range of human experience.

5. The work of Jeffrey Mitchell and Beverly Raphael formed the foundations for the recognition of the psychological hazards associated with emergency services and disaster response functions.

6. Conceptually, the risk of psychological discord is equal to the number of traumatic events times the severity or magnitude of the traumatic events, times the personal relevance of the traumatic event, times any pre-existing factors. This risk is mitigated by the level of pre-trauma preparation, the level of support services available and the speed of intervention.

7. Statistically, risk of post-traumatic psychological discord among emergency service personnel is roughly 15-18%.

8. Critical incident stress management (CISM) is the term that is most commonly applied to organized efforts to prevent and mitigate posttraumatic stress among emergency and disaster personnel.

REFERENCES

American Psychiatric Association (1980) *Diagnostic and Statistical Manual of Mental Disorders, Third Edition*. Wash. D.C.: APA Press.

American Psychiatric Association (1987). *Diagnostic and Statistical Manual of Mental Disorders, Third Edition, Revised.* Washington, D.C.: APA Press.

American Psychiatric Association (1994). *Diagnostic and Statistical Manual of Mental Disorders, Fourth Edition.* Washington, D.C.: APA Press.

American Red Cross (1991). *Disaster Services Regulations and Procedures: Disaster Mental Health Services* (3050M). Wash. D.C.: Author.

Armstrong, K., O'Callahan, W., and Marmar, C. (1991). Debriefing Red Cross Disaster Personnel: The Multiple Stressor Debriefing Model. *Journal of Traumatic Stress*, 4, 581-594.

Corneil, D.W. (1993). *Prevalence of post-traumatic stress disorders in a metropolitan fire department*. Dissertation submitted to the School of Hygiene and Public Health, The Johns Hopkins University, Baltimore, Maryland.

Dunning, C. (1985). Prevention of stress. In NIMH, *Role Stressors and Supports for Emergency Workers*, (pp. 126-139). DHHS Publication No. ADM 85-1408. Rockville, MD: NIMH.

Dunning, C. and Silva, M. (1980). Disaster induced trauma in rescue workers. *Victimology*, 5, 287-297.

Everly, G.S. (1995). Psychotraumatology. In G. Everly and J. Lating (Eds). *Psychotraumatology: Key Papers and Core Concepts in Post-traumatic Stress* (pp. 3-8). NY: Plenum.

Everly, G.S. and Lating, J.M. (1995). *Psychotraumatology: Key Papers and Core Concepts in Post-traumatic Stress.* NY: Plenum.

Helzer, J., Robins, L. and McEvoy, L. (1987). Post-traumatic stress disorder in the general population. *New England Journal of Medicine*, 317, 1630-1634.

Jones, D. (1985). Secondary disaster victims. *American Journal of Psychiatry*, 142, 303-307.

Killian, L. (1952). The significance of multiple group membership in disaster. *American Journal of Sociology*, 57, 309-314.

Lifton, R.J. (1967). *Death in Life:Survivors of Hiroshima.* NY: Simon and Schuster.

Mitchell, J.T. (1982). The psychological impact of the Air Florida 90 disaster on fire-rescue, paramedic and police personnel. In R. Crowley, et at. (Eds). *Mass casualties: A Learned Lesson Approach.* Wash. D.C.: U.S. Dept. of Transportation.

Mitchell, J.T. (1983). When disaster strikes ...... The critical incident stress debriefing process. *Journal of Emergency Medical Services*, 8, 36-39.

Mitchell, J.T. (1985). Helping the helper. In NIMH, *Role Stressors and Supports for Emergency Workers* (pp105-118). DHHS Pub. No. ADM 85-1408. Rockville, MD: NIMH.

Mitchell, J.T. and Everly, G.S. (1993). *Critical Incident Stress Debriefing: An Operations Manual*. Ellicott City, MD: Chevron.

Mitchell, J.T. and Everly, G.S. (1995). *Critical Incident Stress Debriefing: An Operations Manual, 2nd Ed*. Ellicott City, MD: Chevron.

Ravenscroft, T. (1994) *Going Critical : GMB Report on the Growing Crisis in the London Ambulance Service for the Select committee on Health*. London: GMB-APEX and TNG Unions.

Raphael, B. (1975). Crisis and loss: Counseling Following a Disaster. *Mental Health in Australia*, 1, 118-122.

Raphael, B. (1977). The Granville train disaster. *Medical Journal of Australia*, 1, 303-305.

Raphael, B. (1986). *When Disaster Strikes*. NY: Basic Books.

Raphael, B., Singh, B. and Bradbury, L. and Lambert, F. (1983-1984). Who helps the helper? The effects of a disaster on the rescue workers. *Omega*, 14, 9-20.

Robinson, R., (1994). *Follow-up study of Health and Stress in Ambulance Services*, Victoria, Australia, Part 1. Melbourne: Victoria Ambulance Crisis Counseling Unit.

Schlenger, W.E., Kulka, R., Fairbank, J. Hough, R., Jordan, B., Marmar, C. and Weiss, D. (1992). The prevalence of post-traumatic stress disorder in the Vietnam generation. *Journal of Traumatic Stress*, 5, 333-364.

Thompson, J. and Suzuki, I. (1991). Stress in ambulance workers. *Disaster Management*, 3, 193-197.

Chapter 2

PSYCHOTRAUMATOLOGY: AN INTRODUCTION

GEORGE S. EVERLY, JR.

"First study the science, then practice the art."-Leonardo DaVinci

In Chapter One, it was stated that exposure to an unusually adverse event, outside of the usual range of human experience, had the potential to psychologically traumatize those who might experience such event. It was further noted, that psychological traumatization could occur to those who directly or vicariously experienced the traumatic event. This concept of vicarious traumatization, or "secondary victimization" was introduced with the intention of having the reader entertain the notion that those individuals who vicariously experience traumatic enents by virtue of repeated close proximities to trauma are at extraordinarly high risk for becoming a vicarious, secondary victim of psychological trauma. Emergency services personnel, public safety personnel and disaster workers, including humanitarian aid workers should be considered prototypic examples of individuals, in non-combat related roles, who are continually at extraordinary risk of becoming secondary victims of psychological trauma. Most notably these individuals are at risk for developing sympotoms of post-traumatic stress disorder (PTSD) or

George S. Everly, Jr. • International Critical Incident Stress Foundation, Ellicott City, Maryland.
In G.S. Everly, Jr. Innovations in Disaster and Trauma Psychology, Volume One: Applications in Emergency Services and Disaster Response. Baltimore: Chevron Publishing Corp, 1995.

some related syndrome. Finally in Chapter One, it was posited that the risk of emergency personnel developing symptoms of PTSD may be as high as 15 to 18 times that of the general population.

As the study of psychological trauma, as a formal discipline, is a relatively new endeavor, there are relatively few homogenizing themes within the field. The purpose of this chapter is to introduce the reader to certain core constructs that may be of value in the quest to illuminate and better understand this rapidly expanding and critically important field.

PSYCHOTRAUMATOLOGY

The successful growth of virtually any new endeavor is often predicated upon identification and recognition. Although it may sound pedestrian, identification and recognition are usually predicted upon a recognizable imprimatur, ie, a name or term which serves as an umbrella for purposes of recognition and for the definition of boundaries so as to avoid semantic confusion.

As noted in Chapter One, it has been proposed that the study of psychological trauma be referred to as "psychotraumatology" (Everly,1993). More specifically , psychotraumatoogy is the study of processes and factors that lie antecedent to, concomitant with, and subsequent to psychological trauma" (Everly, 1993, p270). The term "psychotraumatology" was suggested over the simpler term "traumatology" due to 1) the fact that "traumatology" already denotes a subspecialty within medicine, ie, the study of wounds; and, 2) "psychotraumatology " literally means the study of psychological trauma(see Everly and Lating, 1995 for a discussion).

TWO-FACTOR FORMULATION OF POST-TRAUMATIC STRESS

The practice of any skill or artform should be predicated upon an understanding of phenomenology. As Leonardo da Vinci noted

"First study the science, then practice the art." In clinical science, then, it maybe argued that treatment is the natural corollary of phenomenology (Everly and Lating, 1995). Let us briefly examine the putative foundations of post-traumatic stress, and of course, post-traumatic stress disorder (PTSD). In doing so, we shall review evidence that suggests that there exists a two-factor costituency for PTSD.

FACTOR ONE: NEUROLOGIC HYPERSENSITIVITY

It has been proposed that posttraumatic stress may be best conceptualized as a "disorder of arousal" (Everly, 1990), The "disorders of arousal" model of pathogenesis was first proposed by Everly and Benson (1989) in an effort to better understand and categorize anxiety and stress-related disorders. They argue that all anxiety and stress-related disorders exist as variations on a theme of pathognomonic neurologic hypersensitivity and sustained arousal within the subcortical structures of the limbic system. The amygdaloid and hippocampal centers, as well as the noradrenergic projections of the locus ceruleus seem likely candidates to sustain these pathognomonic arousal qualities and seem especially relevant as key structures in the phenomenology of post-traumatic stress.

Several lines of evidence support the notion that the phenomenology of post-traumatic stress is based upon pathognomonic neurologic hypersensitivity.

Ernst Gellhorn writing 3 decades ago suggested that the human nervous system was vulnerable to changes in both its tonic status as well as its characteristic patterns of paroxysmal activation(Gellhorn, 1965; Gellhorn and Loofbourrow, 1963). Gellhorn (1965) noted:

> ...in the waking state the ergotropic division of the autonomic nervous system is dominant and responds primarily to environmental stimuli: If these stimuli are very strong or follow eachother at short intervals, the tone and reactivity of the sympathetic system increases"(pp 495-495).

The increased tone and reactivity of the sympathetic nervous system, Gellhorn called "ergotropic tuning." Gellhorn and Loofbourrow (1963) concluded that the limbic system-based "ergotropic tuning" process was the biological basis for many anxiety and stress-related disorders.

Similiar to Gellhorn, Robert Post (Post, 1985; Post and Ballenger, 1981) has argued that excessive stimulation of the limbic system could result in a condition whereby the neural substrates themselves develop a functional hypersensitivity. Post calls this phenonenon "behavioral sensitization"

Historically, Kardiner (1941) observed in victims of post-traumatic stress exaggerated startle reactions and propensities for explosive and aggressive behavior. These observations lead him to conceptualize post-traumatic stress as a "physioneurosis."

Thus, it seems clear from various convergent lines of evidence that post-traumatic stress represents a pathophenomenon which rests largely upon a condition of neurologic hypersensitivity.

As for the basic foundational constituency of the proposed neurologic hypersensitivity, several mechanisms have been implicated by Everly(1993) based upon his review of related lines of research:

1) an augmentation of available excitatory neurotransmitters,
2) a functional decrease in available inhibitory neurotransmitters, and
3) changes in the neuron's micromorphology which serve to functionally enhance excitability.

Thus, in our quest to understand the nature of PTSD and related syndromes the first core homogenizing theme is posited to be that of a sustained pathognomonic neurologic hypersensitivity. Germane to that assertion is the perspective that PTSD and related syndromes may be best understood as "disorders of arousal" consistent with the formulations of Everly and Benson(1989).

FACTOR TWO: PSYCHOLOGIC HYPERSENSITIVITY

Master psychotraumatologist Pierre Janet writing in the early 1900's is said to have believed that psychological traumatization was somehow related to the trauma victim's psychological interpretation that he/she was helpless in the context of the traumatogenetic events (see van der Kolk, Brown, and van der Hart, 1989).

Psychological factors, especially interpretational, or appraisal, mechanisms go a long way in helping to explain the wide range of variability in response to traumatogenetic stressors.

Indeed, Epictetus noted, "Men are disturbed not by things but the views which they take of them." Even endocrinologist Hans Selye said, "It is not what happens to you that matters, but how you take it." It may well be that to some extent "stressors, like beauty, lie in the eye of the beholder."

With regard to psychological trauma, the clinician must be careful not to take this notion too literally, however, for this might lead us to "blame the victim" for his/her disorder. Clearly there exists devastating conditions that would serve to traumatize virtually anyone, eg, torture, rape various mass disaster conditions, violent life threatening conditions, etc., but appraisal mechanisms seem to serve to augment and sustain, or mitigate and diminish the severity and chronicity of post-traumatic stress syndromes.

In concert with this notion of the important role that appraisal plays in the development of PTSD and related post-traumatic syndromes, the major psychiatric nosologies appear sensitive to interpretational mechanisms in their formulations of what constitutes a traumatic event. For example, the American Psychiatric Association (1994) describes a traumatic event as an event that:

1) "involved actual or threatened death or serious injury, or a threat to the physical integrity of self or others" and,

2) "involved intense fear, helplessness, or horror. "

Clearly, the threat of death or injury is an interpretation of environmental conditions, further, the states of fear, helplessness, or horror are the results of appraisals made by the person experiencing the event.

If we search deeper, however, to discover what aspect of the interpretational process appears to be most pathogenic, we discover the concept of Weltanshauung, or "worldview."

Simply stated, it may be argued that psychological trauma represents a contradiction, or violation, to some key psychological assumption, belief, expectation, or phenomenological construction about the world (Janoff-Bulman, 1992; Everly, 1994). This assumption may be thought of as a worldview, or as it may be conceived of from a rhetorical perspective, Weltanschauung. More specifically, the trauma may be conceived of as representing a violation or contadiction to the worldview as it pertains to one's belief about oneself, and/or one's belief about the relative safety of the immediate environment, or the world in general(Everly,1994).

Viktor Frankl (1959) has argued that the failure to find self-responsibility as well as meaning, or understanding (which yields a sense of safety), lies at the root of psychopathology.

Similarly, Maslow (1970) has written that the quest for safety represents the most fundamental of all human drives beyond the quest for basic physiological needs.

Thus, violations or contradictions to one's worldview regarding a sense of safety and a sense of self represent negative, disabling cognitions which possess powerful traumatogenetic properties (see Everly and Lating, 1995).

Therefore, we see that the second factor in our phenomenological construction of post traumatic stress is a psychologic hypersensitivity consisting of a violation or contradiction, or at least a disruption, to one's worldview(Weltanschauung) as it pertains to one's sense of safety and/or one's very sense of self.

It may be argued that in the emergency services professions, the maintenance of a protective worldview, albeit sometimes an illusion, serves to allow these professionals to enter high risk venues without Lesitation, to repeatedly face danger, and to unselfishly put themselves at risk in their eforts to save others. Several of the more common worldview themes held by those who pursue the emergency services are:

1. The world is fair.
2. If I try my best I will always succeed.
3. If I care for others, they will care for me.
4. Human life is precious.
5. My training and experience will insulate me from harm.
6. If I know what I'm doing, I won't get hurt.
7. My effort to help others are appreciated.
8. There is a reason for everything.
9. There is always a clear "right" and "wrong"
10. Only "weak people suffer from stress.

When a trauma occurs that, in the view of the individual, convincingly contradicts one of these deeply held beliefs, some posttraumatic stress syndrome seems a likely consequence.

SUMMARY: AN INTEGRATIVE MODEL OF POST-TRAUMATIC STRESS

The DSM-IV diagnostic criteria for PTSD have been reviewed earlier in Chapter One. In addition, Chapter Two presented a two-factor model of posttraumatic stress offered for further phenomenological clarification. It will be recalled that in addition to the traumatic event, the DSM-IV indicated there exists three symptom clusters: persistent recollection of the event, avoidance and numbing

FIGURE 2.1

AN INTEGRATIVE MODEL OF POST-TRAUMATIC STRESS

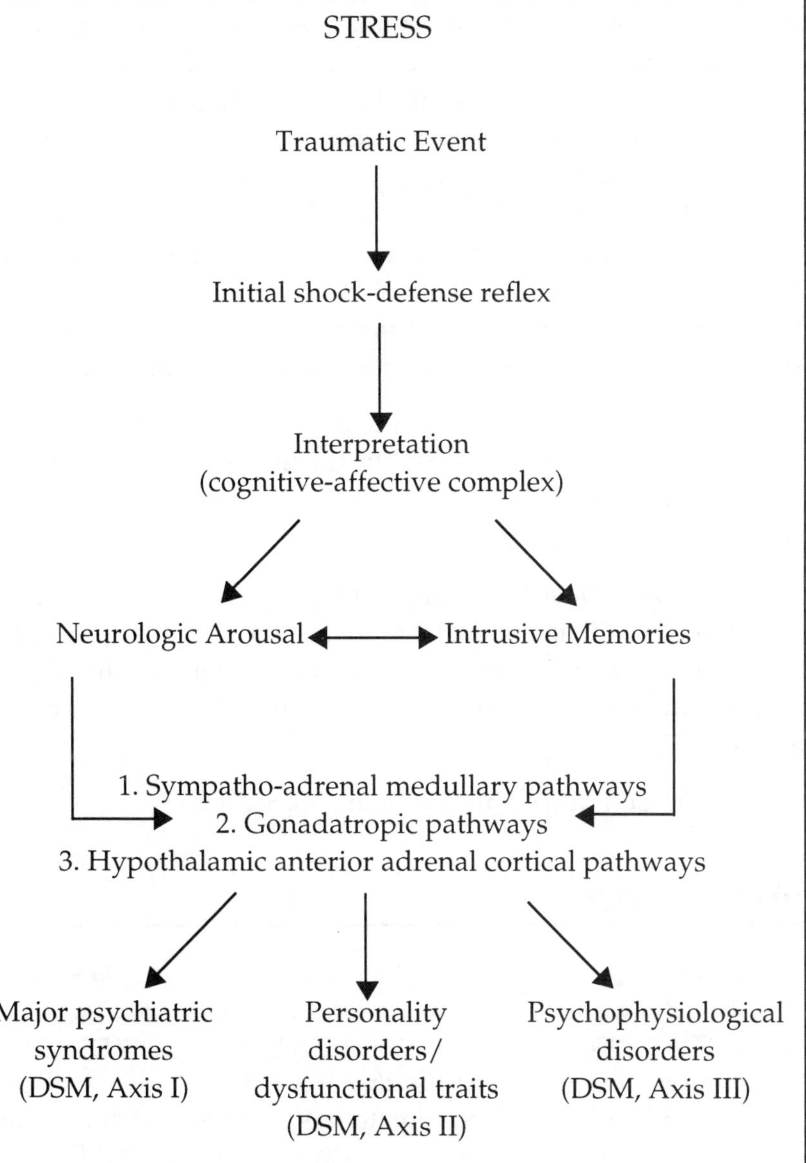

symptoms, and symptoms of increaed arousal. But these symptoms alone do not necessarily define all of the reactions that may arise as a result of a trauma.

Consistent with an extreme "fight or flight" response, trauma initiates an accentuation of sympathetic nervous system activity and adrenal medullary response (Kosten, etal.,1987). Further, there may be increased levels of adrenal cortical function especially in the glucocorticoid - cortisol pathway (Rahe, etal.,1990). Finally, there is evidence that the gonadotropin - testosterone pathway may be accentuated(Mason, etal.,1990) as a result of psychological trauma. All of these factors are consistent with Selye's (1956) notion of increased "somatic wear and tear." Thus, we would not be surprized to discover that victims of post-traumatic stress would also suffer from stress-related physical disorders affecting bodily function.

As a result of this "wear and tear" on the body, internists and family medical practitioners may be the first to see many victims of psychological trauma. This is likely to be true for emergency services personnel who are disinclined to utilize mental health services.

In sum, we believe that post-traumatic stress has the capability of affecting its victim in many ways, not just the presentation of PTSD. The World Health Organization has even recognized that psychological trauma may result in enduring changes to one's basic personality (WHO, 1992).

These notions are summarized in Figure 2.1.

REFERENCES

American Psychiatric Association. (1994). *Diagnostic and Statistical Manual of Mental Disorders, 4th Ed.* Wash. DC: APA Press.

Everly, G.S. (1990). Posttraumatic Stress Disorder as a Disorder of Arousal. *Psychology and Health*, r,135-145.

Everly, G.S.(1993). Psychotraumatology: A two-factor formulation of post-traumatic stress. *Integrative Physiological and Behavioral Science*,28, 270-278.

Everly, G.S.(1994). Short-term psyhotherapy of acute adult onset posttraumatic stress. The role of Weltanschauung. *Stress Medicine*, 10, 191-196.

Everly, G.S. and Benson,H.(1989). Disorders of arousal. *International Journal of Psychosomatics*, 36, 15-22.

Everly, G.S. and Lating, J.M.(Ed.)(1995). *Psychotraumatology: Key Papers and Core Concepts in Posttraumatic Stress*. NY:Pleaum.

Frank, V. (1959). *Man's Search for Meaning*. Boston: Beacon.

Gellhorn, E.(1965). Nurophysiological bases of anxiety. *Perspectives in Biology and Medicine*, 8, 488-515.

Gellhorn, E. and Loofbourrow, G.(1963) *Emotions and Emotional Disorders*. NY: Harper and Row.

Janoff-Bulman, R. (1992). *Shattered Assumptions*. NY: Free Press.

Kosten, T.R., Mason, J, Giller, E. etal. (1987). Sustained urinary norepinephrine and epinephrine elevation in post-traumatic stress disorder. *Psychoneuroendocrinology*, 12, 13-20.

Maslow,A.(1970). *Motivation and Personality, 2nd ed. NY*: Harper and Row.

Mason, J.,Giller, E., Kosten, T.&Wahby, Y. (1990). Serum testosterone levels in posttraumatic stress disorder patients. *Journal of Traumatic Stress*, 3, 444-457.

Post, R. (1985). Stress, sensitisation, kindling and conditioning. *Behavioral and Brain Sciences*,8,372-373.

Post, R. and Ballenger, J. (1981), Kindling models for progressive development of psychopathology. In H. van Pragg(Ed) *Handbook of Biological Psychiatry* (pp. 609-651). NY: Marcel Dekker.

Rahe, R. , etal. (1990). Psychological and physiological assessments on American hostages freed from captivity in Iran. *Psychosomatic Medicine*, 52, 1-16.

Selye, H. (1956). *The Stress of Life*. NY: McGraw-Hill.

van der Kolk, B., Brown, P. and van der Hart, O.(1989). Pierre Janet on posttraumatic stress. *Journal of Traumatic Stress*, 2, 365 - 378.

World Health Organization (1992). *ICD-10*. Geneva: author.

Chapter 3

EFFECTS OF TRAUMATIZED CHILDREN ON THE RESCUER

ATLE DYREGROV

Helpers generally, and rescuers more specifically, are concerned, compassionate, dedicated and committed. They have a great desire to be helpful to others (Raphael, 1981). By and large, many helpers seem to possess the same abilities that Samuel and Pearl Oliner (1988) have described in ordinary men and women who risked their own life on behalf of others, when they rescued jews in Nazi Europe. These helpers had a sense of internal control believing that they could succeed when others foresaw failure, they had stronger feelings of closeness to others, had a greater sense of responsibility toward them, and had a heightened empathy for pain. Such a personality predisposes the helper to altruistic behavior, and I believe that these traits are common among most rescuers, that is, emergency services, disaster response, and public safety personnel.

In the literature concerning critical incident stress and the effect on rescuers, it seems that the presence of children is regarded as especially stressful (Hershiser & Quarantelli, 1976; Jones, 1985; Rayner, 1958). In a study of ambulance employees, Robinson (1984), found

---

Atle Dyregrov • Senter for Krisepsykologi, Bergen, Norway.

In G.S. Everly, Jr. Innovations in Disaster and Trauma Psychology, Volume One: Applications in Emergency Services and Disaster Response. Baltimore: Chevron Publishing Corp, 1995.

Portions of this chapter have been previously published in the *Journal of Traumatic Stress*, vol. 5, 1992. Used with permission of Plenum Press.

"dealing with death of children" the situation that caused the greatest stress among the employees. Interestingly, disasters workers comment on how relieved they feel when there are no children involved in a disaster (Taylor & Frazer, 1981). Why do rescuers react so profoundly when children are involved?

THE PSYCHOLOGY OF WORKING WITH TRAUMATIZED CHILDREN

Rescue work with traumatized children often evokes several core psychological processes. Let us briefly examine them. First of all, working with traumatized children ***potentiates motivating forces in the helper's personality*** (Table 3.1). Since children are considered innocent and unable to protect themselves, these motivating forces seem to be more intense when rescuers are working with children. This creates an extreme level of personal involvement. Unfortunately, this may also cause helpers to put aside concern for their own welfare, and they may work beyond their point of exhaustion.

TABLE 3.1

BASIC PSYCHOLOGICAL PROCESSES ASSOCIATED WITH HELPING TRAUMATIZED CHILDREN

- Potentiates motivating factors in the helper's personality
- Activates the child within:
  * separation anxiety
  * basic fears of childhood
- Breaks down natural defenses
- Intensifies identification

Another important factor contributing to the helper's propensity to react to situations involving children is what I will term the activation of ***"the child within"***. When helping traumatized children, conscious and unconscious layers of memories and fantasies of our own childhood modulate our reactions. We who care for children in our work were once children ourselves, and our vulnerability in situations involving children is a resonance of our own separation anxiety and other fears of childhood. Our childhood fantasies of losing or being separated from our parents, of being alone or deserted, with the helplessness involved, are to my mind strongly influential in creating the sense of helplessness and frustration we experience when children are traumatized. These shadows from our past are not readily acknowledged in adult life, when we want to appear rational and controlled in all settings. We should also acknowledge that some traumatized children have become adult rescuers to reverse or counteract their childhood feelings of helplessness. Thus, layers of the helper's own memories may interfere with or influence the helping relationship, making it easy to identify with the traumatized child's anxieties and fears.

Sometimes a person's own attachment history will bring him or her into role conflicts, and the helper may adopt a role as a surrogate parent or sibling, rather than as a helper. The danger of this is most pronounced in long-term caring relationships. When rescuers face dead children this upturns the orderliness of life. Our outlook on life and the basic cognitive schemata on which we rely to understand the world are ruptured.

Thirdly, when children are involved, there is often a breakdown of ***natural defenses.*** While helpers ordinarily are able to distance themselves psychologically from emotionally challenging situations, they can become overly involved, almost instantly identifying with a traumatized child or it's parents. The emotional barriers or our usually conscious efforts to keep thoughts away from the emotional aspects of the situation fail, and we can become overwhelmed by our own emotional reactions. Exposure to childhood victims of trauma renders our usual coping mechanisms less useful.

For example, consider humor. Humor is a universal coping mechanism among helpers, used to gain emotional distance, secure a tension outlet, mobilize energy and reinforce team identity and cohesion. Several studies have found humor very helpful in disaster situations. Alexander & Wells (1990), in an unpublished study of morgue-workers following the Piper Alpha disaster, found humor the most common coping strategy used by those involved in identifying the bodies and the bodily remains. As many as 98% of the workers found humor helpful in mastering their situation. Hetherington & Guppy (1990) studied road patrol officers in England and also found the use of humor to be the most common coping mechanism when facing trauma. Here, 93% used humor to deal with traffic accidents. However, when we studied helpers following a 1988 Norwegean bus disaster where 12 children died and many were seriously wounded, we found only 2% who found humor useful to a high extent and 20% who found humor helpful to some~extent. Although humor was used as an example, it is also difficult to employ other coping mechanisms such as distancing, dehumanizing or other means of suppressing thoughts and reflections where children are involved.

This breakdown of natural defenses is most evident in the acute setting, such as the emergency department or critical care unit, where helpers often describe strong emotional reactions when children are the patients. In disaster areas, emergency personnel often report that they function adequately until they come upon a child's body or a child's toy (Hershiser & Quarantelli, 1976; Jones, 1985; Rayner, 1958). From the moment helpers encounter children or their toys, many function less effectively or, at times, not at all. Material objects take on great symbolic value, and sometimes they are more powerful in triggering emotional reactions than are human bodies or remains.

This breakdown of natural defenses interacts with another psychological dynamic which is frequently experienced by health care, law enforcement and rescue personnel. This is the **identification** with the victim or the victim's family. Identification with the victim is exceptionally strong when the helping relationship involves children. Helpers have different relations to children in their personal lives. They are parents, siblings, grandparents, uncles, aunts, and so forth. They easily imagine how the trauma could have happened to one of their own loved ones. Since most helpers occasionally worry that something disastrous could happen to the children they love, they can easily and vividly replace the traumatized or dead child with the images of their own beloved children. One rescuer in the Norwegian bus crash stated:

"I have a son the same age as the children involved. I have followed him on a bus-trip. The impression of happy children on a holiday instantly triggered thoughts about my own son. It became so intensely close and real to me."

The combination of the helpers' personality, the child within, the challenge to existential order, and the strong identification with the child, explains why helpers react so strongly when children are traumatized.

EFFECTS OF WORKING WITH TRAUMATIZED CHILDREN

Exposure to traumatized children can surface at the scene or during the immediate work with the child, although most reactions will occur in the time following an incident. Some develop more gradually as a consequence of long-term exposure to traumatized children. Some common reactions should be mentioned.

HELPLESSNESS

Rescue and health care personnel are eager to help, are action oriented and like to be in control. When working with traumatized children, they often feel utterly helpless, knowing there is little they can do to alter the situation. They feel overwhelmed by the trauma affecting innocent children, and often feel there is nothing they can do to console the victims or survivors. As many as 85% of the helpers

TABLE 3.2

COMMON EFFECTS OF WORKING WITH TRAUMATIZED CHILDREN

- Helplessness
- Fear and anxiety
- Existential insecurity
- Rage
- Sorrow and Grief
- Intrusive Images
- Self-reproach, shame and guilt

who responded to the bus-disaster mentioned ealier acknowledged feelings of helplessness at not being able to do more at the scene. What do you say to a surviving child whose mother has been killed in an auto-accident when he asks: "How is my mother? Emotions from our childhood are easily reactivated, bringing forth the emotional tone from situations where we were unable to prevent negative things from happening.

FEAR AND ANXIETY

Perhaps the most important consequence of exposure to traumatized children is an alteration of the helpers' sense of vulnerability and security regarding their own children or other children they love. The illusion of invulnerability is often shattered when children are victims, and this creates an increase in intense feelings of vulnerability and fear that something similar will happen to oneself or to one's loved ones. A badly burnt child will stimulate thoughts like: "Could this have been my child?"

Following the bus disaster almost 3/4 of the personnel on scene had, to some degree, experienced anxiety for their loved ones in the month following the disaster. Their increased vulnerability led them to increased surveillance and protection of their children:

> "I have felt very insecure when sending my own children by bus after the accident."
>
> "I find myself nagging my children about being careful in the traffic. "

Rescuers often feel the need to visit their children's bedrooms after bedtime just to look at them, be there with them, or to hold them in their arms and hug them.

EXISTENTIAL INSECURITY

More than any other situation, pediatric trauma and death triggers thoughts about life's meaninglessness and unfairness. It is a direct insult to a helper's assumption of an orderly and just world. Since children are unable to protect themselves, their suffering is seen as unjust and unfair. When children die as a result of illness or trauma or when they are murdered, the sequence of life's cycle is distorted. Children are supposed to outlive their parents, and their deaths shake a basic assumption about life. As a helper stated after a fatal accident involving children, "They died at the wrong end of life". Some helpers may question the meaning of life in a manner similar to that of bereaved parents. The death of, or deliberate injury to, a child makes it difficult to find a successful cognitive framework around which the event can be integrated into one's life experience. When so many rescuers spontaneously report events concerning children when they are asked to state the worst event encountered in their work history, it reflects the difficulties with integrating such events in one's assumptions of the world.

RAGE

Children's trauma is often directly caused by adults. Helpers frequently express feelings of rage and anger toward those seen as responsible. When there is daily exposure to traumatized children, helpers may experience changes in their values regarding parents and adults. Public safety and health care professionals may grow more critical, intolerant and less trustful of others. Another more gradual change related to this is a general increase in irritability towards others. While listening to people talk about trivial things such as having a cold, the lack of sleep, or the stress of having small children, helpers may feel annoyed or irritated that such details and trivial circumstances could upset anyone.

SORROW AND GRIEF

Sorrow and grief are commonly experienced in the helping professions following the death of a child. This is especially true when there has been a long caring relationship. In pediatric house officers following a child patient's death, Behnke et al. (1987) found reactions similar to grief responses experienced after the death of a loved one. "I have grown used to adults dying, but I can never get used to a child's death". The death of a child almost always triggers sadness, frustration and helplessness.

It is not uncommon for helpers to start crying when they return home from a critical event involving children. Tears may come when they see their own children:

> "My reaction started when I returned to my wife and children. Then I started crying."

Sometimes helpers openly react at the scene of a child's death. Since it seems more acceptable when children are the victims, fellow workers do not see such an open display of emotions as unusual.

INTRUSIVE IMAGES

Intrusive images seem to be more easily formed in those who work with traumatized, dying or dead children. When helpers are asked what traumatic event they most vividly remember from their professional career, they are likely to describe events that include children. The mental images can be formed in all sensory modalities, although the visual mode seems to be the most dominant:

"Gradually the color of his skin changed. I could see he was dying. He died in my arms."

"We carried two dead children in our ambulance. From one of the stretchers a leg with a yellow sock was visible.

Now I see yellow socks everywhere."

"The size of the shoes was what got to me. The sight returns to me, and I keep thinking about my own child who uses the same shoe size."

"I still feel the curly hair of a small dead child in my hands."

SELF-REPROACH, SHAME AND GUILT

Self-reproach, shame and guilt are reactions that can be potentiated when children are involved as victims. Emergency and other helpers contemplate about what more could have been done, what could have been done differently, or how they could have been more effective in the performance of their duties.

On the other hand, positive consequences can also result from working with traumatized children. Many helpers experience a shift in values after working in such situations. Approximately 1 month following the bus disaster, more than 1/3 of the helpers in the bus disaster acknowledged a change in life's meaning. They came to a greater sense of appreciation and care for their loved ones, particularly for children.

WHAT CAN HELPERS DO?

In this part, I will focus on some of the ways that helpers can actively help traumatized children and, at the same time, help themselves.

HELPING RESCUERS

It is essential that helpers are ***emotionally prepared*** for facing traumatized children. Besides knowing about possible reactions from being exposed to traumatized children, helpers need to be aware of how their usual coping mechanisms can fail to function when children are involved, as well as learn strategies that will be useful in dealing with situations involving children. Unfortunately, experienced helpers seldom provide newcomers with useful strategies in this respect. It is strange to see how well we let others take part in our technical skills while we keep our more personal skills for coping with trauma to ourselves.

By being mentally prepared, one is able to keep from reflecting while at the scene. This is vitally important to keep from identifying with victims while engaged in on-scene operation. However, these on-scene coping mechanisms are detrimental if used to cope over time. It is important to have **standard procedures or routines** (Dyregrov, 1989; Mitchell, 1983) to secure a talk-through of the impressions formed in and thoughts and reactions triggered by the event. While distance is needed at the scene, contact with one's own emotions is vital for keeping one's emotional life intact over time. Critical Incident Stress Debriefing (CISD), on scene crisis intervention, and preincident education programs are all highly recommended as formal critical incident stress management interventions which assist rescuers in coping with traumatized children.

I would like to emphasize the use of *"peptalk"* or *self- enhancing comments* when one gets involved with traumatized children. Remember, rescuers are important to the psychological life of a traumatized child for several reasons:

- Rescuers meet the child shortly after what may well be the most important event of his/her lives.
- Rescuers possess the qualities to help the child physically, furthermore, they have access to facts that may be of vital importance to the child.
- Rescuers have the authority to psychologically communicate these facts in a way that children will believe them.

However, this places a responsibility upon the rescuers. Rescuers have to be *honest, direct and open* to prevent the secondary traumas that can result from not being honest. Furthermore, a lack of trust can develop toward adults after being prevented from knowing the facts or being told distorted facts or lies regarding a given trauma or disaster.

HELPING CHILDREN

At the scene, emotional first-aid for children should follow the same principles as for adults. It is the climate of support, security and care that one is able to establish that is of importance, more so than what one says, In disaster situations, support and comfort, as well as providing for food and rest, may be needed. The opportunity to play or draw and the opportunity to verbalize feelings and complaints are both important, but the primary task is of securing protection and safety around the child.

Children should be shielded from impressions that can lead to further trauma, as well as the Press or curious bystanders. At the same time, children should be united or reunited with their family as soon as possible or provided with information about how their parents and family fare. Children's concern over the safety of significant others can be extreme (Pynoos & Nader, 1988).

If there is one thing I would like you to remember from this chapter it is to include children in follow-up and rituals following traumatic events. Children are so often excluded from important events that concern their trauma. Let me illustrate this. When it comes to viewing the body of their dead parent or sibling, the adult world often excludes children. This is especially so following sudden death causing bodily harm or mutilation. Police, funeral directors, and health professionals alike join forces in saying: "A child should not see this" or "The deceased will be better remembered as he or she was". We think that children can't take it, that viewing the body will cause permanent harm.

To be included, children must be properly prepared, both for the sight of the dead, how the room will look and how adults will behave. They need to be accompanied by adults who can explain to them what is happening, and they need opportunities for expressing their thoughts and feelings afterwards (Dyregrov, 1990). If we exclude children, we leave them alone with their fantasies and fears, and they will miss both the opportunity to make the unreal real, as well as the possibility to bid farewell to their loved ones. Having had the opportunity both to counsel and follow many families through such rituals, I can say that I have yet to see problems arising from including children in these ceremonies, with the exception of some adolescents who have become afraid that the dead one will come back to visit them. How small can the children be at such ceremonies? There is no downward limit. Remember that although a 1 1/2 year old will have very little understanding of what goes on, this child will be an adult some day. Having been present at the wake or funeral of his or her mother or father can then be of great symbolic value to the child.

I would also suggest that different groups of helpers recognize children as family members when parents or siblings are seriously ill. Although pediatric units by nature are good at this, emergency wards, ICU-wards and other adult wards often take a very passive attitude towards children, not necessarily prohibiting their presence, yet not securing the more active presence of children. Toys or drawing material is often unavailable. Children need to get medical information that will help them process what happens, and they need to be able to bid concretely farewell when someone they love is dying.

For emergency helpers outside the hospital, there are some very important needs that can be met for children. Being present at accident or murder scenes or other places where critical events happens, one may have access to important facts that the child may lack or have wrong. In order to grasp what has taken place, children have the same need as adults to know the facts of what happened. In my experience, this need is often overlooked by adults. Children need to know what happened, what is known about why it happened, and what was done. As rescuer or helper, you are able to address common rumors, fears and misconceptions. Many traumas that affect children do not necessarily happen when they are present. You possess relevant facts that can be of immense use to children. By meeting children following critical incidents and by helping children getting to know these facts, your own feelings of helplessness will simultaneously be counteracted, and you also get the opportunity to see that children can cope with these events in extraordinary ways as long as adults provide the basis for this.

This active involvement should also include following the child back to the scene of the event. Let me give you an illustrating example from a colleague of mine (Grønvold Bugge, 1990):

Two men tried to swim ashore when their boat was broken down by the rough Norwegian sea. One survived the other drowned. The twelve year old boy whose father drowned insisted on seeing his father. He brought his camera and let his mother take pictures of him. He had many direct questions about the different marks on his father's body. He also met the rescue personnel manning the ambulance that had brought his father to the hospital. They demonstrated the ambulance for him. This was important, and at one point, he said: I did not know that you did so much to save my father. I have been so angry because I thought that you must have accepted that he was dead".

The paramedics, together with the police, took the family on board the pilot vessel out to where the boat had gone under. There they threw spring flowers from their own garden into the sea. The policeman and the diver stood by the boy and informed him about the rescue work done for his father. They pointed out to the boy where his father was found, and the boy finally understood why his father's friend had not been able to save him. Previously he had said: "I have been so angry with him. I thought that he did not care about my father."

This example illustrates an important aspect of childhood trauma, namely that children often lack the relevant prior knowledge necessary to organize disparate elements into a cohesive whole or to set related events into an organized structure. Having been shown how the ambulance functioned and by seeing how rough the sea could be, this child was able to "grasp" what had happened and what efforts had been made to save his father. When children draw, play out or visit/revisit the scene of events, this enhances their ability to structure and grasp what has happened. Children need contextual support and concrete anchor points for their understanding and mental clarification of an event. The child's mind is very active in dealing with traumatic events. Facts tie them to reality and counteract fantasies and misconceptions. Two other examples also illustrate the importance of giving facts to help processing emotions and thoughts:

A young man fell or threw himself from a highway bridge onto a road where he was instantly killed. His 16 year old sister and his fiance had tried to control him but in vain, and had finally gone to fetch the police for help. When they returned, they could not find him, but when driving underneath the bridge, the police saw what they suspected was a body. The police would not let the sister or fiance near the scene, and although they saw the body at the hospital after he was washed, both girls had many guestions and fantasies about how he must have looked and what position he was found in. To help reduce these fantasies and repetitive thoughts, a meeting was arranged with the ambulance personnel who could describe in detail how he was lying and how he looked when they picked him up. This helped them set their thoughts at ease in a very short time.

A seventeen year old girl slipped on the ice and fell under the rear wheels of a bus and was pulled around the wheel by the non-skid chains. Half a year into the follow-up of the immediate family, I was asked to see the 16 year old best friend of the deceased because she could not function in her ordinary life. When she came to my office, it was clear that her main problem was the fantasies about how her friend must have looked after being pulled around by the wheel. Instead of starting therapy focusing on her fantasies, contact was made with a policeman who had been at the scene of the event and who could describe in detail how she had looked. Although the back of her head was gone, her face had remained relatively intact, and the rest of her body was not as damaged as she had imagined in her fantasies. By providing her with facts, she was able to produce one concrete image of her dead friend instead of being plagued by ever changing fantasies.

These examples illustrate how helpful it can be for child and adolescent victims to get information concerning facts from those involved at the scene of an event. By providing children with facts, their fragmented, often uninterpreted images and fantasies about an event are given structure. Children are helped to understand and tolerate a traumatic event, and a more coherent memory can be formed. By providing this kind of help, helpers can reduce their helplessness by engaging in meaningful tasks, and at the same time victims, be they primary, secondary or tertiary, are provided with invaluable help. Important measures to help children following accident scenes are listed in Table 3.3.

Our feedback from helpers is that although more active involvement with children after a trauma can sometimes be time-consuming and somewhat anxiety-provoking the first time, it adds meaning and closure to events, reduces helplessness, and at the same time is extraordinarily important for the affected child.

TABLE 3.3

HELPING CHILDREN COPE WITH TRAUMA

- use honest, direct and open communication
- let children get the facts
- go through what happened with them
- let children visit the scene of the event
- let children meet the rescuers and helpers
- let children be part of follow-up meetings

REFERENCES:

Alexander, D. & Wells, A. (1990). Post-traumatic stress reactions among police officers after the Piper Alpha Disaster. *Paper presented at the Second European Conference on Traumatic Stress", Noordwijkerhout, the Nederlands*, September 23 - 27.

Behnke, M., Reiss, J., Neimeyer, G., and Bandstra, E. S. (1987). Grief responses of pediatric house officers to a patient's death. *Death Studies*: 11, 169-176.

Dyregrov, A. (1989). Caring for helpers in disaster situations: Psychological debriefing. *Disaster Management*, 2, 25-30.

Dyregrov, A. (1990). *Grief in children: A handbook for adults*. London: Jessica Kingsley Publishers.

Gronvold Bugge, R. (1990). Sudden death: accident and suicide. *Paper presented at the Second European Conference on Traumatic Stress, Noordwijkerhout, the Nederlands*, September 23 - 27.

Hershiser, M. R. & Quarantelli, E. L. (1976). The handling of the dead in a disaster. *Omega*, 7, 195-208.

Hetherington, A. & Guppy, A. (1990). Post traumatic stress in British police. *Paper presented at the Second European Conference on Traumatic Stress, Noordwijkerhout, the Nederlands*, September 23 - 27.

Jones, D. R. (1985). Secondary disaster victims: the emotional effects of recovering and identifying human remains. *American Journal of Psychiatry, 142*, 303-307.

Mitchell, J. T. (1983). When disaster strikes.... The Critical Incident Stress Debriefing. *Journal of Emerqency Medical Services*, 8, 36-39.

Oliner, S. P. & Oliner, P. M. (1988). *The altruistic personality*. New York: The Free Press.

Pynoos, R. S. & Nader, K. (1988). Psychological first aid and treatment approach to children exposed to community violence: research implications. *Journal of Traumatic Stress*, 1, 445-473.

Raphael, B. (1981). Squibb Academic Address. Personal disaster. *Austr N Z J Psychiatr*. 15: 183-198.

Raphael, B., Singh, B. & Bradbury, L. (1980). Disaster helper's perspective. *Medical Journal of Australia*, 445-447.

Rayner, J. F. (1958). How do nurses behave in disaster? *Nursing Outlook*, 6, 572-576.

Robinson, R. (1984). Health and stress in ambulance services. *Report of evaluation study - part 1. Research report 84-2.* Social Biology Resources centre, Carlton.

Taylor, A. J. W. & Frazer, A. G. (1981). Psychological sequelae of operation overdue following the DC10 aircrash in Antarctica. *Victoria University Publications in Psychology* No. 27, Department of Psychology, Victoria University of Wellington, New Zealand

Chapter 4

FAMILIAL PSYCHOTRAUMATOLOGY AND EMERGENCY SERVICE PERSONNEL

GEORGE S. EVERLY,JR.

Earlier chapters in this volume have attempted to speculate on the nature, or phenomenology, of psychological trauma from both physiological as well as psychological perspectives(psychotraumatology). Having offered such psychotraumatological speculation, it seems important to extend such speculation into the realm of the systemic effects of psychological trauma. The most fundamental of all systems relevant to the study of mammals, especially homo sapiens, is of course the family system; hence the present chapter is Familial Psychotraumatology. The symptoms of post-traumatic stress upon the family have been described (McCubbin and Figley, 1983) and intervention models have been constructed (Figley, 1995, Harris, 1991).

This paper speculates on the phenomenology of familial discord in the wake of psychological trauma. Emphasis is placed upon the integration of biological and psychological processes as they may be relevant to the families of emergency services and disaster response personnel.

George S. Everly, Jr. • International Critical Incident Stress Foundation, Ellicott City, Maryland.

In G.S. Everly, Jr. Innovations in Disaster and Trauma Psychology, Volume One: Applications in Emergency Services and Disaster Response. Baltimore: Chevron Publishing Corp, 1995.

BIOLOGICAL ROOTS OF FAMILIAL AFFILIATION AND ATTACHMENT

Henry and Stephens (1977), in their masterful treatise on sociobiology, describe two primary sociobiologic drives which emerge from the mammalian subcortical limbic system. The first is the drive for social/familial affiliation and attachment (see also MacLean, 1985).

The affiliative/attachment drive is purported to consist of socially-related behaviors such as affiliation, attachment, nurturing, affection, and even play. In humans, this drive may manifest itself in various forms of interpersonal collaboration, reliance, dependence, and related behaviors, extending even to the sociologic concept of the family. This behavior pattern is referred to by Henry and Stephens (1977) as "the cement of society."

The affiliative drive appears to reside primarily in the anatomy of septum and the cingulate gyrus, a portion of the subcortical limbic system (Henry and Stephens,1977; Murphy, MacLean, and Hamilton, 1981; MacLean, 1985). Ablation of the cingulate gyrus tends to eliminate affiliative behavior and grooming behavior (Murphy, MacLean, and Hamilton, 1981). So apparently fundamental is this affiliative drive that Maclean has argued that the roots of "family" may be phylogenetically coded in the limbic thalamocingulate areas of the mammalian brain (MacLean, 1985). Furthermore, disruption of the natural attachment mechanism in infants of many species reportedly leads to profound behavior and physiological indices of distress, e.g., dysfunctional behavior patterns, anxiety-like and other signs of excessive arousal, cardiac and respiratory dysfunctions, and extreme dependence and clinging-like behaviors (van der Kolk, 1987). This complex of signs and systoms indicative of interference with normal attachment and bonding in infants has been called the "separation cry." Similarly, disruption of the normal ontogenetic evolution of the affiliative/attachment drive, such as through premature separation or trauma, may lead to dysfunctional affilative, collaborative, dependence, and even nuturing/child-rearing behaviors in later life (van der Kolk, 1987).

BIOLOGICAL ROOTS OF INDIVIDUALITY, AGGRESSION, AND SOCIAL SEPARATISM

As Henry and Stephens (1977) described the attachment drive, they also described another primary sociobiologic drive, this is the drive which fuels autonomous and aggressive behaviors. MacLean (1986) has viewed this drive as the drive for self-preservation.

The autonomy and aggression drive is purported to consist of behaviors such as exploration, the acquisition of territory, aggression, defensive behavior, fighting, the need for control, and other behaviors considered to be useful in self-preservation. This self-preservation complex includes the well-known "fight or flight" response. In humans, this drive may manifest itself as aggressive propensities, territorialism, the need to control oneself and one's environment, and a diminished propensity for trust. In general, this drive may manifest itself in the form of an independent interpersonal posture and withdrawal from affiliative behavior, social bonding, communication, and family-related behavior. If the affiliative drive can be seen as the cement of society, then this drive of autonomy and aggression-related behaviors may be thought of as that which provides "order" to society. In concert with this notion, in mammals, including nonhuman primates, this drive appears to be very much responsible for mediation of the social hierarchy (Pribram, 1962) social order, social separatism, and defensive social posturing.

The amygdaloid complex appears to serve as the anatomical core of the autonomy and aggression pattern (Henry and Stephens, 1977, MacLean, 1986). Ablation of the amygdala imparts a noted docility effect (Kluver and Bucy,1939), yet perhaps even more interesting is the fact that when a nonhuman primate undergoes amygdalectomy, its position in the social order (hierarchy) is diminished (Pribram, 1962). Therefore, there is compelling evidence that the amygdala plays an important role in defining social order and hierarchies among primates. The amygdaloid complex is not only involved in social hierarchy formation and aggression, but it is involved in fear responses as well (see Henry and Stephens, 1977). It would probably be an oversimplification to state that the amygala initiates the fear response. A more appropriate interpretation would most likely be that the amygdaloid complex modulates the aggression response vis-a-vis the fear response, i.e., the "fight" vis-a-vis the "flight" response through some complex mechanism capable of appraising the magnitude of threat posed within the confrontational situation. There is clear evidence that both the fight and flight responses have neurological bases in the amygdaloid complex (see Henry and Stephens, 1977: MacLean, 1949, 1986 for discusssion).

BIOLOGICAL ROOTS OF FAMILY DYSFUNCTION FROM PSYCHOLOGICAL TRAUMA

Given the aforementioned reviews of biological mechanisms as a basis, we may extend this discussion into the sources of behavioral dysfunction as a result of psychological trauma.

Perhaps over simplistically, it has been argued that extreme stress and psychological trauma appear to inhibit tthe basic biological drives for affiliation, communication of affectively-ladened information, interpersonal affection, and family-related behaviors (Henry, 1993). The physiology of such suppression or inhibition may be the proposed stress-induced blocking effect that cortisol may exert on certain neural substrates in the brain (Sapolsky, Krey, and McEwen, 1984).

Similarly, it has been suggested that extreme stress and psychological trauma may serve to sensitize and augment the biological drives for aggression, control, individualism and the "fight or flight" response (Everly, 1990, 1993).

Thus, the net effect of psychological trauma, upon the trauma victim from a biological point of view, may be a biologically-based disturbance in limbic system function which serves to:

1) inhibit interpersonal communications
2) augment aggressive, rageful, and control-oriented behavior, and
3) inhibit effective functioning in social units of all kinds, but especially the family.

These reactions may emerge even more floridly among individuals who work or volunteer in the fields of emergency services and disaster response because of the habitual action-oriented , control-oriented, emotionally-suppressing nature of their job functions. It also be that certain aspects of their core personality structure may bias these individuals toward such stress-related reactions.

Thus, trauma may serve to exacerbate these environmental and personologic propensities for control, emotional suppression, diminished emotionally-ladened communications and independence.

BASIC PSYCHOLOGICAL PATTERNS

MacLean (1985) notes that 45 years of evidence points to two primary psychological/behavioral themes emerging from the neurology of the limbic system:

1) preservation of the species, and
2) self-preservation.

Preservation of the species, from a psychological and behavioral perspective, requires the individual to focus upon the needs of others. Preservation of the species involves nuturance, communication modes conducive to sociability, and attendance to the affective states of others.

Self- preservation, on the other hand, from a psychological and behavioral perspective, requires the individual to focus upon oneself. Self preservation usually requires hypervigilance, low thresholds for "fight orflight" activation, aggressive propensities, and egocentricism often to the point of requiring solitude and withdrawing from others.

Maslow (1970) discusses the basic motives that drive human beings. He notes that human motivation is first based upon the satisfaction of ***physiological needs***. However most fundamental of all drives, outside of the need for meeting the physiological requisites of life, is the need for a sense of ***safety***. Once the need for safety has been satisfied, and only then, the individual is motivated by the quest for ***social affiliation***, interpersonal bonding, love, and perhaps familial bonding. Once these 3 foundational needs have been satisfied according to Maslow (1970), humans may then strive for enhanceing ***self-esteem*** and ***self-actualization***. Thus the motivational hierarchy may look as represented in figure 4.1 below:

FIGURE 4.1

MASLOW'S HIERARCHY OF NEEDS

Self-actualization

Self-esteem

Social Affiliation

Safety

Physiological Needs

PSYCHOLOGICAL ROOTS OF FAMILIAL DYSFUNCTION FROM PSYCHOLOGICAL TRAUMA

To reiterate, Maslow (1970) argues that until the basic lower order needs are satisfied, eg, physiological needs and the quest for safety, the attainment of higher order needs such as social affiliation/interpersonal bonding, self-esteem, and self-actualization are impossible.

Trauma forces the victim to regress back to lower order needs regardless of what pretrauma motivational needs had previously been satisfied. The trauma victim then becomes fixated at the attainment of the lower order need. The self-preservation quest for safety is the level of motivation most likely to entrap the trauma victim after the actual traumatic threat to one's life has resolved. Thus, safety, security and self-preservation may become the dominating motives for trauma victims.

If one's sense of safety is continually in doubt, as with many trauma victims, the traumatized individual may be thought of as abandoning the need for interpersonal affiliation and living in a chronic, unrelenting quest for a sense of safety.

Thus, it becomes clear as to why the family and interpersonal affiliation of the trauma victim are likely to suffer discord and tension. The trauma victim, by virtue of the traumatic experience, has been forced to shift from the basic drive of preservation of the species to a drive dominated by a theme of self-preservation. The trauma victim has seen the need for interpersonal relationships become subordinate to the egocentered quest for safety with all of its aggressive, self-defensive oriented characteristics.

RESOLVING THE FAMILIAL DYSFUNCTION

Despite the powerful determinants of familial discord that may plague many emergency services personnel who suffer from trauma, resolution of the familial discord is achievable.

The first step in resolving the familial discord is understanding. Both the victim of the traumatic experience and his/her family must be educated as to the roots of the psychological distance and tension in the family. It should be explained that although difficut to cope with, such reations are normal expressions of a self-preserving orientation in the wake of a traumatizing experience.

Secondly, patience is emphasized. Recovery takes time.

Thirdly, family counseling becomes a cornerstone of the recovery process. This may be in addition to any counseling or professional support that the traumatized emergency service worker may obtain.

Fourth, in some instances the individual family members of the emergency service worker may have to seek professional or informal support of their own outside of family counseling to assist them in the recovery process. They too have become victims of psychological trauma, albeit indirectly.

CONCLUSIONS

Clearly, emergency service and disaster response personnel are at increased risk for psychological traumatization by virtue of their job descriptions. Psychological trauma is well known to be capable of extracting a heavy toll from these dedicated individuals. However, often neglected is the realization that the family unit of the rescuer will virtually always be a victim of the same traumatic event that adversely impacts the traumatized rescurer. The greater the severity of the impact upon the rescuer, the greater the severity of the impact upon the rescuer's family.

Despite the powerful sources of famillial tensions, discord, and dysfunction as reviewed in this chapter, the family can successfully recover from psychological trauma as can the rescuer. It was beyond the scope of this chapter to detail specific thereputic methods, for family rehabilitation (see Figley, 1995; Brende and Goldsmith, 1991; Harris, 1991), rather, the goal of this chapter has been to provide insight, albeit speculative, into the origins of familial dysfunction in the wake of psychological trauma. Understanding and normalization are virtually always foundations for the recovery processs from psychological trauma.

REFERENCES

Brende, J.O. (1991). Post-traumatic stress disorder in families. *Journal of Contemporary Psychotherapy*, 21, 115-124.

Everly,G.S. (1990). Post-traumatic stress as a Disorder of Arousal. *Psychology and Health*, 4, 135-145.

Everly, G.S.(1993). Psychotraumatology: A two-factor formulation of post-traumatic stress. *Integrative Physiological and Behavioral Science*, 28, 270-278.

Figley, C. (1995). Systemic PTSD: Family treatment experience and implications. In G.Everly and J. Lating (Eds). *Psychotraumatology: Key Papers and Core Concepts in Posttraumatic Stress* (pp341-358). NY: Plenum.

Harris, C.J. (1991). A family crisis intervention model for the treatment of posttraumatic stress reaction. *Journal of Traumatic Stress*, 4, 195- 207.

Henry,J.P. (1993,Feb). Alexithymia and PTSD. *Invited paper presented to the Fifth Montreux Congress on Stress*, Montreux Switzerland.

Henry,J.P. and Stephens,P.M.(1977). *Stress, Health, and the Social Environment*. NY: Springer.

Klüver, H. and Bucy, P. (1939). Preliminary analysis of functions of the temporal lobes in monkeys. *Archives of neurology and Psychiatry*.42,979-1000.

MacLean,P.D.(1949). Psychosomatic disease and the visceral brain. *Psychsomomatic Medicine*,11,338-353.

MacLean,P.D.(1985). Brain evolution relating to family, play, and the separation call. *Archives of General Psychiatry*, 42, 405-417.

MacLean,P.D.(1986). Culminating deevelopments in the evaluation of the limbic system. I. B. Doane and K. Livingston (Eds). *The Limbic System*(pp1-28).NY:Raven.

Maslow, A. (1970). *Motivation and Personality*, 2nd Ed.NY: Harper and Row.

McCubbin,H. and Figley,C. (1983) *Stress and the Family, Vol.* 1.NY: Brunner/Mazel.

Murphy,M.R., Maclean, P. and Hamilton, S. (1981). Species-typical behavior of hamsters deprived from birth of the neocortex. *Science*, 213, 459-461.

Pribram, K. (1962). Interrelations of psychology and the neurological disciplines. In S.Koch(Ed). *Psychology* (pp.119-157).NY: McGraw-Hill.

Sapolsky, R.,Krey,L. and McEwen, B.(1984). Stress down-regulates corticosterone receptors in a site specific manner in the brain. *Endocrinology*, 114, 287-292.

van der Kolk,B.(1987). *Psychlogical Trauma*. Wash.D.C.: APA Press.

Chapter 5

TRAUMATIC STRESS: A PERSONAL VIEW FROM COMBAT

COLONEL RICHARD L. JAEHNE, USMC

What follows is my personal account of the effects of traumatic stress disorder as it is caused by the effects of combat. I tell it in the first person because it is the most effective way to emphasize the highly personal, traumatic nature of combat stress and because it is my own story. I have endeavored to explain how combat stress occurs, what happens to the individual as a result and how a person can recover from its effects. I offer my story because I think that there are thousands of men who have been in offensive combat, who may have lived my life, but who have not had the opportunity to tell their story about why they hurt.

As a young man I had many advantages — a caring supportive family, stable home, and many personal successes as an athlete and in school. Unfortunately, all that had little to do with surviving in combat.

Some say that stress disorder is genetic or induced by social circumstance. That has not necessarily been my experience. I am no medical expert, but I am someone who recently celebrated something of an anniversary — 24 years ago I killed myself. I found through personal experience that stress disorder in combat is about killing yourself — emotionally — and then living with it.

Colonel Richard L. Jaehne• United States Marine Corps, Washinton D.C.
In G.S. Everly, Jr. Innovations in Disaster and Trauma Psychology, Volume One: Applications in Emergency Services and Disaster Response. Baltimore: Chevron Publishing Corp, 1995.

DEFINING COMBAT STRESS

I believe there are two kinds of combat stress: That induced by indirect threats and that induced by direct combat.

INDIRECT-INDUCED COMBAT STRESS.

One type of combat stress occurs in those kinds of circumstances where you are faced with a non-descript threat to your life. Someone or thing may be sniping at you, or you are convinced that someone may be preparing to attack you. These circumstances cause a kind of response which may have been seen in the trenches of World War I, Khe San in Vietnam, or Beirut as the young Marines occupied the airport. In all of these cases, individuals were targets who lacked the ability to respond effectively to the threat. This type of stress is numbing and disorienting. It deadens the spirit but does not necessary alter the individual. One <u>can</u> recover from this type of stress with some assistance and I think that traditional types of stress therapy can have a positive effect on an individual with this kind of combat stress.

DIRECT COMBAT INDUCED STRESS.

There is another kind of stress which is induced by actual combat. It happens in a <u>moment</u>. It doesn't happen over time. It happens in that instant when your entire character is filled to overflowing with the feelings, emotions, and the death that your senses say you must confront. It happens to privates and to officers. It happens to each person in a very personal and unique way. However, the outcome is that you must choose to either survive within yourself or simply go off the "deep end"; i.e., check out of the situation and say, "I can't fight anymore."

All have heard the famous George Patton story where he slaps a young soldier in a hospital who just cannot fight anymore. It is possible that the soldier was faking; however, it is also possible that his condition was real. It could have been a response to that indirect threat or it could have been a response to direct combat. Both types of stress exist but they are very different in effect and recovery.

MY PERSONAL STORY

In 1968 I joined the Marine Corps. It was a year of headlines and traumatic personal decisions for thousands of young men of draft age. I was a volunteer who chose to go to Vietnam to serve in combat. A parade of combat veterans spoke to all of new second lieutenants about combat, what it was like, and what you had to face as you went to war. As I finished training, I believed that I knew about combat. I was wrong — not so much in the skills required to fight but in understanding the residual emotional trauma that the fighting left behind.

In 1969, I was sent to Vietnam. I waited for a month in Okinawa with thousands of other Marines for another TET offensive to occur. We were to be instant replacements. One night in February 1969, we were ordered to pack our gear, and by the next morning we were in Vietnam. We had gone from peace to war in a moment.

As I joined my battalion, which was heavily engaged in fighting with North Vietnamese Army (NVA) forces, I discovered that my roommate from training was also in the battalion. He had arrived earlier than I and was now the senior officer left alive in his company. He was a young lieutenant but that did not matter, he was all they had. In my first few days with the battalion, we braced for attack, spent sleepless nights on alert, and listened to radio conversations as friends and fellow Marines fought and died. We began to live with combat.

Soon, I took command of my first platoon and shortly thereafter was involved in my first direct combat. The Marine Corps had sent all new lieutenants through an exhaustive training program to prepare us for that moment and I had great confidence in my personal ability to face an armed enemy.

FIRST COMBAT, FIRST DEATH

The first combat I experienced was a night ambush with a small squad. It was one of those nights which I soon learned was like many nights in war when nothing goes as it should. We saw eight enemy soldiers entering a village and triggered the ambush on them. We soon found that our position prevented the use of mortars and other indirect fire weapons, so we engaged the enemy with just the weapons we had in our hands.

Our position was in sand and soon our M-16 rifles and then our machine guns began to fail. In no time, we twelve marines had two working weapons. So, just like in the movies, two of us "went around" to take care of the enemy who were still shooting at us. As I moved, I threw a hand grenade and a piece of the pin stuck.

The spoon popped but the trigger did not ignite. When the hand grenade landed, the man I threw it at shot back at me and bullets came very close. You can see bullet tracers at night and it appeared to the squad that I had been hit. A young corpsman jumped up and he ran to help me. He was killed trying to reach me. That was my first death.

What you must understand is that *every single person lives with shame* in combat about something he did or failed to do. Each person feels personally responsible for something which caused a death.

The platoon I commanded was supposed to be 46 men in strength. We replacements joined twelve who remained of the original forty six. You see, the day I arrived in Vietnam that platoon had discovered, engaged and laid for three days some 300 meters from a NVA regiment, fighting literally day and night for survival. One of those remaining Marines was a nineteen year old machine gunner who-had black hair when he started the fight. He was gray at the end of those three days. Each of these twelve men had combat stress. They did not want fight anymore. Now, all of a sudden, this new lieutenant had killed one of their own...a comrade who had survived those three days of hell. I can tell you they were not too happy with me.

We finished the fight that night but the deed was done. They were apart from me. I did not have combat stress. They did. They had mentally "killed" each other. They learned as individuals and as a group to survive on their own terms and I was not part of those terms. I learned that *combat stress creates groups of people that share a common bond.*

In combat, you have to make awful choices. Two months later we were off in an extended operation designed to search out NVA in their own territory. Three weeks into the operation, after having seen a number of men die in close combat, we got to a hill. As we reached the hill, the path narrowed, with steep cliffs on either side. We had to get up the hill and the NVA knew it. For 24 hours, we tried to scale that hill. We used air strikes, artillery, mortars and fought up the hill twice — only to be repulsed. Frankly we ran out of options. So, in the best tradition of "when you don't have a choice you go for it," we did just that. We launched the third assault.

As we attacked up the hill, the NVA started rolling cans full of explosives down at us. Machine gun fire was raking our path and a can full of explosives landed next to one of my squad leaders. He was one of the original twelve men who had survived the three nights of hell months before. Both of his legs were blow off.

In the middle of the assault, as my squad leader lay dying, I faced an awful choice: Either stop the assault and evacuate him right then to have any chance of saving his life but face a fourth assault attempt, or keep going and finish the assault. Neither was a very good choice... We kept going ... He died ... and so did I.

In that instant, I reached inside myself and found ***the switch***. There is an emotional switch that accompanies combat stress. It is a switch that allows you to become an animal. When we finished the assault there was nothing left alive between the bottom and top of that hill. Once you find the switch, it is like Adam and the Garden of Eden, you cannot undo it. I can find the switch which turns off my humanity any time night or day. I can be back on that hill any time night or day. Today, I do it voluntarily. For 20 years, I had no choice.

LIVING WITH COMBAT STRESS MEANS LIVING WITH YOUR OWN DEATH

In my opinion, the only way most people can live with this knowledge, this SWITCH, is to kill themselves emotionally. A person says: "I'm dead and it doesn't matter what happens to me after this." When I did this, I chose to be dead emotionally. I did not want anymore friends in combat. I did not want any emotional attachment to someone I was responsible for. I would suggest that there are many young men who came back from Vietnam with similar experiences.

WHAT IS UNIQUE ABOUT OFFENSE-INDUCED COMBAT STRESS

I believe there are some unique things about the type of combat stress with which I have lived. Offensive combat is about willful, sanctioned violence that results in death. It exists in an environment of total emersion in violence, not for days but for weeks and months at a time. To a person in combat, the vacation known as R&R leave is literally a surreal experience. Such a person who goes to Hawaii, often has no concept of where he is or what is happening to him. In combat, a person has no alternatives. He cannot just opt out of a patrol or a mission. Of course, some choose to do so; however, most do not.

INCREASED SENSORY SENSITIVITY

After a time, many individuals in combat develop a "sixth sense." Their body is fine tuned beyond normal limits. One of the horrible things that happened to us when we came back from Vietnam was that we were simply thrown back into the United States. Three days after we left combat, we were standing on a Main Street somewhere in America. I would challenge you to go out on your Main Street and attempt, just attempt for one minute, to see ... hear ... smell ... and feel everything around you, simultaneously. You will go into sensory overload.

Now, if you choose to do this, you can simply stop. When we came home from combat we could not stop receiving and processing that level of sensory input which we had needed to survive. On Main Street, we were confronted by an explosion of sensory inputs which sent us into sensory overload and emergency emotional shutdown. We had to block all feelings in order to survive. There is only so much one can take.

THE QUESTION IS — WHY?

The ***switch*** is found at a moment in time in combat when you have ***total emotional release***. When the "***switch*** is flipped" you find a personal dragon that has been living within you and which civilization has spent countless generations trying to slay. You live with Super Bowl emotions every minute of your life in combat. I believe that every person who comes home from combat asks the question "Why?"..."Why did I come home and why did he not come home?"...and each person who asks this question lives with the answer..."I do not know, but perhaps it was something I did."

LIVING WITH SHAME

There is not a man who comes back from this type of experience who is not ashamed of something he or she did or failed to do. My first shame was a piece of hand grenade pin. There were many others. I was in a fight one day and two radio operators on either side me were killed and I did not even get a scratch. I still have no idea why I lived and they did not. I pray is was not something that I did. So you ask "Why?" You look at yourself and ask "Did I do something that saved my life and cost them theirs?" You relive these moments of death over and over again try to determine what you could have done differently to prevent the death. This scene is repeated in the minds of countless combat veterans, again and again.

I believe that those who have fought in offensive combat live with the self-doubt of "Why?" and a sense of unavoidable shame. In battle, you do not have time for shame. You must continue to function. After the battle is over, you must face your personal "dragon", that switch which allows you to live outside civilization. You look inside yourself and see you own face staring back at you with that knowing look of one who is capable of doing such horrendous violence that you terrify yourself. You know precisely where your switch is and do not want to touch it. Yet, you know you have to be able to touch it to survive in combat. I believe that among young combat leaders this problem is even more acute. As a platoon commander, I felt personally responsible for everything that happened to each person under my command. As a brand new lieutenant I was taught that I was responsible not only for my own actions but for the actions and lives of all of the people assigned to me. I, and I believe-all lieutenants, lived by a code of conduct which demanded that I not ask anything of my men which I was personally unwilling to do.

I can also remember young enlisted Marines in Vietnam who refused promotion because they did not want to be personally responsible for someone else's death. It was acceptable for a Marine to face his own death. He was prepared to deal with that; but, he was not going to be responsible for making a mission decision which led to another's death.

RECOVERY

I have recovered to some extent from my own combat stress; however, every time I think about this issue I have tried to understand why I have recovered and what helped me to do so. I do not fully understand the healing process, but would offer some insights into it.

I think that each person who recovers from combat stress, particularly offense-induced combat stress, has made a choice to die and then has made another choice to rejoin the living. It is not a choice one makes instantaneously.

There is some anecdotal information about people who have had near-death experiences. Maybe you have met someone who has had such an experience or had one yourself. Those who have, describe it as being peaceful, serene, and light. They speak of being compelled to remain in that place beyond life. Those who come back from such an experience say they felt that something drew them back to life but *they themselves had to make the personal effort to return to the world of the living*.

I think that this is how I recovered. No one-brought me back. No one could. I had to make that choice myself. For many years I preferred to live as an emotionally dead person because, as such, I did not have to face all those things that made me want to make that choice in the first place.

A counselor or loved one can help a person who chooses to be dead emotionally by helping him strip away some of the impediments to feeling. However, the "dead" person must choose to come back himself. I would offer two thoughts to those who seek to help someone recover from combat stress:

1. DO NOT BE JUDGMENTAL

A person who lives with combat stress has lived in the outer envelope of civilization. He knows what he has been asked to do and has done is outside civilized norms. He has constantly asked himself the question "Why?" and judged himself lacking in response. He is hypersensitive to external, judgmental inferences. Anything said to him which is judgmental is going make him withdraw. He is already his own most severe judge.

2. VALIDATE HIS EXPERIENCE AND EMOTIONS.

The person returning from combat requires validation of his feelings and experiences. When we came back from Vietnam it was traumatic. It was judgmental. It invalidated our experiences. We were told by word and the reactions of people we met that we had done something wrong. I am encouraged that Americans were much more supportive of those who returned from Desert Storm, but that was a popular war and a "victory." Validation is a critical component to healing, particularly for those who fight in unpopular wars or come home without a victory laurel. Without validation they will withdraw into their own dead world.

MY PERSONAL RECOVERY

From a personal stand point, I think I recovered over time as a result of a number of factors. What I have are feelings about the healing process, not hard empirical data. All I can say is that I feel again and I had not done so for a very long time. In my opinion, there are several factors which helped me to recover. They are listed below.

1. VALIDATION AND SUPPORT

I belonged to organization which saw fit to keep me, reward me for my service and validate my experiences on a continuous basis. I have been asked to be a commander and an instructor. I have been given the opportunity to teach thousands of young Marines how to survive in combat. The Marine Corps asked me to do that and the Marines listened to what I said with great interest. Every time I spoke about combat, I had to open myself up and relive the combat experience again. I cannot talk about combat without being instantly transported back. All of this helped to validate who I was and what I had live through.

2. SHARING COMBAT EXPERIENCES

Men who have shared combat experiences find that a gathering of them where they tell stories about combat is real therapy. It validates the individual and his own traumatic experiences. Mutual sharing of experiences helps each individual understand that fears, shame, and emotions are common to all. Sharing the horrible things inside helps a person believe that it is "OK to feel this way." I don't think that either family or therapist can make this happen. Effective sharing requires the validity and bond of common combat experience.

3. FAMILY, FRIENDS AND PROFESSIONAL THERAPISTS

I do believe that family, friends and professional-therapists have an important role to play. There is a support role to sponsor and encourage those types of activity which bring buried feelings to the surface.

4. FAITH IN GOD

I was fortunate as a young man to have a deep faith in God. I believe that this also has been a significant part of my recovery. It certainly helped me in my darkest moments. My favorite parable is about God walking along a beach with a young man. The life of this man is revealed out on the beach. The man is angry with God and says, "For awhile there are two sets of prints, but look there is only one and that was the most difficult point in my life. You left me!" God looks at him and says, "Son, when there was only one set of footprints I was carrying you." I have felt that support. It is an important thing to have.

5. OPPORTUNITY TO GIVE BACK

Because of inherent feelings of shame and guilt, I believe that each of us who have combat stress needs the opportunity to give something back to those who may go the next time. I had the extraordinary privilege of commanding an Infantry Battalion for two almost years. I was given the chance to pay back to hundreds of young men in some small way that piece that I left in Vietnam.

6. FACING YOUR DRAGON

All of these things helped. Ultimately I made visits back to life emotionally, I don't think I came back on any given day. I have now chosen to live more on this side than on the other side. Part of this healing process was when I was forced, in a time of war again, to face my dragon and to share my combat experiences to help others prepare for combat. Each time I talked about my personal combat experiences I was emotionally drained but I had to reach deep within myself to live again.

7. ROLE OF INTERVENTION

One day, during the Gulf War, I was asked to talk to a whole group of new Chaplains that were getting ready to go into the Gulf. I believe that it was that day which caused me to finally decide to live on this side rather than just visit. As I spoke, I faced 45 ministers and priests who were going to have to go help men and women in combat for the first time. I wanted to tell them what they would face. I told them about an experience that helped define the role of intervention in combat stress healing.

In Vietnam one day, I was arguing with a village chief about where my platoon was going to string some barbed wire. (Parenthetically, we found out later that this village was a Viet Cong district headquarters with an underground bunker complex. Of course, we did not know this at the time.) It was Sunday, so we had a group of new chaplains coming out to visit us. As they turned off the road a command detonated mine exploded killing three of them. The only survivor was the Battalion Chaplain.

There were three hundred people in that village. I am certain that they are only alive today because that Chaplain stopped me from acting. I flipped the ***switch***, having long since killed myself. I was going to destroy that village and everyone in it. That did not happen because the Chaplain touched my arm and said "No. It will not bring the chaplains back." In that moment, he brought me back to life and civilization. I could never have recovered had he not done this.

This is the razor's edge were you live in combat. You bring it home and you can not put it away. You know exactly where the ***switch*** ... the razor's and you have to choose to live on one side or the other. Emotionally, sometimes, it is just too much, so you shut down emotions in order to survive.

CONCLUSION

I would hope that what I have shared with you is helpful in understanding combat stress and the people who live with it. I believe that my experiences are not unique...that they are valid ... that they are real. There are many kinds of stress and many types of related stress disorders. I believe that combat stress, both directly and indirectly induced, is real. Maybe someone you know has it.

There are many young men among the police, firemen and paramedics who have served in the military who may have combat stress. If so, they are living with two kinds of stress, the stress from their current high-risk job and the combat stress they brought with them from combat. I believe that those who take high risk jobs gravitate to danger. They find solace in danger. They understand it and are at home with it.

As you talk with such people, I would ask you to remember that when an young man comes back from combat he is not a killer but he has learned to kill. He is not animal but he has had to learn to live like an animal, survive like animal. He is seeking somehow to put these two pieces of his life into perspective. He takes his life apart in a moment and will spend the rest of his life putting it back together. Remember how combat stress disorder occurs. It is not something that grows. It is something that explodes inside of you! Once it explodes, it is hard to take all those pieces and put them back together.

As our great country continues to send its young men and in its young women into combat, we must be prepared to help them while they are there and to help them and their families when they return. Help them to rejoin the living and place their combat experiences in proper perspective with the rest of their lives. Otherwise, many will never be able to return.

I hope that what I have offered is a helpful perspective on traumatic stress, not only as it relates to combat, but as it relates to any cause. Traumatic stress is a highly personal experience and is best understood with the aid of a personal perspective. To that end, I offer this personal account.

Chapter 6

A CHILDHOOD DREAM

JOHN HAVENHILL

I had a dream, a childhood dream that has come true.
That of being a Firefighter and helping a child or saving a life or two.
It's an exciting profession, one filled with joy tempered with times that can make you sad,
Like experiencing the loss of a comrade, someone's son, mother or dad.
Every time the bell rings a question comes to you, will this be my last call;
Or will there be others too?
It's a profession filled with dedication and pride, motivated by team work, stimulated by fear.
Then there are those calls where you have to struggle to fight back your tears.
So if I don't come back from a call. Please tell my family and friends that I loved them all, fore I was happy living this dream come true.
God Bless my comrades and citizens too,
For I gave my life for you, fulfilling this childhood dream that had come true.

John Havenhill • Firefighter, Emeryville, California.
In G.S. Everly, Jr. Innovations in Disaster and Trauma Psychology, Volume One: Applications in Emergency Services and Disaster Response. Baltimore: Chevron Publishing Corp, 1995.

John Havenhill has been a firefighter for the city of Emeryville in California for 15 years and is a member of the CISD team for the county. During the Eastbay Firestorm in 1991, John and his engine company were overrun by fire five times while protecting citizens as they escaped from the firestorm. The loss of Battalion Chief Riley inspired him to write this poem. This poem was dedicated to Battalion Chief Riley, his family, and fellow firefighters in Oakland.

PART II

INNOVATIONS IN PROGRAM DEVELOPMENT

PART II

INNOVATIONS IN PROGRAM DEVELOPMENT

The purpose of Part I of this volume was to provide the reader with a basic foundation as to the nature of traumatic stress and its potential impact upon emergency service personnel, disaster response and humanitarian aid workers, as well as public safety personnel (including military). This foundation was provided in the form of both academic and personal discussions. In Part II, we shall review important innovations in program development designed to prevent or mitigate traumatic stress for the aforementioned professional groups.

In Chapter Seven the overarching field of critical incident stress management (CISM) is reviewed by one of the individuals who pioneered and developed the CISM field. Chapter Seven offers brief definitions of the interventions which are the primary constituents of CISM. A brief historical perspective is provided as well.

Chapters Eight through Eleven represent discussions of pioneering CISM programs. These chapters include discussions of relevant rationales as well as various intervention techniques employed in the programs under discussion. Chapter Eight describes a CISM program developed in Australia. Chapter Nine describes a CISM program created in Western Canada. Chapter Ten specifically examines the unique challenges associated with the development of a CISM program for law enforcement personnel. Finally, Chapter 11 provides a useful view of stress management for disaster workers written by one of the key architects of the field.

Chapter 7

ESSENTIALS OF CRITICAL INCIDENT STRESS MANAGEMENT

JEFFREY T. MITCHELL

INTRODUCTION

In the course of the last two decades, the Critical Incident Stress Debriefing (CISD) has become an extremely popular group intervention for individuals exposed to powerful traumatic events. Today there exists over four hundred specially trained (combination mental health professional and peer support personnel) teams which operate in a dozen countries. With the proper training and supervision, these teams can provide the CISD process as well as other support services to groups of traumatized people after work place trauma or major community wide traumatic events or disasters. Estimates are that in excess of twenty thousand of the seven phase, structured Critical Incidents Stress Debriefings have been provided and the anecdotal reports of successes along with some recent standardized empirical studies are quite encouraging (Dyregrov, 1989; Dyregrov and Mitchell, 1993; Mitchell, 1983, 1988a, 1988b; Mitchell and Everly, 1993, 1995; Burns and Harm, 1993; Leeman-Conley, 1990; Meichenbaum, 1994: Ravenscroft, 1994; Robinson and Mitchell, 1992; Robinson, 1994; Shalev, 1994).

Jeffrey T. Mitchell • University of Maryland Baltimore County, Catonsville, Maryland.

In G.S. Everly, Jr. Innovations in Disaster and Trauma Psychology, Volume One: Applications in Emergency Services and Disaster Response. Baltimore: Chevron Publishing Corp, 1995.

The popularity of the CISD, unfortunately, has overshadowed the fact that *the CISD process is only one technique within a comprehensive system of interventions* called comprehensive "Critical Incident Stress Management" (CISM). There are many processes in a comprehensive CISM program which have been designed primarily to achieve three objectives. CISM aims to prevent traumatic stress whenever possible, mitigate it should it occur, and accelerate maximal recovery from psychotrauma with the goal of restoring traumatized people to full function in their work and personal lives. The use of the CISD outside of the context in which it was developed (that is , CISM) may be helpful, but it lacks the significant power it could have when used in conjunction with other important and powerful prevention and intervention approaches. Additionally, the use of the CISD instead of psychotherapy where such therapy may, in fact, be required is an inappropriate and potentially dangerous application of the CISD method.

This chapter will provide an important and useful overview of a comprehensive approach to prevention, intervention, and recovery strategies for the management of traumatic stress. Indeed, this chapter should be considered the core around which most of the other chapters in this book revolve.

THE HISTORY OF CRITICAL INCIDENT STRESS MANAGEMENT

Contrary to popular belief, the Critical Incident Stress Debriefing (CISD) did not come first. Rather, Critical Incident Stress Management (CISM) was developed first. Later, CISD was developed within the context of CISM to meet the specific needs of emergency services personnel who were encountering extremely stressful events. In fact, the developer of seven phase CISD process, which is so widely used today, was teaching the principles of CISM long before the first article on CISD was published in 1983 (Mitchell, 1976, 1981, 1982).

CISM has its roots in the field of crisis intervention which was initiated by such luminaries as Gerald Caplan and Eric Lindemann, who developed the theory base and general principles and practice of crisis intervention in the aftermath of the tragic Coconut Grove fire in Boston in 1942 (Lindemann, 1944; Caplan 1964, 1976; Canning, 1976; Parad, 1965; Aquilera et al., 1974). Those very same principles, which were developed by Caplan and Lindemann, have been utilized during the last five decades as a basis for traumatic intervention and recovery in a broad spectrum of settings including disaster work, telephone counseling, family interventions, rape and incest trauma, just to name a few (Berg, 1970; Mc Gee, 1974; Burgess and Baldwin, 1981; Dyregrov, 1989; Slaikeu, 1984).

The development of an organized, systematic approach to critical incident stress management (CISM) arose as a direct result of the author's work with emergency personnel who rely on logical structures, team work and organization, and a systematized and carefully facilitated approach to bringing order to chaos. CISM was more likely to be used by the emergency services personnel if it too was systematized and structured in a manner which was very similar to every other procedure they must learn to do their jobs.

One of the key elements of a comprehensive approach to CISM is education. It was certainly one of the very first CISM components put into place for emergency personnel. Stress education programs were developed to provide prevention oriented information before traumatic stress occurred. It was also important to provide stress information after psychotrauma. Stress education after the fact is important because good information helps to lower anxiety and put the entire situation into its proper perspective. Education in the CISM field entails information which can be used to assist others as well as information which could be used to assist an individual to take better care of him or herself. Both features of a CISM education program were in place in the mid seventies (Mitchell, 1976, 1981, 1982).

There were several other significant features of CISM in place in the mid seventies and early eighties. These included peer counseling programs, significant other support programs, community and disaster outreach programs, demobilizations, defusings and on-scene support services. From the earliest development of CISM services there has been a need to provide effective follow up for every intervention provided (Tindall, 1985; Harvey et. al., 1991; Mitchell. 1992; Mitchell and Bray, 1990, Mitchell and Everly, 1993; Robinson, 1994).

Now that the CISD process was placed within an historically accurate position in the context of a broader program of stress prevention and intervention processes (CISM), we will now review the core elements of Critical Incident Stress Management.

COMPONENTS OF CRITICAL INCIDENT STRESS MANAGEMENT

Any stress prevention or intervention program which relies exclusively on one specific intervention or process is not likely to achieve maximal effects. It is impossible for any one intervention to be equally effective to all people at all times under all circumstances. Excessive reliance on stress education alone or only on the CISD process, for example, can easily set the stage for a failure which could negatively effect the confidence of the provider of the "help" and, more importantly, damage the recipient of that assistance. Warnings about the over-reliance on one specific intervention have been made frequently in the past (Mitchell and Bray, 1990; Raphael and Wilson, 1993; Mitchell and Dyregrov, 1993; Mitchell and Everly, 1993,1995; Meichenbaum, 1994; Moran and Britton, 1994; Shalev, 1994; Mitchell, 1994; Sloan et al., 1994).

When a traumatic stress management program is being developed, the word, "comprehensive" should be kept in mind. A comprehensive approach is a multi-faceted approach. A comprehensive approach requires a range of interrelated and connected processes which are carefully managed to assure the greatest potential for the achievement of the goals of prevention of or recovery from psychotrauma.

The following sections of this chapter will outline and describe the various components of a truly comprehensive Critical Incident Stress Management program. It should be noted that the components of CISM have been loosely divided into three main segments. Pre-deployment or pre-exposure includes components which occur before people are exposed to traumatic events. The deployment or exposure section describes interventions which can be utilized during the traumatic situation to maintain the health and function of those involved in the incident. The post stress or post exposure section explores interventions which can mitigate the impact of the event and encourage people to achieve maximal recovery. Some CISM strategies transcend the somewhat arbitrary boundaries which have been presented in this paragraph and are found in all three segments.

PRE-EXPOSURE STRATEGIES

THE CISM TEAM

To achieve practically anything in stress management within an organization, individuals must commit themselves to the intense work associated with the formulation of new and specialized programs and procedures. Interested individuals may soon lose focus and tire of the work unless they are guided by specific goals and by enthusiastic leaders. Team work is the very best approach to the development of a critical incident stress management program.

It will take a team to provide the education to the other members of the organization. Team members will be the ones with the additional special training it takes to maintain the stress management programs. It will be teams who provide the defusings and debriefings, community outreach programs and disaster services. Trained team members will be the ones who provide the peer counseling services, advise the management and who assist in many other stress management processes.

An organized CISM team is required to keep a CISM program going. Most CISM teams are combination teams. That is, they have members who are drawn from the personnel in the organization (peer support personnel) and from mental health services as well. Efforts should be made in the very beginning of a stress management program to recruit the best possible team members and to provide them with the best available training. The team should pick its leadership carefully. Mental health professionals need to be chosen to provide the supervision and expertise to the team. The team should be tasked with the full development and continuation of the CISM services.

Once organized, a team should meet regularly and plan its activities. It is important that the team be seen as an on-going entity, not just a group of people who respond when there is trouble. Good CISM teams are active with the health and welfare issues of the organizations they serve. They teach, they advise, they support all members of the organizations they have been designated to serve (Mitchell and Everly, 1995).

SCREENING

Pre-exposure stress management strategies include the careful screening and selection of personnel who will work in positions in which they might be exposed to significant stress. If traumatic stress exposure is expected as a routine in certain jobs such as law enforcement, fire fighting or nursing or emergency medical services, then some effort should be made to select candidates who have a better chance of survival in those specific fields. It takes emotionally strong and healthy people to withstand the rigors of a career in a field frequently exposed to traumatic events. Employers would be wise to match the requirements of the job with the personalities, capabilities and limitations of the employees.

ORIENTATION

One way to reduce stress is to fully orient a person to their job before they enter into a situation in which they are expected to perform their duties. It is well known that job ambiguity and job conflict are sources of considerable work place stress (see Everly and Girdano, 1979). Employees should also be made aware of the usual stressors they are likely to encounter in the performance of their duties.

When faced with unusual events such as disasters, it would be helpful for those entering the situation to obtain thorough briefing concerning the event so that they might mentally prepare themselves to manage the situation effectively. Two things which usually cause a considerable stress reaction are surprise and underestimation. Situations which catch people off guard and cause a period of mental confusion may result in injury or a reduction of their performance abilities.

EDUCATION

As mentioned earlier in this chapter, stress education is one of the most important elements of a comprehensive CISM program. It is most helpful when it is provided before people are exposed to the events which produce psychotrauma. The experience of the professionals in the stress management field is that stress knowledge helps people prepare for the potential of stress in their work or in personal lives. They can make arrangements to protect themselves better with stress knowledge and thus mitigate the impact of certain experiences on their lives. Even in situations in which they cannot protect themselves from the impact of traumatic stress, they can recognize their reactions earlier and choose to obtain help more rapidly.

Stress education should begin in the recruit schools, training academies, or orientation programs for professions with a high risk for exposure to traumatic stress. Early education helps to establish the proper attitudes for stress management for the person's entire career. Stress education, however, should not stop with the completion of the academy or recruit school. It should continue over the course of the career by means of periodic continuing education or in-service education programs. The maximum effect of stress education can be achieved in this manner.

The typical topics covered in a Critical Incident Stress Management education program would be:

- Nature of stress
- Critical Incident Stress
- Types of events most like to cause distress
- Immediate effects of stress
- Long-range effects of stress
- Signs and Symptoms of general stress
- Signs and Symptoms of Critical Incident Stress
- Survival techniques for general stress
- Survival techniques for Critical Incident Stress
- The functions of a Critical Incident Stress Team
  - defusings
  - debriefings
  - peer counseling
  - significant other support
  - community outreach
  - follow up services
  - etc.
- Finding help when it is needed
- Utilizing personal and professional resources

(Mitchell and Everly, 1994)

The main idea behind stress education is the establishment of a protective barrier against psychotrauma and to point out the mechanisms by which people can quickly reduce and conquer significant stress generated by work place trauma or disturbing events in their personal lives.

Even though the experience of stress experts supports the concept that stress knowledge helps to reduce the impact of stress and assists in rapid recovery, some groups fear that knowledge about stress would cause trouble for their organizations. These groups felt that knowledge of stress reactions would establish an environment in which people would know enough about stress to take advantage of their organizations by means of false stress disability claims and other harmful actions. Even today, some groups actively resist the introduction of comprehensive stress management programs into their organizations. Thankfully, the number of resistors is decreasing as the success of stress education programs is repeatedly demonstrated.

PREPLANNING

The management of the organization has an obligation to preplan the organization's response to traumatic events. Policies should be established for emergency operations, communications, death notification processes, managing the media, using the CISM team, coping with dignitary visits, and providing debriefings and / or other services. On matters which relate specifically to Crisis Intervention and CISM, the CISM team should be brought into the preplanning sessions.

Established preplans should be tested by means of drills and detailed discussions. Any required improvements should be made and everyone in the organization should be advised of the changes. Written policies should be drawn up and copies should be distributed throughout the organization. No preplans should be allowed to gather dust for a year without being tested and / or reviewed.

One effective written policy of an organization would be that "Good management equates to good Critical Incident Stress Management" or "Good Critical Incident Stress Management *is* good management". When such a policy is endorsed by top management, it is easier to have it accepted and used by people at lower levels of management.

CISM STRATEGIES DURING TRAUMATIC EXPOSURE

When a traumatic event occurs, members of the CISM team swing into action. But their efforts alone may be less than effective unless the organization has participated in preplanning sessions like those described in the paragraphs above. If the organization is unprepared to accept CISM, it will not work as effectively as it might.

Assuming that a crisis plan is in effect, the CISM team can achieve a great deal. Initial services it provides are often called "On scene" support services or "mid-action" support services. These services are a form of "emotional first aid". The services are practical, common sense actions which lower stimuli, remove people from highly stressful conditions and enhances people's abilities to cope with traumatic situations. The SAFE-R model of crisis intervention discussed in Chapter 12 is an effective mid-action support mechanism.

Here are some other support services provided by CISM team members during a distressing situation:

- briefings before deployment to the situation
- assignment of specific tasks
- clarification of leadership
- appropriate rest breaks
- food and fluids for long events
- rotation of work crews
- updated briefings as conditions change
- rest / sleep areas in prolonged incidents
- lavatory facilities
- one-on-one contacts to those showing obvious distress
- necessary advice to supervisory and management staff
- temporary removal if individual stress unresolved
- alterations of tasks
- orientation to time passage
- controlling media access
- clean changes for soiled clothing / gloves
- stimulus reduction
- emphasis on safety
- etc.

(Mitchell and Bray, 1990)

POST STRESS INTERVENTIONS

DEMOBILIZATION

Demobilizations are always associated with a disaster or a large scale event. They are short (ten minute) informational presentations which are usually made during the first and second shifts at a disaster. Demobilizations are given to small teams of workers who have worked together during a disaster. The ten minute informational mini-lecture is then followed by about twenty minutes of rest, food and fluids before the personnel are returned to routine duties (not back to the disaster site). Once a working team is sent to the demobilization center, they do not return to the disaster site. They may go to other routine duties elsewhere in the community, but not at the disaster site until at least twelve hours have passed. Demobilizations are always followed several days later by a Critical Incident Stress Debriefing (CISD).

The main goal of a demobilization is to provide everyone who worked the disaster or large scale incident with some information which might help them to cope with their stress for a few days until a full debriefing (see below) can be provided. A secondary goal is to observe the participants to see if there is anyone who has special needs. If any are identified they are offered the opportunity to briefly discuss the incident with a CISM team member. They of course may refuse to speak if they choose not to. No one is ever obligated to speak during or after a demobilization.

During the demobilization a CISM team member makes the ten minute presentation. Generally the demobilization reminds the participants that some may have stress symptoms after working such an awful scene and some may not. A list of possible cognitive, physical, behavioral, and emotional symptoms are given to the participants. Then they are also given advice as to how to keep their stress reactions under control. They are usually advised to eat properly, get rest, exercise, reduce caffeine intake, and watch out for alcohol use which has a great potential to make things worse.

Demobilizations are very brief and very action oriented. The small working groups are processed through the demobilization center one after another until every one has been processed through the center. Sometimes, two or three groups are being given the same information at the same time by two or three CISM team members. One CISM team member works with one small group at a time, but multiple groups may be going on in different parts of the room simultaneously.

When all of the personnel have been processed through the demobilization center one time the CISM team members begin to plan for the CISD's which will occur during the next week to ten days. A CISD is a follow up service for a demobilization. Other services may also be necessary for some individuals. For example, some might benefit from a one-on-one peer counseling session. Others may need psychotherapy (this is a relatively rare occurrence among emergency personnel).

Demobilizations are very limited processes. They provide useful information only and in no way are they to be considered a substitute for debriefings, counseling or other support services. They should only be presented by trained CISM team members to avoid the complication which arise when untrained people attempt to provide services to distressed personnel (Mitchell and Everly, 1995).

DEFUSING

Defusings, along with mid-action crisis intervention services, are among the most frequently employed CISM techniques. In essence, defusings are shortened debriefings. Most often defusings are led by a team of two or three peer support personnel. A defusing usually takes under one hour to provide. They are relatively easy to direct and although they are not time consuming, they results can be very powerful.

For best results, a defusing should be held within about eight hours from the resolution of a traumatic event. The shorter the time frame between the ending of the event and the beginning of the defusing, the better the results are likely to be.

A defusing is aimed at a small working group which experienced a traumatic event together. Defusings are conversational in tone.

There is no demand on the participants to discuss anything which they wish to avoid. The team members can ask a wide range of questions about the traumatic experience of the group. If the responses get too deep and personal, team members will shift the focus of the questioning to lighter questions.

There are three parts to a defusing. They are:

- Introduction
- Exploration
- Information

In the introductory remarks phase of the defusing, the CISM team members introduce themselves, describe the defusing, set forth the guidelines for the process, and encourage the participants to actively discuss the traumatic experience. The second phase of the defusing is initiated when the peer support team members ask the participants to describe their experience of the traumatic event. The team lets the individuals in the group freely talk while they monitor the comments of the participants. They then ask any questions which they feel are appropriate to bring out the most important information about the traumatic experience. When the discussion of the experience begins to fall off and the team has no further questions, a decision is usually made to enter the third and final phase of the defusing which is the information phase. In this phase, the team members provide information which can be helpful to the participants during the next few days until the distress resolves on its own or until the team can organize a full CISD (see below) if one is necessary. The information provided in the third phase of the defusing suggests rest, proper food, exercise, and many other stress control strategies.

A properly run defusing will usually accomplish at least one or two main objectives. A defusing will either eliminate the need to do a CISD or it will enhance a CISD if one is still necessary. In addition stress reduction information is usually well received by the participants. At the very least everyone in the defusing comes away from the experience with more information about the incident than they had before the defusing. That information typically lowers the level of tension in the group which has been stirred by individuals focusing too heavily on their own unique perspective (Mitchell and Everly, 1995).

CRITICAL INCIDENT STRESS DEBRIEFING (CISD)

The CISD is the most complex of the interventions utilized after a traumatic incident. It is not psychotherapy or a substitute for psychotherapy. Instead, it is a group discussion of a traumatic event designed to mitigate the impact of a severe stress experience. It is designed to be used as a prevention process against the development of traumatic stress reactions. And, the CISD has been developed to accelerate the recovery process of a "normal" population which has been exposed to severe stress (Mitchell, 1983).

The CISD process is conducted only by trained CISM team members who have taken at least a two day basic Critical Incident Stress Debriefing course, or its equivalent. CISD's have seven phases (Mitchell and Everly, 1995). Those are:

- Introduction
- Fact
- Thought
- Reaction
- Symptoms
- Teaching
- Re-entry

The CISD process can take up to three hours to complete. The length of time for the debriefing varies according to group size and the intensity of the material to be processed. Only those who were directly involved in the traumatic event are brought into the debriefing. Observers are simply not allowed.

In the introduction phase the ground rules are explained and the group members are encouraged to actively participate. The fact phase is the phase in which group members can briefly describe, from their own perspective, what they experienced during the traumatic incident. The thought phase of the CISD helps the participants focus in on their own thoughts which occurred while they were engaged in the incident.

The fourth phase of the CISD process is the most important phase. It is called the reaction phase. During this phase, the group members discuss the parts of the situation which they found hardest to cope with. Participants are asked what part was the very worst for them personally. The participants describe the aspects of the situation which caused them the most distress. Elements of the CISD process especially the reaction phase may be therapeutic. However, the reader is reminded that the CISD process is prevention oriented, not treatment oriented.

The fifth phase of the debriefing is the symptoms phase in which the participants describe their own cognitive, physical, emotional, and behavioral signs and symptoms of distress. The teaching phase immediately follows the symptoms phase. The CISM team now teaches the group a number of helpful stress reduction strategies and emphasizes some common sense approaches to staying healthy in the midst of stress. The team then leads the debriefing into its final phase, the re-entry phase. The participants are asked if they have any questions or if they have any statements to make before the debriefing concludes. The CISM team members then make final statements and the group is released.

Debriefings are usually followed by some simple refreshments. This is an ideal time for CISM team members to approach individuals who might be in need of one-on-one counseling or other services (Mitchell and Everly, 1995).

INDIVIDUAL CONSULTS

There are many times when individual consults are more appropriate than group processes. After the CISD, as described briefly above, individuals may gain substantial benefit from one-on-one contacts with peer support members of the team or with CISM trained professionals such as mental health professionals or clergy personnel. The SAFE-R crisis intervention model discussed in Chapter 12 is, once again, an excellent model for one-on-one intervention.

If only one or two people are distressed by the traumatic experience calling an entire group together is not a wise idea. Those who are not affected by an incident will resent the few who are. A one-on-one support is indicated in these circumstances. In many cases, individuals will contact members of a CISM team for assistance with non critical incident stress situations such as conflicts with a supervisor or marital discord. This is one major reason why peer counselor training is highly recommended for peer CISM team members (Mitchell and Everly, 1995).

OTHER CISM SERVICES

The key CISM services were listed in the sections of this chapter above. The list is not complete, however, and it cannot be adequately completed in this chapter. One reason is the fact that space does not permit a complete presentation of all of the CISM services within this chapter. It would, in fact, require a moderate sized book to cover the details necessary to adequately cover each of the items on list of CISM services.

Another reason why a complete coverage of CISM services is not possible in this chapter is that the list continues to expand over time. Creative thinkers who see needs in the people they serve are constantly adding new services to CISM list. The following items are some of the items which currently hold a space on the CISM list of services:

- ***Chaplain services***. No one should underestimate the spiritual needs of individuals who are exposed to traumatic events. CISM trained clergy personnel play a vitally important role in the management of psychotrauma.

- *Significant other support services.* The significant others of operations personnel are often hurt indirectly by the traumatic events which affect their loved ones. They need support and guidance. This can be provided by trained CISM team members. Support of the operations personnel without simultaneously supporting the environment in which the operation person lives is indicative of poor support for the personnel in the organization. One type of support goes hand in hand with the other.

- *Family support services.* Families of emergency personnel are very important in the overall support of the services personnel. Families and children have special needs which must be addressed by the CISM services. To neglect these people is equivalent to neglecting the personnel themselves. Family support services are a logical extension of significant other support services.

- *Community outreach programs.* In many places tragic events have occurred and there were little to no organized services to assist the community members. It has frequently happened that CISM teams were called upon to assist such communities. Trained CISM teams of both professional and peer support personnel have been very successful in reaching out to provide a wide range of support services to the communities. These services went well beyond the provision of debriefings or defusings.

- *Research and development.* Since the CISM services list is capable of expansion as described earlier, it is important that the CISM services which are rendered are evaluated for their effectiveness and that new services be developed as the needs are identified.

(For additional information on all of the CISM services described in this chapter see Mitchell and Everly, 1995.)

FOLLOW UP SERVICES

CISM teams have an obligation to follow up on each and every service they provide to make sure that they have achieved the basic goals of CISM which have been presented earlier in this chapter. Without follow up some traumatized people might continue to suffer unnecessarily. Follow up services are provided by a number of means. They include, but are not limited to:

- One-on-ones contacts
- Home visits
- Work site visits
- Telephones calls
- Small group meetings
- Referrals for professional services
- Education programs after psychotrauma
- Etc.

Peer support and clergy team members tend to do more of the follow up services than mental health team members because they are generally more available than the mental health professionals.

Follow up services are always required at least to check to see that stressed people are doing all right and are returning to full function (Mitchell and Everly, 1995).

GUIDELINES FOR EFFECTIVE CISM

Effective CISM programs are never an accident. They are carefully planned and managed efforts. They take committment, leadership resolve and dedication. A frequent mistake is to think that a CISM is a mental health professional's task. CISM services are, instead, an organizational committment which is part of good management. Mental health professionals are vital to a Comprehensive CISM program. But the development, coordination and administration of a CISM program is the responsibility of the organization.

The utilization of peer support personnel is another key element in effective CISM programs. This is especially so in emergency services organizations. Most stressed personnel are more likely to listen to one of their own than a mental health professional. Peers have been a key to success in almost all CISM programs.

Multiple CISM teams which cover the same jurisdictions are not always healthy nor effective. Instead, there is usually unnecessary competition between the groups which causes resentment and in-fighting. Coordination between teams which border each other is very desirable. Mutual aid support is also desireable since the provision of services to people who are too emotionally close to the providers is a potentially dangerous process. Communication between teams is very important.

Every person who works on a CISM team should have the proper training to do so. Peers, clergy and mental health professionals should complete a minimum two day approved CISD basic course before serving on a team.

CISM programs should have at least some standardization. One set of guidelines has been proposed by the International Critical Incident Stress Foundation which is headquartered in Ellicott City, Maryland.

CONCLUSION

Psychological trauma is not likely to disappear. The health and safety of workers in a variety of professions is jeopardized by traumatic events. CISM services offer a new hope that traumatic stress can be mitigated and overcome. Effective and inexpensive programs now exist and more are being developed to assure that stressed workers do not have to suffer in silence.

Human being are the most valuable resource in any organization. The time has come to take much better care of them through CISM services. The following chapters within this section discuss pioneering CISM programs.

REFERENCES

Aguilera, D.C., Messick, J.M., and Farrell, M.S. (1974) *Crisis Intervention: Theory and Methodology*. St. Louis, MO: C.V. Mosby.

Berg, D. (1970). Crisis intervention concepts for emergency telephone services. *Crisis Intervention*, 4, 11-19.

Burgess, A. W. and Balwin, B.A. (1981). *Crisis Intervention Theory and Practice, a clinical handbook*. Englewood Cliffs, NJ: Prentice Hall, Inc. 1981.

Burns, C. and Harm, N. (1993). Emergency Nurses' Perceptions of Critical Incidents and Stress Debriefing. *Journal of Emergency Nursing, 19,* (5), 431-436.

Caplan, G. (1964). *Principles of Preventive Psychiatry*. New York: Basic Books, Inc.

Caplan, G. (1976). *Support Systems and Community Mental Health*. New York: Behavioral Publications, Inc.

Canning, J. (ED.) (1976). *Great Disasters*. New York: Gallery Books.

Dyregrov, A. (1989). Caring for helpers in Disaster situations: Psychological debriefing. *Disaster Management, 2,* 25-30.

Dyregrov, A and Mitchell, J.T. (1992). Work with traumatized children, *Journal of Traumatic Stress*, 5, 5-18.

Everly, G.S. and Gidano, D.A. (1979). *The Stress Mess Solution*: Bowie, MD: R.J. Brady.

Harvey, J.H., Orbuch, T. L., Chwlisz, K.D., and Garwood, G. (1991). Coping with sexual assault: the role of account making and confiding. *Journal of Traumatic Stress*, 4, 515-532.

Leeman-Conley, M. (1990). After a violent robbery.... *Criminology Australia*, April / May, 4-6.

Lindemann, E. (1944). Symptomology and management of acute grief. *American Journal of Psychiatry*, 101, 141-148.

Mc Gee, R.K. (1974). *Crisis intervention in the community*. Baltimore: University Park Press

Meichenbaum, D. (1994). *A Clinical Handbook / Practical Therapist Manual for assessing and treating adults with Post Traumatic Stress Disorder (PTSD)*. Waterloo, Ontario, Canada: Institute Press.

Mitchell, J.T. (1976). Rescue crisis intervention. *EMS News*. Maryland Institute for Emergency Medical Services Systems, vol 4, 4.

Mitchell, J.T. and Resnik, H.L.P. (1981). *Emergency Response to Crisis*. Bowie, MD: R. J. Brady Co.

Mitchell, J.T. (1982). The psychological impact of the Air Florida flight 90 disaster on fire-rescue, paramedic and police personnel. In R A Cowley, S. Edelstein and M. Silverstein (Eds.), *Mass casualties: a lessons learned approach, accidents, civil disorders, natural disasters, terrorism*. Washington, DC: Department of transportation (DOT HS 806302).

Mitchell, J.T. (1982). Recovery from Rescue. *Response*. Fall, 7-10.

Mitchell, J.T. (1983). When disaster strikes: The critical incident stress debriefing process. *Journal of Emergency Medical Services*, 8, 36-39.

Mitchell, J.T. (1992). Comprehensive traumatic stress management in the emergency department. In MacPhail, E., and Moore, S., *The Emergency Nurses Association Monograph Series: Leadership and Management in Emergency Nursing, 1*, 3-16.

Mitchell, J.T. (1994). Too much help too fast. *Life Net, a Publication of the International Critical Incident Stress Foundation, Inc., 5* (3), 3-4.

Mitchell, J.T. and Bray, G.P. (1990). *Emergency Services Stress: Guidelines for preserving the health and careers of emergency services personnel.* Englewood Cliffs, NJ: Brady / Prentice Hall, Inc.

Mitchell, J.T. and Dyregrov, A. (1993). Traumatic Stress in Disaster and Emergency personnel: Prevention and intervention. In J.P.Wilson and Beverly Raphael (Eds.), *International Handbook on Traumatic Stress Syndromes*. New York: Plenum Press

Mitchell, J.T. and Everly, G.S. (1993). *Critical Incident Stress Debriefing (CISD): An operations manual for the prevention of traumatic stress among emergency services and disaster workers*. First Edition. Ellicott City, MD: Chevron Publishing.

Mitchell, J.T. and Everly, G.S. (1994). *Human Elements Training for emergency service, public safety and disaster personnel: an instructional guide to teaching debriefing, crisis intervention and stress management programs*. Ellicott City, MD: Chevron Publishing Corporation.

Mitchell, J.T. and Everly, G.S. (1995). *Critical Incident Stress Debriefing (CISD); an operations manual for the prevention of traumatic stress among emergency services and disaster workers*. Second Edition. Ellicott, City, MD: Chevron Publishing Corporation.

Moran, C and Britton, N.R. (1994). Emergency Work Experience and Reactions to Traumatic Incidents. *Journal of Traumatic Stress, 7*, 575-585.

Parad, H., ED. (1965). *Crisis Intervention: Selected Readings.* New York: Family Service Association of America.

Raphael, B. and Wilson, J. P. (1993). Theoretical and intervention considerations in working with victims of disaster. In J.P. Wilson and B. Raphael (Eds.), *International Handbook of Traumatic Stress Syndromes.* New York: Plenum.

Ravenscroft, T. (1994). *Going Critical: GMB / Apex and T&G Unions 1994 survey of occupational stress factors in accident and emergency staff in the London ambulance service.* London: GBM / Apex and T&G Unions

Robinson, R. (1994). *Follow-up study of Health and Stress in Ambulance Services Victoria, Australia, Part I.* Melbourne, Australia: Victorian Ambulance Crisis Counselling Unit.

Robinson, R and Mitchell, J.T. (1993). Evaluation of Psychological Debriefings. *Journal of Traumatic Stress, 6* (3), 367-382.

Shalev, A.Y. (1994). Debriefing following traumatic exposure. In R.J. Ursano, B.G. McCaughey and C.S. Fullerton (Eds.), *Individual and Community Responses to Trauma and Disaster: The structure of Human Chaos.* Cambridge, UK: Cambridge University Press.

Slaikeu, K. A. (1984). *Crisis Intervention: a handbook for practice and research.* Boston, MA: Allyn and Bacon, Inc.

Sloan, I.H., Rozensky, R.H., Kaplan, L. and Saunders, S.M. (1994) A shooting incident in an elementary school: Effects of worker stress on public safety, mental health and medical personnel.*Journal of Traumatic Stress, 7,* 565-574.

Tindall, J.A. and Gray, H.D. (1985). *Peer Power: Becoming an Effective Peer Helper.* Muncie, IN: Accelerated Development, Inc.

Wilson, J.P. and Raphael, B., (Eds.) (1993). *International Handbook of Traumatic Stress Syndromes.* New York: Plenum Press.

Chapter 8

CRITICAL INCIDENT STRESS MANAGEMENT IN AUSTRALIA

ROBYN ROBINSON

BACKGROUND

Australia is no stranger to disasters. On Christmas evening 1974, a cyclone descended on the city of Darwin killing 65 people, injuring 1000 and destroying 90 per cent of houses. Most of the population, some 45,000, were left homeless. Although there had been warnings of the impending disaster, no one really believed that the tragedy which was about to unfold would really eventuate. In 1977, 83 people died when a train plunged into a bridge support at Granville in New South Wales, bringing down layers of concrete on the carriages below and the people inside.

In more recent times, 55 people were killed and a further 62 injured in two separate bus accidents which occurred within eight weeks of each other on the north-east highway of Australia (Grafton and Kempsey 1989). Australia has also been unfortunate enough to experience several senseless mass murders; for example nearly thirty lives were lost in three separate events at the hands of gunmen who

Robyn Robinson • Trauma Support Consultants, North Carlton, Australia.
In G.S. Everly, Jr. Innovations in Disaster and Trauma Psychology, Volume One: Applications in Emergency Services and Disaster Response. Baltimore: Chevron Publishing Corp, 1995.

went berserk (Hoddle Street Melbourne, 1987; Queen Street, Melbourne, 1987 and Strathfield Plaza Sydney, 1991). Attacks also have been focused on Police; for example in 1986 a bomb was planted outside the Russell Street Police Complex in Melbourne, from which a female police officer eventually lost her life; several years later two police were gunned down (Walsh Street, Melbourne).

Sections of Australia pose very high fire risks. The well-known 1983 Ash Wednesday bushfires spanned three States (New South Wales, Victoria and South Australia). Prior to 1983, there had been several seasons of rich winter underbrush growth followed by dry hot summers. When the fires started - fanned by high winds - they were unstoppable. Seventy-two people died, over 2,000 homes were destroyed and there was massive destruction to stock and wildlife. Tragically, the casualties included firefighters, which contributed to the then Chief of the Country Fire Authority in Victoria resigning his position, with media reports stating that he could no longer bear the responsibility for the loss of life of his staff.

It falls predominantly on emergency service workers to manage these disasters and, nowadays, assistance is available to help the workers themselves in dealing with traumatic aspects of their job. It has been recognized, in Australia, for many years that disasters can impact on emergency service workers, and there are descriptions of support to them following Cyclone Tracey (Raphael, 1986), Granville (Raphael, 1977; Raphael, Singh, Bradbury & Lambert, 1983-4), and Ash Wednesday (Berah, Jones & Valent, 1984). In addition, there have been short and long term follow-up studies of the firefighters who attended Ash Wednesday (Innes & Clark, 1985; McFarlane, 1984,1986,1988) and study of emergency and rescue workers following the Mount Erebus air disaster (Taylor, 1983). The literature also contains studies which identify day to day traumatic events for workers, such as dealing with the death of children (Robinson, 1984; 1993) and there are personal accounts by emergency service workers of the impact of traumatic events on them (Edwards, 1990). A comprehensive account of the social and psychological impact of disasters on people, including emergency service workers, is presented by Raphael (Raphael, 1986). Also, a literature review of studies of post-traumatic stress disorder in Australia (including studies of emergency service workers) is given by Burges-Watson (Burgess- Watson, 1987).

Since the late eighties, there has been a strong increase in awareness about the effects of traumatic or critical incidents on emergency service personnel and, concurrently, a rapid introduction of programs of psychological support (or CISM) to assist staff and their families. Most emergency service agencies throughout Australia have had some form of debriefing/peer support program in place since the early nineties.

The development of these programs has been an innovation by emergency services and has been carefully watched by other workplaces and professional bodies. Hence, in Australia in 1995, psychological support programs have been established in hospitals (general and psychiatric), defense force services, protective services (e.g. prisons), youth services, welfare departments, departments of education (at primary, secondary and tertiary levels), rehabilitation services, social security departments, banks, petroleum companies, airlines and other industries such as mines. More recently, there has been interest shown by the private sector (e.g. through occupational health and safety) and high risk sports (such as sky diving and surf rescue). There is also provision for psychological assistance to members of the community following disasters. Most States and Territories have legislation which facilitates counseling support to the community once a disaster has been declared.

It is beyond the scope of this chapter to detail the above developments. However, it is important to recognize the positive impact which emergency services have had on other workplaces, and through this to the general community in terms of developing our understanding of trauma and how to best deal with it.

Rapid and effective change has occurred such that, today, it is expected (and not the exception) that there will be assistance to people following major traumatic incidents.

The developments described above do not mean that the task of assisting people following their exposure to a traumatic incident has been completed. Research on the efficacy of support programs and of particular interventions (such as debriefing and defusing) has only commenced (Robinson & Mitchell, 1993) and there is a need to develop theoretical understanding of "normal" trauma response. We are only beginning to understand cumulative trauma and its management, and there are indications that this may be more prevalent than single major incidents (Robinson, 1993). Also, there needs to be better understanding of the different ways in which various kinds of people may be affected by traumatic incidents (e.g. emergency service workers, victims of assault/accident, disaster-struck communities).

This chapter describes the rationale for introducing critical incident stress management programs into emergency services, traces the historical development of this movement then describes its current status including strengths and weaknesses.

Many people have been part of this development. I attempted to describe the major influences and contributors in this chapter and apologize for any omissions.

RATIONALE FOR CRITICAL INCIDENT STRESS MANAGEMENT PROGRAMS

Emergency service personnel can, on a regular basis, be exposed to traumatic situations of the kind which were once described as "beyond the range of usual human experience" and by definition potentially traumatizing (DSM-III). It is therefore interesting to reflect on why there has been the need to so carefully and persistently argue the case for the introduction of psychological support systems to assist workers when necessary. Some people retain the belief that support programs are not needed and these views are often reflected in comments such as "we didn't need this (support)in my day", "these programs will make people less able to cope" and "people who can't cope with trauma should get out of the job".

It is now believed that all human beings have the capacity to show a highly distressed response (with emotional, cognitive, behavioral and physiological components) if they are subjected to a sufficiently distressing or frightening situation. The 1994 definition of post-traumatic stress states that simply learning about a terrible situation (without direct exposure) is sufficient to create a traumatic response (DSM-IV).

There seems to be a common tendency to underestimate the impact of trauma and its duration on people. One reason may be that some traumatic experiences are unusual and uncommon. Thus, it can be difficult for people who experience traumatic events to understand what is happening to them, and it can also be difficult for friends, relatives or colleagues to appreciate the degree of impact or its duration over time. Our general understanding of trauma, as a community, has been limited and we are still in the process of developing knowledge and education about this important area of human functioning.

For emergency service personnel, who pride themselves on their capacity to deal with traumatic incidents, it is not always easy to accept the fact that some situations may have an emotional impact on some staff. Further, recognition of the need for psychological support programs has often come only after tragedy has struck. For example the New South Wales Police peer support program was implemented following the suicide of a police officer who is reported to have been affected by the Grafton bus accident; The Victorian Ambulance Crisis Counseling Unit was established in 1986 following the Russell Street bombing and the first debriefing team in the Northern Territory was created following a hot air balloon accident near Alice Springs in which 13 people were plunged to their death. It is indeed unfortunate when it takes a tragedy to stimulate action.

The first rationale for work-based psychological support programs derives from the understanding that all human beings can be affected by exposure to traumatic events. While pre-employment selection and post-employment training may assist employees to cope with traumatic situations, it is essentially a human condition that even the most skilled and experienced employee can be affected by or have a reaction to a particular traumatic event. These reactions are seen as a normal response to an abnormal event (Mitchell & Bray, 1990). If a workplace exposes an employee to trauma, then that organization has a responsibility to undertake measures to assist the worker.

The second rationale for psychological support programs is economic. Money can be lost through sick leave, early retirement, staff replacement (including education and training) and accident. Further, stressed staff who remain at work may show low morale, anger or withdrawal. They may function below their capacity and/or disrupt others. There may be personal costs in terms of family dysfunction, anxiety, depression, alcohol/drug abuse et cetera, which in turn will become hidden costs to the organization.

Cost-benefit studies on psychological support programs are in the process of being undertaken and reported.

These will test the common sense view that happy, healthy employees work more productively and stay in the workplace longer than do their more stressed colleagues.

HISTORICAL DEVELOPMENT

Professor Beverly Raphael was a pioneer in developing understanding of the impact of disasters on emergency services personnel. She was one of the first people to recognize the need for debriefing of workers such as was organized following cyclone Tracy and the Granville train crash (Raphael 1986).

A major and concerted period of growth began in 1986 with the visit to Australia by Dr. Jeffrey Mitchell, sponsored by the then Social Biology Resource Center in Victoria. Dr. Mitchell toured three States and addressed many audiences of emergency service personnel, mental health workers and people involved in disaster planning. A three day conference was conducted and attended (by invitation) by senior emergency service staff from around Australia. This conference provided the impetus for many delegates to instigate workplace education on trauma management and to develop support services in their own agencies. The clear role and structure of debriefing teams, developed and described by Dr. Mitchell, provided guidelines for many Australians to develop their own programs.

Following this conference, the first Combined Emergency Services Critical Incident Stress Debriefing team in Australia was trained in Melbourne and began functioning in July 1987. This was followed closely by the Adelaide Fire Services Debriefing team and within four years every State or Territory had at least one emergency service debriefing team in place. With this development of teams came a cohesive group of practitioners (mental health practitioners and emergency service personnel) who were at the forefront of developing support services in the emergency services. They were in regular contact with one another through phone and teleconferencing and they shared teaching and resource materials with each other much of which had been forwarded from America. They consulted with one another on how to set up programs and how to solve program implementation problems so that the newer systems were created with a minimum of mistakes. Most teams were trained by a small group of people following the outline provided by Dr Mitchell, and this provided consistency of approach and maintenance of standards. Not everyone followed the "Mitchell model" as it came to be known, and there were logical and sensible changes in some programs which were in keeping with cultural and geographic factors as well as agency needs.

In 1988 a second conference was held, with key speakers from five nations who were expert in this field. Over 300 people attended. The Australians reported on the establishment of debriefing teams and shared many experiences about their activities over the past two years.

The years from 1988 to 1990 were to see many developments including:

1. The establishment of debriefing teams and rudimentary systems of support in almost all emergency services in all States and Territories of Australia.

2. The development of a professional association - the Australasian Critical Incident Stress Association (ACISA). The Australasian Society for the Study of Traumatic Stress (ASTSS) also formed during this time.

3. The development of broad peer support programs in addition to or instead of debriefing teams. Emergency service peer support members were given functions of providing one-on-one counseling as well as group interventions such as debriefing and defusing.

4. The development of systems of psychological support (some but not all based on the emergency service model) in such diverse organizations as defense force services, protective services, hospitals, education department, welfare organizations, banks and industries which experience industrial accident.

A third international conference was held in 1990. Australia was in the middle of a recession, however, the conference still managed to attract over 300 delegates. This conference, unlike the previous two, highlighted Australian speakers and experiences . At this conference the Australasian Critical Incident Stress Association was officially formed and its draft constitution accepted by a general meeting of interested persons. ACISA currently has nearly 400 members (some from New Zealand) and is now incorporated. There are regional divisions in all States and Territories which organize educational meetings, trainings and similar activities. An annual conference is held (hosted by different States/Territories) and a regular newsletter is produced. The national Management Committee of ACISA comprises representatives from all States and Territories and it has an executive which is elected at the Annual General Meeting of the Association.

THE CURRENT STATUS OF CISM PROGRAMS

A brief description of Australia's population and the structure of its emergency services is given as background to understanding the development of CISM programs.

Australia is approximately the same size as the United States of America but much less densely populated (approximately 17 million). Most of this population is concentrated in coastal areas and in the major cities. There are extensive outback and remote areas with minimal or no population.

The emergency services are comprised of police, fire, ambulance and state emergency: these agencies are organizationally independent from one another - though in some States/Territories the emergency services come under the umbrella of a Bureau of Emergency Services or its like. A National Federal Police Agency exists. Fire Services for each State/Territory tend to be divided into Metropolitan and Country Services. Ambulance services are State/Territory organized and function independently. For example they are not, in the main, run from hospitals or fire stations. Very few private ambulance companies exist, though there are indications of changes towards privatization.

Many of the emergency services agencies have developed psychological support services which combine debriefing teams and peer support (Robinson, 1994). Programs often, but not always, operate under a Clinical Director (mental health professional) who may be an employee of the agency or an external, contracted consultant. Some agencies also now have a Peer Coordinator (emergency service personnel) and this position is usually half or full time.

Many programs provide both one-on-one counseling as well as group interventions as described below.

One-on-one counseling One-on-one counseling has traditionally been provided by mental health professionals. For example, many of the police departments have psychology units which have been established for many years. Other emergency services (more recently) have developed social work, psychology and/or welfare positions- though some of these are on a part-time or voluntary basis.

Over the past few years, peer support personnel have been trained to undertake one-on-one counseling and many agencies now have a dual system such that staff may speak either to a mental health person or a peer support person if they require individual assistance. (Robinson & Murdoch, 1991).

The roles of peers in providing counseling has been an innovation in emergency services. Though variations exist in the ways in which peer systems operate, the general parameters are as follows:

1. To provide basic counseling for staff
2. To refer staff, where appropriate, to mental health practitioners
3. To assist mental health practitioners by receiving referrals from them
4. To teach colleagues about critical incident stress and how to access support services
5. To liaise between local mental health professionals and agencies (especially in rural areas)
6. To work on teams with mental health professions following major incidents (e.g. to conduct defusings and debriefings).

The selection of peers requires much care. Selection generally occurs prior to training, though in many programs peers also may be selected out at the conclusion of a training program if either the person or the Clinical Director deems him or her to be unsuitable for the role. There are basically two sets of criteria which are utilized in selection. The first is clinical (peers need to be suitable for this role, have good listening skills, good group work skills, and be substantially free of emotional problems at the time of entry into the program). The second set of criteria is that they be acceptable to their peers in terms of credibility, trustworthiness and ability to maintain confidentiality. Mental health and emergency service personnel work together in selecting peers using a variety of sources of information including observation of participation during training sessions, interviews, references and field reputation. In addition to these considerations, it is recommended that the appropriate senior staff within an agency approve the final set of names and that the team of peers, when considered as a whole, have a diversity of rank (biased towards lower rank), and adequate coverage of geographic locality. Other criteria may be employed to develop the required balance of team members.

Peers operate under the following guide-lines:

1. Confidentiality is always maintained (unless there is an immediate threat to life)

2. Clients are seen on a self-referral basis only

3. Peers may not become advocates for staff nor have the authority (in their capacity as a peer) to endorse stand-down or other entitlements: peers may in some circumstances speak on behalf of a client or suggest leave

4. Peers work on a voluntary basis

The peer system has been particularly successful in States/Territories with large outback areas, where access to mental health professionals is limited or non existent. Following a little apprehension by the field that peers might become "stress assessors", most peer systems are now progressing smoothly and are being well utilized.

Group intervention procedures Group intervention, in most instances, follows the principles developed by Dr. Jeffrey Mitchell. Not all agencies have adopted this approach and some have incorporated elements of his approach into their programs.

In recent years, there has been a trend towards conducting more defusings and less debriefings. The need for more follow-up has been recognized and, following a major incident, it has been found that it may be necessary to maintain contact with staff for many months.

Many of the currently operating CISM teams serve one emergency service only. While several early teams commenced and trained as combined emergency services, this focus has mainly been maintained in the smaller cities and States (for example, Tasmania). Some combined emergency service teams operate independently or semi independently of police services (e.g. South Australia and Canberra), and this situation may have developed because many police agencies already had some form of psychological support service in place (police psychology departments) when the debriefing teams were being developed.

Evaluation data on the outcomes of debriefings has been collected in Tasmania and other places (Robinson & Mitchell 1993; Eeles 1991). Findings are that debriefings are helpful to staff, and that the greater the impact of the event on personnel the greater the perceived benefit. Talking about an incident, especially to others who have been through that same situation, has been reported to be the most useful aspect of the debriefing, together with an opportunity for staff to see that they and their responses are "normal".

Other activities Many emergency services have developed educational programs which have been introduced into recruit and continuing officer education. Also, many agencies have developed "teaching packets" which are used by peers to educate their colleagues about critical incident stress and available support services. There have been training programs for mental health professionals on the clinical management of trauma and working within the emergency services. CISM team training programs have been conducted in all States and Territories of Australia.

Spouse support programs have been initiated with an early success reported by the Western Australian Fire Service.

STRENGTHS AND WEAKNESSES

In reflecting on our developments, it is possible to identify both strengths and weaknesses. The major strengths are as follows:

(i) On a national level, a highly collaborating approach was established between those people involved in establishing support programs in emergency services. Consequently, it was possible to develop a fairly high degree of consistency in protocols and standards in the important early days.

(ii) The combined peer support/debriefing approach has suited the particular geographical and cultural needs of this country and it has fleshed out the ways in which mental health and peer support personnel can productively work together to the benefit of all parties concerned.

(iii) A strong professional network (through the Australasian Critical Incident Stress Association) has developed which now forms a major vehicle for professional development and communication between like minded people in this area.

(iv) There has been rudimentary and ongoing evaluation of the outcomes of debriefing together with an emphasis on the need for research; this has promoted understanding of the debriefing process and other interventions and stimulated research.

THE MAJOR WEAKNESSES AND DIFFICULTIES

(i) The securing of appropriate and sufficient senior management support for programs has been important and a major factor in both the initiation and termination of programs. Positive support ensures healthy programs and lack of support leads, at best, to minimally functioning programs. The quality of service providers (mental health practitioners and peers) has the same potential to affect the success or otherwise of support programs. However, in practice, it has been management factor which has varied. Management support is particularly vital for group interventions, which often have resource implications in terms of staff release to attend debriefings et cetera or peer training.

(ii) Support programs need to provide more information and feedback to senior management on program activities and outcomes. This can be achieved without jeopardizing client confidentiality.

Managers need this information in order to continue their financial and moral support; we have moved past the era when managers can or should take the effectiveness of these programs solely on trust.

(iii) Adequate funding must be secured in order to enable programs to function. This has been particularly difficult given the tight economic constraints which have operated throughout the country in recent times. Increased awareness of occupational health and safety issues has assisted in giving priority to support programs.

(iv) The voluntary nature of program services has not been adequately rationalized. Until this point, many support services were given on a voluntary basis by both mental health practitioners and peer support personnel. Now, most mental health practitioners are paid for all services, and there is divided opinion as to whether or not peers' time should be voluntary. Arguments are becoming more frequent for peers to receive time in lieu (or similar) for their off-duty peer work. There is a need for program service providers and senior management to clarify and resolve these matters.

(v) Inter-agency team liaison needs to be developed. Since most emergency services are organized on a State/Territory basis, support services for any particular agency needs to accommodate a large number of personnel sometimes spread over a large geographical area (such as Western Australia). Between-agency services may not be feasible on a regular basis, nevertheless, a combined emergency service response will likely be necessary in the event of a major disaster.

CONCLUSION

Australia has seen a very rapid growth in psychological support services for emergency service personnel in the late eighties and early nineties. The innovation of the emergency services has been observed by many other workplaces and professional groups which, in turn, have developed programs based on the emergence service experience. Thus the benefits of the psychological support systems developed by the emergency services, have spread to many other workers in the community.

The main emphasis over the past five years has been on establishing programs, training teams and trying to secure minimal budgets. The next decade will almost certainly see a greater focus on accountability and research which examines programs to see whether they deliver what they promise and whether they are cost effective.

This is a field where there is a particular need for collaboration, within emergency services, between services at State/Territory level and also between nations. It is important that open lines of communication be established in the interests of the overall well-being of the people for whom these programs are designed to assist.

There are good reasons for Australians to be proud of their achievements. Special acknowledgment is due to those pioneers around Australia who have ensured that these programs got off the ground and that they continue to function today. We owe much to people from many other countries, such as Dr. Mitchell, for sharing their knowledge, time, and expertise. From these sources, Australians have shaped their own system of psychological support for emergency services and many thousands of people have been assisted as a result. There is much more that we can learn and do. It is a very exciting and rewarding time and one can only speculate on where the next decade will lead us.

REFERENCES

American Psychiatric Association. (1994). *Diagnostic and Statistical Manual of Mental Disorders (Fourth Edition).* Washington DC.: American Psychiatric Association.

Berah,E., Jones,H.J., & Valent,P. (1984). The Experience of a Mental Health Team Involved in the Early Phase of a Disaster. *Australian and New Zealand Journal of Psychiatry*, 18, 354-35.

Burger-Watson, P. (1987). Post-traumatic stress disorder in Australia and New Zealand: A clinical view of the consequences of inescapable horror. *The Medical Journal of Australia*, 147,443-447.

Creamer,M., Burgess,P., Buckingham.W., & Patterson,P. (1989). *The Psychological Aftermath of the Queen Street Shootings*. Melbourne: Department of Psychology, University of Melbourne.

Edwards,G. (1990). What Price Pain: A Personal Report of Stress. *The Australian Firefighter*, 26, 20-23.

Eeles,D. (1991). *Tasmanian Emergency Services: CISD Team Review*. Hobart, Department of Police & Emergency Services.

Innes,J.M. & Clark,A. (1985). The Response of Professional Fire-Fighters to Disaster. *Disasters*, 9/2, 149-153.

McFarlane,A.C. (1984). The Ash Wednesday Bushfires in South Australia: Implications for Planning for Future Post-Disaster Services. *Medical Journal of Australia*, 141, 286-291.

McFarlane,A.C. (1986). Long Term Psychiatric Morbidity after a Natural Disaster: Implications for Disaster Planning and Emergency Services. *Medical Journal of Australia*, 145, 561-563.

McFarlane,A.C. (1988). The Phenomenology of Post Traumatic-Stress-Disorder Following a Natural Disaster. *Journal of Nervous and Mental Disease*, 176, 22-29.

Mitchell,J. (1988). Stress: The History, Status and Future of Critical Incident Stress Debriefing. *Journal of Emergency Medical Services*, 44,47-52.

Mitchell,J. & Bray,G. (1990). *Emergency Services Stress*. New Jersey: Prentice-Hall.

Mitchell,J. & Everly,G. (1993). *Critical Incident Stress Debriefing*, Ellicott City M.D.: Chevron Publishing Company.

Raphael,B. (1977). The Granville Train Disaster: Psychological Needs and their Management. *Medical Journal of Australia*, 1, 303-305.

Raphael,B. (1986). *When Disaster Strikes*. Syndey: Hutchinson.

Raphael,B., Singh,B., Bradbury,L., & Lambert,F. (1983-4). Who Helps the Helpers? The Effects of a Disaster on the Rescue Workers. *Omega*, 14, 9-20.

Robinson,R. (1984). *Health and Stress in Ambulance Services: Report of Evaluation Study Part I*. Melbourne: Social Biology Resources Centre.

Robinson,R. (1993). *Follow-up study of health and stress in Ambulance Service Victoria*. Melbourne: Victorian Ambulance Crisis Counselling Unit.

Robinson, R. (1994). Developing psychological support programs in emergency service ageqqncies. In *Coping with Trauma* by R. Watts & D. Horne (Eds), Brisbane: Australian Academic Press.

Robinson,R. & Mitchell, J. (1993). Evaluation of Psychological Debriefings. *Journal of Traumatic Stress*, 3, 367-382.

Robinson,R. & MurdochP. (1991). *Guidelines for Establishing Peer Support Programs in Emergency Services*. Melbourne: Waterwheel Press.

Taylor,A.J.W. (1983). Hidden Victims of the Human Side of Disaster. *Undro News*, Mar/Apr, 6-12.

Chapter 9

WHAT ABOUT THE PROXY VICTIMS OF A DISASTER?

THE ALBERTA CANADA EXPERIENCE

ROBERT VAN GOETHEM

When emergency service personnel and rescue/response workers are called to the scene of a disaster or major emergency, they become potential victims of an environment that may be filled with pandemonium, confusion, pain, fear and shock. The intensity of what they must cope with at the scene depends upon the scope and magnitude of the emergency and their role in it. They are immediately thrust into the rescue/response ethic and are confronted with a multitude of activities associated with assisting those in danger, assessing the situation and participating in the efforts to mitigate the impact of the event; they may also be involved in providing comfort and support to bereaved as well.

These heroic and, in some cases, dangerous tasks must be carried out amidst the sights and sounds of the emergency. Responders must act quickly and decisively in the face of pain, fear, anger and in some cases, hostility from those whom they are trying to help.

Robert van Goethem • Disaster Services, Alberta Public Safety Services, Edmonton Alberta, Canada.
In G.S. Everly, Jr. Innovations in Disaster and Trauma Psychology, Volume One: Applications in Emergency Services and Disaster Response. Baltimore: Chevron Publishing Corp, 1995.

EFFECTS OF TRAUMATIC STRESS AND CRISIS

Involvement in major emergencies and disasters exposes all participating rescue/response and recovery personnel to significant sources of stress. The effects of being exposed to these distressing, unexpected sights and sounds, combined with less than desirable working conditions, have been known to lead to physical illness or emotional problems (Everly, 1989).

Rescue/response personnel who have been exposed to prolonged emotional contact with severely traumatized survivors may also experience that trauma vicariously (Mitchell & Bray 1990). This is especially true if there is an identification with the survivor or some personalization with the event (Mitchell and Everly, 1993). A study conducted on pre-hospital care personnel in Australia, identified responsibility as a high stressor due to the likelihood of knowing the victims of multi-casualty incident (Robinson and Mitchell, 1993). Knowing the victims can produce powerful, sometimes debilitating reactions which, in some cases, can render the responder too overcome to respond effectively (Robinson and Mitchell, 1993).

Many rescue/response personnel develop protective strategies to deal with their exposure to most gruesome events. In spite of this, many will eventually become involved with a tragedy that is difficult to deal with. Following the San Diego air crash of 1978, in which 145 people lost their lives, approximately 250 body bags were used to recover 10-15,000 body parts (Mitchell and Everly, 1993). Police officers who responded to the disaster scene, experienced a variety of symptoms which included nightmares, difficulty sleeping, loss of appetite. They also reported experiencing heart attack symptoms, migraine headaches, stomach aches, colitis, and musculoskeletal discomfort (Davidson, 1979). As late as August 1986, some 36 persons involved in recovery operations admitted that they were still having difficulties in dealing with their activities at the crash site (Mitchell, 1986).

Regardless of the level of experience and training, it is doubtful that anyone can be completely insulated against the effects of participating in a gruesome rescue/recovery task. One of the after-effects of being witness to carnage connected with disasters is called "death imprint" (Lifton, 1967) which can cause severe feelings of anxiety, being overwhelmed, feelings of vulnerability and a sense of being out of control. Rescue operations have been identified as extremely stressful when extraordinary carnage is involved, particularly when there are no survivors (Robinson and Mitchell, 1993).

The immediate physical consequences of exposure to a stressful event may be increased heart rate, blood pressure and muscle tension, all of which speeds up metabolism, Increases energy expenditure and heightens concentration (Everly 1989). If these physiological changes are extended for too long, occur too frequently, or become too intense, physical discomfort can become quite severe (Everly 1989).

Following an event perceived as highly stressful, physical illness or symptoms, especially nausea and gastrointestinal disorders are fairly common (Everly 1989). For example, within two days following the Coliseum disaster which occurred in Cincinnati, Ohio, in December 1979, "two thirds" of the mental health team members who assisted family members at the temporary morgue became physically ill; they were victimized by their proximity to post disaster activities (Umbenhauser, 1980). A study of 180 workers who had to deal with the gruesome task of repeatedly handling bodies through several stages of the recovery process following the Mount Erebus crash showed that a number of the workers were severely traumatized by their encounter with massive death and mutilation. An initial assessment of that group revealed that 80.5% experienced changes in sleep patterns, 76% reported changes in appetite, 48.9% dazed feelings, 40% changes in interaction and 33% changes in social activities; only 18.5% appeared to be free of symptoms (Taylor & Frazer 1982).

The most frequently observed immediate reactions are anxiety, fatigue (Frederick 1981), hopelessness and moments of melancholy (Taylor 1983).

In a survey of 102 disaster responders, which included 48 rescue and on-site workers, it was found that 90% suffered repeated recall of the event and in 20% of these, recall was severe enough to interfere with daily functioning. About 50% complained of fatigue, anxiety or depression; half of the subjects reported sleep disturbances, 25% had nightmares and almost 45% reported guilt related to the event. Most guilt feelings have been associated with a specific situation, an injured person who could not be kept alive or a rescue effort that was performed too late to be effective (Wilkinson, 1983).

A study of rescue/response and recovery personnel involved in a major rail disaster identified significant endorsement for a post incident support system that provided Critical Incident Stress Debriefings; 90% of the front line personnel reported that CISD's would be "important" or "very important" (Roberts, 1987).

PLANNING AND INTERVENTION STRATEGIES

A strategy needs to be developed within industry and emergency response organizations to mitigate the impact of stressful events on response personnel and protect them from the short term and long term effects of stress associated with emergency response and the stressful day-to-day job activities. Ideally, this strategy would consist of a wellness program which provided education (prevention), post incident stress debriefings (intervention), and confidential follow-up counseling support. The benefit of such a program would be the strengthening and enhancement of the health and coping mechanisms of emergency personnel and personnel exposed to a stressful work environment.

A wellness program must respect the importance of planning and the development of strategies to deal with the impact of repeated exposure to dramatically stressful events (see Everly and Feldman, 1985). Pre-incident stress awareness training can be provided as part of the existing Employee Assistance Programs, using "in-house"" resources. The inclusion of training and awareness would assist personnel in becoming less vulnerable to the harmful effects of stress. A capability must be established which can provide Critical Incident Stress Debriefings (CISD's), while at the same time, establishing a solid "peer support" network and access to outside debriefing resources (Mitchell and Everly, 1993).

Personnel need to be aware of which kinds of stressors are typical to their work environment and the kinds of stress reactions which normally follow exposure to gruesome rescue/recovery activities. They should also be taught techniques and skills for coping with stress. Practice in defining or expressing one's feelings and sharing them with co-workers would help them to be less sensitive about their own stress levels and more willing to seek help and provide assistance to co-workers.

In the absence of "in-house" CISD resources, the most likely support would come from mental health clinicians or properly credentialed social workers. The stigma related to seeking this kind of professional support can be best eliminated and dealt with through affiliation with local resources and including them in the planning and training activities so that a mutual understanding and respect can be nurtured. Response personnel also need to be apprised of the benefits derived from post-disaster stress debriefings.

Early intervention at the scene and immediately after an incident will help personnel cope with the event by interrupting negative processes and minimizing their influence (Mitchell and Everly, 1993).

Intervention at the scene of the emergency may include actions by the incident commander to prevent prolonged exposure to gruesome sights by rotating response personnel to minimize exposure. The availability of an on-site professional to carry out assessment, consultation and remedial intervention appropriate to the interests of the distressed individual and the needs of the response team would be an appropriate role for a mental health clinician or social worker trained in critical incident stress debriefings, provided that role receives the full cooperation of the response organization.

Any intervention on-site, by a professional who is not part of the response organization, must be sanctioned by plan and policy. Interventions that are not acknowledged and approved will not only interfere, but may create added stress for response personnel. It is essential that the need for on-site intervention and post disaster stress counseling be recognized and agreed upon by the response organization in advance.

The major goal of post-incident stress counseling support is to minimize the severity and duration of emotional trauma by helping rescue/response personnel understand and cope more effectively with their own and each other's reactions.

The function of a stress debriefing is to help those who have been traumatized by a major event deal with their emotions by encouraging and allowing the expression of emotions and helping their peers to understand that having such feelings is not only normal, but part of the healing process (Mitchell and Everly, 1993) .

Those who have yet to begin the emotional reconciliation process can be helped to anticipate the psychological effects they may yet experience in the weeks to come. A structured debriefing program delivered to the response group following the incident would be extremely beneficial.

A post-event stress debriefing offers many advantages for emergency personnel. It is an incident specific, focused intervention procedure for releasing pent-up emotions when the intensity of such feelings is likely to be quite high (Mitchell and Everly, 1993). Further, the debriefing process can aid distressed workers by teaching them how to use specific skills for coping with stress and providing support for one another. Most important, it provides an opportunity for personnel to request further confidential professional help if they feel it would be helpful.

Since the normal adjustment process following exposure to an intense, distressing experience may take many weeks and not all people can adjust satisfactorily without some assistance, there must be a means of monitoring the adjustment progress of individuals.

Such monitoring aids in assessment, provide additional opportunity for personnel to express their feelings and be reassured of their normality and make professional support available on an on-going basis.

A well established working relationship between a response organization and professional counseling support resources operates to the advantage of both parties. Working together on a continuous basis increases trust, broadens the perspective and knowledge of both sides and makes for greater efficiency when professional support is required.

Organizing such a support system requires the complete endorsement of the response organization. This can be best accommodated through an education process which reinforces what is already known and removes the suspicion and uncomfortable feelings associated with bringing professional outsiders inside the organization.

Personnel at the sharp end of emergency operations must be educated about the positive benefits of participating in stress workshops and taking advantage of stress debriefings.

It will be important to emphasize within the response organization that preventive measures such as stress management training, on-site and post-disaster intervention (CISD's) followed by confidential follow-up counseling is a necessary involvement against unnecessary loss in morale, capability and efficiency. It may be necessary to develop within existing Employee Assistance Programs, the capability to conduct CISD's and then to identify operational personnel who would function as "peer support" personnel and who would be trained to recognized if and when post disaster debriefing sessions should take place. During these debriefings, those "peer support" personnel would act as facilitators and assist professionals in conducting the debriefings.

Alternatively, linkages could be established with existing CISD resources. However, It would still be necessary for the organization to establish and develop a strong "peer support" network to assist those local resources in conducting debriefings. It has been found that without "peer support" who are familiar with the incident which has necessitated the CISD, debriefings are not quite as successful. It is therefore necessary to develop solid "peer support".

If local resources are used, those resources should be included in exercises and be provided some cross training so as to have a basic understanding of the way the organization functions. In this way, they can earn the respect and confidence of those with whom they will eventually carry out confidential debriefings. This extra-curricular activity of those outside resources would have to be sanctioned by both groups.

In Alberta Canada, the Disaster Social Services Branch of Alberta Public Safety Services functions as the Provincial coordinator for the Alberta CISD Program which was developed and established by the Branch, based upon protocols established by the International Critical Incident Stress Foundation. This Branch has been organizing Critical Incident Stress Debriefing training for mental health professionals from both the public and private sector as well as for emergency services personnel. This training has also been provided for the transportation and petrochemical industries, as well.

DEVELOPMENT OF A CRITICAL INCIDENT STRESS DEBRIEFING PROGRAM IN ALBERTA

The Disaster Social Services Branch, Alberta Public Safety Services (APSS), has, been instrumental in developing a Critical Incident Stress Debriefing (CISD) program for the province of Alberta. Clinical direction and professional support to the program is provided by Alberta Health (Mental Health Services Division). Following the submission of a number of proposals (1986) and follow up meetings, agreement was reached (1990) that Alberta Health would establish a policy concerning their support of a Province wide CISD program which would be Coordinated by APSS.

Alberta Health (a provincial government department) provides its professional support to the program through its mental health division via six geographic areas (regions); each region has a director who is responsible for the operation of approximately eight mental health clinics.

Each Regional Director provides clinical direction and professional support to the CISD program within their region. A coordinator is tasked to coordinate regional activities and to liaise with the Provincial Coordinator (APSS) for program delivery. Clinic managers within the region who have been CISD trained are tasked to function as a Team Leaders under the direction of the regional coordinator. Members of the ambulance and fire service in those communities supported by a Mental Health Clinic are recruited and trained as Peer Support Personnel. The Executive Director for the Mental Health Services Division is responsible for ensuring overall clinical direction to the CISD program province-wide. The role of Alberta Public safety Services Disaster Social Services Branch) is to provide Provincial coordination for CISD program delivery, team development: CISD training workshops, pre-incident stress awareness presentations (ambulance, fire, police), development of a CISD resource registry, and maintain a CISD newsletter to apprise CISD teams of the availability of on-going training, conferences/seminars and literature on the subject of Critical Incident Stress.

Peer supportwithin the various emergency services organizations would identify the need for a CISD and contact APSS/DSS who would then contact the appropriate regional director to set up a debriefing. A CISD Team Leader would be dispatched along with peer support personnel to conduct the debriefing. Following a disaster or major emergency, the Disaster Social Services Branch Director, Alberta Public Safety Services would contact the Emergency Planning Officer for Alberta Health to arrange the deployment of CISD teams to the disaster area should they be required.

It was agreed, following discussions with emergency services personnel, that Alberta Public Safety Services would utilize the services of Dr. Jeffrey Mitchell to conduct CISD training workshops. Candidates would be accepted from Mental Health; Public Health (psychiatric nurses/social workers); and from ambulance, fire and police service (peer support). Debriefers would be selected on the basis of having a group process background, a willingness to be cross-trained, and the desire to participate in the maintenance of a CISD program. It was also expected that trained debriefers would facilitate the development of skills in stress recognition and management amongst designated peer support personnel.

In the beginning, this program was difficult to promote due to firmly held convictions that rescue/response personnel didn't need this kind of support due to their "toughness" and ability to "handle things better than most." Another impediment was some concern that while there were data from studies done on rescue/response in the USA, it could not be assumed that those findings applied to fire, ambulance and police personnel in Alberta. It was suggested that to justify such a program for Alberta, a need for such a program would have to be identified since there were no requests for CISD's being directed to the Mental Health Clinics In the regions.

The Disaster Social Services Branch Director embarked on a project which involved the delivery of Critical Incident Stress awareness presentations to ambulance and fire service personnel. The response to this activity which sought to promote acceptance of CISD teams in Alberta met with considerable success and interest from the ambulance and fire service. A two day workshop entitled "Psychological Response In Disaster Emergencies" was held at the Alberta Public Safety Services Training School; invited speakers were Dr. Michael Blumenfield (New York Medical College), Dr. Vanderlyn Pine (New York State University), Dr. John Keating (University of Washington), and Mr. Mike Reilly (American Red Cross).

Although interest was rapidly growing, there was still the concern that what was needed was hard data that rescue/response personnel in Alberta were also victimized by critical incident stress.

On February 8, 1986, at approximately 8:40 a.m., an east bound VIA Rail passenger train was struck head on by a west bound Canadian National Railways freight train. One of the paramedics at the disaster scene stated, "It's one of the worst I've ever seen ...". This disaster was to be known as the Hinton Rail Disaster.

The Hinton disaster also had a tremendous impact on the residents of both Jasper and Hinton. A news reporter observed that most residents from both communities stayed near radios and television sets to get information on survivors. In Edmonton, friends and relatives converged on the railway terminal to await word and the arrival of survivors who were being bussed into the city.

It has been reported that from an operational perspective, things went extremely well. The town of Hinton had a disaster plan, a plan that worked extremely well. Operations were made easier because of the location of the derailment and access to the disaster site. At the hospital, procedures went smoothly because. like the town of Hinton, the hospital had an emergency plan to deal with the likelihood of a mass-casualty incident.

Something that had not been planned for was follow-up outreach activities and professional counseling support for survivors, bereaved next of kin and stress debriefing counseling for response and recovery personnel. Despite the oversight, Mental Health Services Division of Alberta Health was prepared to respond to the needs of the survivors, the bereaved next of kin, as well as the response and recovery crews. It took but one telephone call from the Director, Disaster Social Services to arrange an information briefing with the Regional Directors to secure the support of Mental Health resources.

Following the rail disaster, sanctions had been obtained to provide Critical Incident Stress Debriefing for the 105 personnel dispatched to the disaster site by Canadian National Railways; unfortunately, the candid remarks of some of the recovery personnel were reported by the press, and sanction was revoked before the debriefings could take place. No amount of assurance regarding confidentiality could turn this situation around; as well, access to rescue/response personnel (fire, ambulance, police) was discouraged due to the perception that it was not really necessary. In spite of a well entrenched stigma associated with seeking counseling support, some rescue/responders (railway personnel, fire, ambulance and police personnel) sought individual support from mental health professionals involved in outreach support.

Problems were encountered in securing the identity and access to survivors and next of kin. Arrangements to get information so as to provide needed outreach had not been obtained from the Medical Examiners Office. Had the mechanics of entry and sanction been addressed, Mental Health professionals could have been dispatched to the hospitals and staging areas to make contact with the survivors to provide counseling support where and when it would have been most beneficial.

Rescue personnel arrived at the disaster site to be confronted by about 100 injured survivors who were described as milling about in a "confused and chaotic state." Some had been heroically trying to rescue others; many had seen fellow passengers literally vaporized before their eyes. Firefighters arrived at the scene and were faced with added dangers of leaking sulfur, diesel fuel and wreckage too hot to approach so that it interfered with any hope of rescuing other persons.

Some of the literature on the subject of disasters and major emergencies suggests that you cannot be in contact with fear, anxiety, pain and chaos without being affected by the pain from witnessing the pain of others (Worden, 1982). I had spoken to some of those on the scene who admitted to being somewhat "overwhelmed by it all"; many admitted to experiencing" unpleasant side effects."

One hundred and five Canadian National Railways (CNR) personnel were sent to the disaster scene to conduct clean-up operations. These personnel would also assist in the recovery of the bodies which were crushed in the midst of the wreckage. Some of those personnel that I had spoken with were quite angry with what they saw; in particular when they were confronted with the remains of railway personnel whom they knew. Some were quite emotional and found it quite difficult to deal with their emotions.

Following the rail disaster, it was decided by Alberta Public Safety Services and Alberta Health (Mental Health Services Division) that a study should be undertaken to identify the perceived needs of rescue personnel and determine if a post-incident program to respond to psychological needs of emergency/response personnel could be justified.

A 30 item form of the General Health Questionnaire (Neuman, Bland & Orn, 1988), to determine the social and emotional needs of persons affected by disaster; as well, a needs inventory were used to learn how rescue/response personnel felt about stress debriefing support systems. This was accomplished by simply asking them to report whether they felt that post-incident debriefings were "important", "very important" or "not very important". In addition, we were interested in learning whether they were looking at changing jobs , whether they had experienced a "change in partnership" and if they were experiencing more visits with physicians due to "physical problems" or "emotional problems". Results indicated that 23 of the 33 Hinton Rail front line respondents (70%) felt that on-site counseling was either "important" or "very important" in terms of perceived need. Further, 30 of 33 front-line Hinton Rail respondents (90%) indicated that post-disaster counseling was either "important" or "very important".

CONTINUED PROGRAM DEVELOPMENT

On July 31, 1987, the City of Edmonton was struck by a tornado that was classed as F-4 in scale (wind velocity in excess of 33 kph). The tornado terrorized residents of the east side of the city for approximately one hour, traveling at a forward speed of approximately 40 kph. In its aftermath were billions of dollars of damage in destroyed property, and 27 deaths.

Within a few hours, Deputy Ministers of the various government departments had arrived at Alberta Public Safety Services HQ (response center) and finalized a strategy to support the city response. Agreement was reached that all existing government programs would be provided at a "one stop" rehabilitation center (e.g. unemployment insurance commission, workers' compensation board, social service, counseling, Alberta housing corporation, central mortgage and housing corporation, insurance, disaster assistance claims, Edmonton telephones, utilities, etc.) so that all of the survivors' immediate needs could be provided as a form of crisis intervention. This plan had been developed by the Disaster Social Services Branch (DSS). As part of this plan, Alberta Mental Health Services Division would provide group counseling support sessions at a pre designated Disaster Rehabilitation Center (DRC) for the direct survivors. Within 8 hours following the onset of the disaster, Alberta Mental Health Service dispatched a Critical Incident Stress trained debriefer to do defusings for Edmonton Ambulance personnel returning from the disaster site(s). Within 72 hours all four shifts of Edmonton Ambulance personnel had participated in a Critical Incident Stress Debriefing. In the weeks that followed, 22 Critical Incident Stress Debriefings had been provided (ambulance service, human services personnel at the Disaster Rehabilitation Center; Red Cross volunteers; Police Victim Support Services Agency; and staff from various small businesses in the industrial park which had been devastated by the tornado).

To deal with the aftermath of the disaster, the DSS Branch arranged for six mental health counselors to be hired and seconded to the Edmonton Board of Health to handle referrals made by Board of Health personnel end conduct outreach activities into the community and at schools.

The availability of Critical Incident Stress Debriefings by Alberta Mental Health Services was due to their support of many of the recommendations which came out of the study of the Hinton train disaster. As a result of this support, Alberta Mental Health Services sent two of their staff to attend a Critical Incident Stress Debriefing training workshop conducted by Dr. Jeffrey T. Mitchell and sponsored by the Commonwealth of Virginia. Arrangements were made by APSS/DSS to send two more staff to a five day workshop on Critical Incident Stress which was held in Cornwall, Ontario the following year.

The Director, Disaster Social Services, Alberta Public Safety Services, continues to conduct educational seminars on Critical Incident

Stress to ambulance and fire services throughout the province of Alberta. Currently, the arrangements are that these in-service seminars will be repeated for each service at two year intervals. Alberta Mental Health Services remains very supportive of this activity in that a CISD trained Mental Health Therapist is tasked to participate in these Awareness Seminars.

The initial strategy was to develop the first Critical Incident Stress Debriefing capability within the Edmonton Region, an area of approximately 12,000 square miles which consists of approximately 50 committees (approximately 19 ambulance services and fire departments), 8 of which have e mental health presence. Servicing this area are 14 psychologists and 59 therapists (psychiatric nurses and social workers).

Alberta Public Safety Services / Disaster Social Service Branch had undertaken the task of securing whenever possible, the services of Dr. Jeffrey Mitchell to conduct two day training workshops on Critical Incident Stress Debriefing. To date, training has been provided in Basic and Advanced CISD and in Peer Support. Candidates for these workshops have been drawn from Mental Health and from the ambulance, fire and police services. Funding for training of Mental Health candidates and selected candidates representing ambulance fire and police service was arranged/provided by the Disaster Social Services Branch of APSS.

Over 60 Alberta Government mental health therapists have been provided CISD training. CISD teams are currently operating in more than 15 Alberta communities; some of the larger communities have more than one CISD team.

The Alberta CISD program has been conducting an average of almost 4 debriefings per month and providing an average of 4 CISD Awareness orientations per month since the development of the program in 1986.

The work of Dr. Jeffrey T. Mitchell towards the development and training of Critical Incident Stress Debriefing teams in the USA has been instrumental in the progress made in Alberta, as we were able to use his efforts, guidelines and progress in the USA as a goal to work towards.

Despite the overwhelming success of the program, it is tragic to note that it has taken a major train disaster to give birth to a CISD program which then acquired its' maturity following a major and devastating tornado; in the aftermath of such destruction, it has been clearly demonstrated that Critical Incident Stress Debriefings do work to the benefit of heroic and dedicated rescue responders.

REFERENCES

Davidson, A. (1979). Air disaster: Coping with stress, a program that worked. *Police Stress*, 1, 20-21.

Everly, G.S. and Feldman, R. (1985). *Occupational Health Promotion.* NY: Wiley.

Lifton, R. (1967). *Death in life: Survivors of Hiroshima.* NY: Random House.

Mitchell, J.T. (1986). Personal communication.

Mitchell, J.T. and Everly, G.S. (1993). *Critical incident stress debriefing: An operations manual.* Baltimore: Chevron Publishing.

Neuman, S., Bland, R. and Orn, H. (1988). A comparison of methods of scoring the GHQ. *Comprehensive Psychiatry*, 29, 402-408.

Roberts, C.A. (1987). *An identification and assessment of the needs of persons affected by a disaster.* Alberta: Alberta Community and Occupational Health.

Robinson, R. and Mitchell, J.T. (1993). Evaluation of psychological debriefings. *Journal of Traumatic Stress*, 3, 367 - 382.

Taylor, A.J. (1983). Hidden victims of the human side of disaster. *UNDRO News*, Mar/Apr., 6-9,12.

Taylor, A.J.W. and Frazer, A.G. (1982). The stress of post-disaster body handling and victim identification work. *Journal of the Human Stress*, 8, 4-12.

Wilkinson, C.B. (1983). Aftermath of a disaster: The collapse of the Hyatt Regency Hotel skywalks. *American Journal of Psychiatry*, 140, 1134-1139.

Worden, J.W. (1982). *Grief counseling and grief therapy: A handbook for the mental health practitioners.* NY: Springer.

Chapter 10

CRITICAL INCIDENT STRESS MANAGEMENT IN LAW ENFORCEMENT

ROGER M. SOLOMON

A critical incident is any situation beyond the realm of a person's usual experience that overwhelms his or her sense of vulnerability and/or sense of control. Common critical incidents for law enforcement personnel include, but are not limited to, line of duty shootings, getting shot, the death or serious injury of other officers, high speed pursuits that end in tragedy, the fight of (and for) one's life, gruesome suicides or homicides, or brutal child abuse cases. Such situations may cause police officers and other emergency personnel to experience unusually strong emotional reactions that have the potential to interfere with their ability to function either at the scene or later (Mitchell, 1983). This chapter will discuss steps that can be taken to mitigate the adverse effects of a critical incident upon law enforcement personnel through the use of critical incident stress management (CISM) programs.

Roger Solomon. • On Site Academy, Gardner Massachusetts
In G.S. Everly, Jr. Innovations in Disaster and Trauma Psychology: Applications in Emergency Services and Disaster Response. Baltimore: Chevron Publishing Corp, 1995.

THE PROBLEM

Two-thirds of all officers involved in shootings experience significant emotional reactions which include a heightened sense of danger, flashbacks, intrusive imagery and thoughts, anger, guilt, sleep difficulties, withdrawal, depression, and stress symptoms (Solomon and Horn, 1986). These reactions are NORMAL REACTIONS TO ABNORMAL SITUATIONS. However, this does not mean that officers automatically or necessarily cope constructively with the emotional aftermath of these events. Without appropriate attention, serious emotional problems, including post-traumatic stress disorder (PTSD), can develop.

Critical incidents include more than shootings. Too often, law enforcement has focused on "the big one" as the incident around which to build programs. Disasters, child victims of violence, doing CPR on a victim who dies, or working a fatal accident where the officer knows the victim, are examples of situations that can overwhelm the officer's sense of vulnerability and lack of control.

In the 1970's, when little was known about critical incident trauma, about 70% of police officers who killed people in the line of duty left law enforcement within five years (Vaughn, 1987). Though a segment of this percentage was, perhaps, due to natural attrition, some of those officers were doubtlessly victims of trauma.

Michael McMains (1991) points out that large departments had reduced that rate to 3% by 1984, while small departments lost two and one-half officers for every one officer involved in a shooting. The major difference between the outcomes was that the large departments had formal policies and procedures to provide psychological support to the involved officers. Programs for resolving the stress caused by critical incidents reduce the loss of trained personnel.

Critical incidents trigger the asking of many soul searching questions and raise stressful issues, such as confronting one's own mortality and emotionally coming to grips with the fact that "it can happen to me." Realizing that he may be relatively powerless to prevent tragedy can be very stressful for the officer who has always coped successfully with the challenge of the job. Dealing with the reality that critical incidents may again have to be confronted may raise questions about whether to stay in law enforcement.

Emotional reactions of guilt, irrationally taking responsibility for events that were beyond his control, and rage that he was involved in the situation are common themes to be worked through. An officer who had to shoot an armed suspect more than a dozen times over a period of several minutes said, "If it was legal, and was necessary, and was righteous, why do I feel like a murderer?" (Flint, 1992). Officers often start questioning their competence and confidence after a critical incident and frequently feel inadequate because they did not achieve an ideal outcome.

The failure to resolve these issues often leads to a variety of negative patterns. Some officers begin to over-react to perceived threats, while others under-react to clear dangers. While some quit prematurely, others become discipline problems or develop increased absenteeism, burn-out, stress disorders, substance abuse problems, or a host of other personal problems that can interfere with functioning at home and on the job.

Officers are given training, firearms, and bulletproof vests to equip them to survive critical incidents. Departments also have a responsibility to equip their officers to constructively deal with and ***Survive*** the emotional aftermath of critical incidents. A Critical Incident Stress Management (CISM) program represents a set of interventions that can help officers cope with the emotional effects of a critical incident (Mitchell, 1983; Mitchell and Everly, 1995).

A CISM program can reduce, and sometimes eliminate, the debilitating effects of critical incidents and cumulative stress. It can promote positive coping behavior, create a more positive work atmosphere, and reduce the emotional isolation often experienced after critical incidents. Although there are little well controlled empirical data, there is widespread agreement among those who address the mental health problems of peace officers that such programs reduce stress symptoms and facilitates emotional recovery (Blak, 1991; Bohl, 1991; Horn, 1991; McMains, 1991; Reese, 1991; Solomon, 1990).

HISTORY AND DEVELOPMENT

Prior to the 1970's, the prevailing police attitude toward psychological stress reactions was, "If you can't stand the heat, get out of the kitchen." Admitting stress symptoms or significant emotional reactions after a critical incident was perceived as a sign of weakness, and threatened one's credibility as a capable officer.

Another reason for the reluctance of officers to admit having reactions was that many thought they were going "crazy." Officers did not know they were experiencing "normal reactions to abnormal situations." Burying emotions, suppressing pain, and keeping up an image of control, were the ways "real cops" dealt with trauma. Unhealthy coping methods such as "choir practice," after work gatherings liberally fueled by alcohol consumption, were common.

Most police agencies did not know how to support officers involved in a critical incident constructively (Solomon, 1988). They were often ignored or treated impersonally and negatively (Solomon, 1988). The stress of such treatment compounded the stress of the incident and created "secondary" injuries (Horn, 1991).

Departments often dealt with officers who had emotional or alcohol problems by "burying" them in some meaningless job and forgetting about them. Quite often, an officer's job was jeopardized by admitting or demonstrating significant problems. One major city chief of police mentioned to the author in the 1970's that "We don't have alcohol or stress problems because as soon as we find one, he's fired."

As a result of those attitudes and actions officers were reluctant to come forward with problems or to seek appropriate treatment. Ignorance about critical incident trauma, poor coping skills, and lack of support or a negative response from the administration caused many officers to leave law enforcement as victims of trauma.

In 1968, the Los Angeles Police Department hired the first in-house police psychologist in the country, Dr. Martin Reiser. Having the availability of psychological services was recognition of the stress inherent in law enforcement and an effort to deal with it constructively. During the next decade, police psychologists and psychological services for law enforcement personnel greatly increased (Reese, 1991).

In 1976, Dr. Michael Roberts, San Jose, California, Police Department Psychologist, coined the term "post-shooting trauma" to illustrate the critical incident reactions of officers involved in line-of-duty shooting situations (Roberts, 1976). He described their reactions and recommended psychological intervention after shooting situations. Others (Solomon and Horn, 1986; Somodevilla, 1986; Stratton, 1984; Shaw, 1981) also started researching post-shooting trauma. This increase in awareness led to programs to deal with post-shooting trauma.

Initially, shooting situations were the main focal point of critical incident programs and were made available primarily to those officers who pulled the trigger. There was little awareness that everyone at the scene potentially had a significant emotional reaction to the incident.

Further, little attention was paid to officers involved in other types of critical incidents. Incidents such as multiple casualty accidents, high speed chases that end in tragedy, gruesome homicides, disasters, traumatic deaths of children, and so on, were not viewed as sufficiently traumatic to warrant immediate psychological intervention. The "macho" image of law enforcement was not ready to recognize that many situations, beyond using fatal force, could trigger an officer's sense of vulnerability. An officer was still expected to "get used" to these tragedies; they were part of the job.

In the 1980's, as knowledge of psychological trauma increased and more officers participated in critical incident stress management programs, law enforcement agencies began to recognize that traumatic incidents included more than just shootings. Post-shooting programs gave way to broader CISM programs that recognized many types of situations as potentially traumatic and as potentially affecting all personnel at the scene.

Prior to the middle to late 1980's, the main thrust of CISM programs was on individual interventions. The value of group debriefings was popularized by Mitchell (1983). Though group debriefings, referred to as a Critical Incident Stress Debriefing (CISD), after critical incidents were conducted prior to Mitchell's work (Wagner, 1979), Mitchell conceptualized a standard debriefing model that applied to, and was well received by, emergency service personnel. The CISD remains the cornerstone of many CISM programs.

As a result of those strides, the number of officers lost to the field after critical incidents is now much lower (McMains, 1991). Also, psychological intervention following a critical incident is now routine in many departments. However, many police administrators and law enforcement personnel are still resistant to recognizing the effects of critical incident stress. Many police agencies still need to initiate the critical incident programs that have salvaged so many careers and lives.

CISM IN LAW ENFORCEMENT

Many county or regional CISM teams across the United States that provide a debriefing after a critical incident. Police officers are often CISM team members and provide peer support during debriefings and other CISM interventions.

If there are no police officers on the team, some should be recruited. Many police officers are more comfortable with other police officers at a CISD than with people from other emergency services. However, the absence of officers from a CISM team does not mean the interventions will not be helpful. Interagency exposure can help officers to learn that their reactions are universal and not limited to their field.

Many departments now have in-house programs that use staff or contract psychologists to provide CISD training, and counseling. Peer support teams, which supplement professional services, are becoming increasingly available. Important considerations for an effective program are discussed below.

Mental health professionals involved in providing CISD must be knowledgeable about critical incident stress, debriefings, and the law enforcement culture. For example, an officer who kills a suspect in the line of duty will not necessarily feel guilty. This officer is not a sociopath and probably feels the action was justified because of perceived life or death jeopardy. An officer who is prepared mentally, emotionally, and physically for the eventuality of a critical incident involving lethal force is less likely to feel guilty than an officer who is unprepared (Solomon, 1988).

Yet, some mental health professionals, lacking a law enforcement background have told officers they should feel guilty or have asked why other options were not taken. These comments and attitudes can be quite harmful.

POLICE PEER SUPPORT TEAMS

Police officers tend to be clannish and are reluctant to talk openly to "outsiders" who may not understand their perspective. Officers are usually more comfortable talking to fellow officers about personal problems than anyone else, including mental health professionals. Therefore, peer support programs which utilize CISM trained officers, i.e. "peers", to provide emotional support to fellow officers experiencing crises are becoming increasingly widespread, particularly for dealing with critical incident stress. Peer support team members are not professional counselors. They are fellow workers willing to be available to their peers after a critical incident and during other times of crisis who offer enlightened, caring human support. Peer support programs are a cost-effective supplement to professional services (Dunning, 1991).

A peer support team can be very helpful in the aftermath of a critical incident (Britt, 1991; Fuller, 1991; Klein, 1991; McMains, 1991; Nielsen, 1991; Schmuckler, 1991; Solomon, 1990; Klyver, 1986). Peer support team members play a significant role in organizing, coordinating, and conducting the CISD and defusings (shortened debriefings). Team members also are valuable in making it "OK" to attend a debriefing or to talk to a mental health professional, and can provide immediate support after a critical incident as well as follow-up after the debriefing. Because peer support team members work regular duty with their fellow officers, they have an excellent vantage point from which to detect stress symptoms and to assess whether to refer an officer for professional counseling.

The blending of professional and peer intervention hastens recovery from critical incident trauma. Professional intervention helps the officer identify and clarify reactions. It also facilitates understanding, integration, and resolution of issues. Peer support team members help fellow officers cope by being there for them and offering caring support during the period of trauma. They can assist their fellow officers to normalize their experiences by helping them talk through the incident informally and by legitimizing their feelings and reactions. They also assist peers in locating additional resources, including referrals to mental health professionals. Professional and peer perspectives complement one another in producing critical incident recovery.

Peer support team members should be carefully selected based on their professional and personal credibility, ability to care for their fellow officers, natural social skills, ability to be empathic, and their respect for confidentiality. A peer support team usually has more credibility if team members are nominated or selected by fellow officers. Otherwise, the team may be perceived as a tool of management and will not be trusted.

While peer support teams exist mainly for the needs of the rank and file, members should also be recruited from the higher ranks. Sergeants, lieutenants, captains, and even higher ranking officers, may experience significant emotional reactions following critical incidents. For example, the responsibility of making critical decisions or a line of duty death, while affecting all personnel regardless of rank, presents different issues for supervisory and command staff.

Comfort levels are likely to be higher when supervisory and command staff have access to someone who shares their perspective.

Furthermore, many officers in the higher ranks have gone through personal traumas and can share valuable experience with younger officers. Their participation in a CISD builds vertical cohesion within the department, demonstrates administrative support of the CISD process, and embodies managerial support for the individuals involved.

Though not mandatory, it is very valuable if team members have critical incident experience. Team members need to have resolved their critical incidents to the point they can talk about them comfortably and can listen to someone else's experience without their own traumatic emotions being triggered.

The "I've been there" perspective provides a credible basis for acceptance among fellow officers and helps to validate and legitimize traumatic reactions. Mental health professionals can say that nightmares and intrusive images are normal reactions to a critical incident, but a stronger impact is made by a peer who can say, "After my incident I had nightmares and intrusive images, and I'm not nuts...If you are experiencing those reactions, you're not nuts either!" Ideally the mental health professional and the peer reinforce each other's credibility in legitimizing reactions.

Team members need training. Instruction should include information about critical incident trauma, coping strategies, how to respond appropriately to a peer who has experienced a critical incident, interpersonal support strategies, CISD, ethics, when and how to refer for professional treatment, and experiential exercises.

Peers must be supervised by a mental health professional. A peer support program or peers trained in CISM are not substitutes for mental health professionals. Without supervision, emotional problems may not be adequately perceived, assessed, or treated. Peers are trained to provide support and to refer to mental health professionals to provide psychological treatment.

ADMINISTRATIVE CONSIDERATIONS

Management support of a critical incident program is vital if a program is to be successfully implemented and utilized. The administrative policy therefore should legitimize critical incident stress and recognize that officers confront overwhelming situations. McMains (1991) points out that a supportive policy acknowledges that police officers are ordinary people doing an extraordinary job, not extraordinary people doing an ordinary job.

Many mental health and law enforcement professionals recommend that there be a policy of mandatory referral to a mental health professional and/or a debriefing for all personnel involved in a critical incident (Horn, 1991; McMains, 1991; Mitchell, 1991; Reese, 1991; Solomon, 1988). Such a policy, focusing on the incident rather than the individual, reduces the negative stigma often attached to seeking help (Reese, 1991).

The needs and experience of the agency should determine which situations should have a mandatory debriefing. The Police Psychological Services Section of the International Association of Chiefs of Police recommends that officers involved in a shooting have mandatory confidential sessions with mental health professionals prior to returning to full duty and that confidential debriefings be made available for all personnel involved in the situation (Solomon, 1990). However, it is important to remember that shootings are not the only critical incidents, as was stated above.

Administrative leave or light duty (whichever the officer prefers) for a few days is also appropriate following high impact situations. The leave allows the officer(s) some time to experience and deal with the emotional impact of the incident.

Administrative leave is particularly recommended following a shooting situation (Solomon, 1990). All personnel at the scene of a high impact situation should be screened for their reactions and relieved for the rest of the shift, or longer, as necessary.

The administrative policy should strongly and unequivocally state that defusings, CISD and peer support meetings are confidential. For example, the policy of the Washington State Patrol is that the interactions of peer support team members are confidential. The only exceptions to confidentiality are a clear and present danger to self or others, or disclosure of a serious crime. Team members are instructed to call the department psychologist or the team coordinator, if possible, when confidentiality cannot be honored. This instruction provides support and supervision to the team member while making additional resources available. Team members who inappropriately violate confidentiality will be removed from the team and may be disciplined. This policy shows that the department is strongly behind the program and respects confidentiality.

The peer support team must be nurtured with regular meetings that include training and a summary of activities since the last meeting. Without regular reinforcement and training, enthusiasm wanes, skills become rusty, and procedures and protocols are forgotten.

The policy and procedures should detail the logistics of the program, including how and when a CISM team is activated. Procedures should define:

1. who calls and informs the team about the incident. (If this is not clearly established the team may not be notified because of all the confusion that typically follows a critical incident.);
2. when and for what situations the team should be notified; and
3. who is called. (In some departments, the mental health professional is called by the department. In other departments, peer support team coordinators are called.)(Nielsen, 1991).

CISD: THE CORNERSTONE OF CISM

Although there is a scarcity of outcome data, clinical experience and anecdotal evidence suggest that CISD provides the following benefits: (see Mitchell and Everly, 1995).

1. CISD SPEEDS THE HEALING PROCESS AND PREVENTS FUTURE EMOTIONAL PROBLEMS. A CISD aims to mitigate the impact of a critical incident and accelerate the recovery process (Mitchell, 1983). A CISD promotes healing in many ways. Some of these are: 1) early intervention; 2) emotional ventilation; 3) placement of reactions in a context of normalcy; 4) education about critical incident reactions and effective coping strategies; and 5) promotion of peer support and group cohesion (see Chapter 7 of this volume).

Early intervention allows officers to understand their experiences in constructive ways before maladaptive, self-critical ways of thinking are solidified (McMains, 1986). Debriefings are conducted soon after the trauma, preferably within 72 hours, when intervention has a maximal effect upon acute trauma situations.

CISD participants talk about what happened and their reactions to the event. They also vent pent-up emotions. Identifying feelings and putting them into words is essential for coping with traumatic incidents (van der Kolk, 1991). Participants receive reassurance that their emotions are normal and that critical incident reactions are not signs of pathology.

CISD is also an educational process instructing participants about critical incident trauma and coping strategies. Knowing what to expect and how to cope with it lowers the risk of prolonged stress reactions.

CISD also promotes peer support, a significant healing factor after a critical incident (Solomon and Horn, 1986). Including all involved personnel in a group format reinforces camaraderie, positive identity, teamwork, and cooperation. Comparing personal reactions with those of others involved in the incident is also very effective in reducing trauma (van der Kolk, 1991).

2. CISD COUNTERS THE LAW ENFORCEMENT CULTURE'S NEGATIVE COPING ATTITUDES. All too typically, police officers build walls around their emotions, suppress their hurt, and deny their pain (Horn, 1991). Many officers, wanting to maintain a strong,

in control image, believe it is important to show that they are unaffected by exposure to danger and tragedy. These officers often think there is something wrong with them when they have deep emotional reactions after a critical incident.

For many officers, talking about emotion is taboo. They perceive admitting hurt, fear, or feelings of vulnerability to be risking criticism from their peers for being weak. This perceived peer pressure causes many officers to suppress their emotions. They may tell the "war story" to peers, emphasizing the glory and the gory. The emotional impact, the personal side, and the private meaning often stay hidden. However hiding one's emotions from oneself does not make them disappear - they are still there, buried alive (Horn and Solomon, 1988)!

CISD provides the knowledge that people are not unique or alone in their emotional reactions and that they are experiencing "normal reactions to abnormal situations." Each participant gains reassurance that it is "OK" to experience emotional reactions after a critical incident and that such reactions do not mean one is going crazy. This reassurance enables officers to deal more comfortably and openly with their reactions, reduces the tendency to suppress their emotions and makes talking to one another and constructively supporting each other easier.

CISD provides a non-threatening way for officers to talk about the emotional impact of critical incidents. Although they often begin talking as if they were confessing to weakness, they are soon surprised to learn not only that no one looks down on them, but also that many others share their feelings. They do not have to play the old game of pretending they are "bullet proof." Just as important, they are prepared to help others recognize and acknowledge their reactions as normal in the future.

3. CISD INCLUDES ALL INVOLVED PERSONNEL. Many personnel may be involved in a critical incident. However, a common mistake is to provide psychological services only to the officer most directly involved, while forgetting other personnel at the scene, as well as the dispatcher.

All personnel at the scene of a critical incident are potentially affected. The officer who shoots a suspect may have a significant emotional reaction. But so may the officer who fires and misses, the officer who does not fire, the officer around the corner who hears the shots and assumes the worst, and the dispatcher who is emotionally on scene.

For example, two officers set up a road block to capture a bank robber who was being chased their way by two other officers. The robber stopped at the roadblock and pulled a gun. One officer fired and killed the suspect. The other officer drew his gun but could not fire because the first officer was in the way.

The officer who fired his weapon was very emotional at the scene. The other officer who did not fire felt he had let his partner down. The officers chasing the suspect felt guilty that they had not been able to capture him sooner. The dispatcher felt she should have done more to prevent the situation. Thus, all personnel involved had significant emotional reactions.

Yet, only the officer who fired the shots was referred for psychological support. It was not until stress reactions and suffering were detected among the other personnel involved in the situation a few weeks later that a group debriefing was held for all.

A CISD includes all personnel at the scene, including the dispatcher, who have the potential for significant reactions. No one is treated as if he/she is not supposed to be upset.

This point is particularly relevant to dispatchers. In many instances, all involved sworn personnel have been provided with CISD services while the primary dispatcher remained in the Communication Center. When those dispatchers later broke down emotionally, they felt an extra burden because they interpreted their exclusion as meaning they should have no problems. Furthermore, being excluded from a CISD leaves dispatchers feeling abandoned, unimportant, and as if their involvement in a critical incident was taken for granted.

4. CISD PROVIDES A SETTING FOR CLEARING UP MISCONCEPTIONS AND MISUNDERSTANDINGS. During moments of peak stress, each involved individual most typically has a different perspective as to what happened. Distortions of time, vision, hearing, and distracted attention combine with strong emotions to create unique perceptual filters for each individual involved in a critical incident (Solomon and Horn, 1986; Blak, 1990). As a result, different interpretations of what happened, different perspectives of what should have happened, and other misunderstandings can occur. The anger and distrust sometimes caused by these misunderstandings can disrupt teamwork.

For example, five officers surrounded a psychotic individual who was brandishing a knife. As the suspect lunged at one officer, another officer on the side, fearing for the life of the first officer, shot and killed the suspect. From the vantage point of the shooter, the knife wielding suspect was only one step away from killing the first officer.

Immediately after the event, all the involved officers questioned why they did not fire their weapons. After thinking about the situation, two officers felt the suspect did not have to be shot. The officer whom the suspect was attacking knew the suspect and wanted to do everything possible to control him without harming him. This officer felt in control of the situation and believed he could take the suspect down with his baton. Another officer, about to strike the suspect from behind with his baton when the first shot was fired, felt he had sufficient time to capture the suspect.

Anger at the shooter came out during the debriefing. A discussion of the differences in perspective enabled the participants to understand each other's perceptions of the situation. All realized the "right" way to handle a situation depends on one's perception. Mutual understanding and respect replaced anger.

A CISD provides the opportunity for everybody to present his/her different perception of the event and enables an accurate picture of what happened to replace misunderstandings. Having an accurate cognitive understanding of what happened enables the officer to feel more in control, reduces stress, and eliminates misinterpretations. Further, it helps stop rumors before they gain momentum.

5. CISD PROMOTES PEER SUPPORT AND GROUP COHESION. Talking about an incident with all others involved fosters trust, generates support, and strengthens group bonds. Support from one's peers is crucial for critical incident recovery (Solomon and Horn, 1986). Horn (1991) points out that officers not only need to debrief the details of an incident, but also need to debrief emotionally and talk out their feelings, fears, and worries **without losing status** (Horn, 1991). The CISD nurtures such peer support.

Many officers involved in the same critical incident have never sat down to talk about what happened. Officers commonly avoid talking with each other about their reactions out of fear of displaying emotions or making other officers feel uncomfortable by bringing up emotional incidents.

For example, two undercover officers observed a gunman attempt to rob a third undercover officer during a stakeout. Shots were exchanged after one officer identified himself and yelled at the suspect to drop his gun. The officers were not injured, but the gunman was killed.

After the initial investigation, the officers went out for a few drinks to talk about what happened. They went over the tactical details, but talked only superficially about their emotional reactions. Over the next four years they referred to the incident, but never talked about their personal reactions to it. They became distant from one another, and never regained the cohesiveness they had prior to the incident.

The officers finally talked about their feelings at a critical incident seminar four years after the shooting. The officer who shot the suspect cried as he disclosed how he feared for the lives of his partners that night. The other officers joined him in tears as they related their sense of responsibility for each other, how much they cared for one another and, most emotionally, how happy they were that all had survived.

These three officers had been reluctant to communicate their feelings to each other out of fear they would be perceived as overly sensitive and fragile. For four years, each officer had lost sleep not only because of his own reaction to the incident, but because of concern for his buddies. All three needed to talk to the others to express their fears, their concern for each other, and their other reactions to the incident. A prompt CISD would have facilitated such expression and strengthened unit cohesiveness, while greatly reducing the suffering of each officer. Interestingly, these officers became the impetus and the backbone for a CISD program in their agency.

The effects of trauma are not necessarily ended by a CISD; in fact, reactions may continue for several weeks or months. Officers may need to talk further with one another about the incident. The CISD "breaks the ice," making it easier for officers to continue to talk informally about the incident, clear up questions, or just check on how the others are doing. A CISD helps develop more open communication among officers involved in the incident, more positive support, and greater group cohesion.

6. CISD PROMOTES A HEALTHY, SUPPORTIVE WORK ATMOSPHERE. The knowledge gained about critical incident stress and constructive coping enables offices to deal more effectively with their own reactions and those of their peers. This creates a healthier work environment than suppressing and hiding one's pain.

For example, a person resisting arrest grabbed the gun of the officer. The officer quickly reacted, took control of his weapon, and subdued the suspect. Other officers arrived and the suspect was handcuffed and taken to jail.

As the officers left the jail to go back in service, the arresting officer realized he was almost killed with his own weapon. Indeed, it is quite typical for the reality of what could have happened to hit once the danger is over. The officer started to cry and shake, and was highly embarrassed that he showed his emotions in front of another officer.

The backup officer, who had gone to a CISD three days earlier, explained to his partner that he was experiencing normal stress "come down" reactions. The shaking was due to stress chemicals working out of his system and the tears were "cleansing." He listened to the officer talk about what happened and his feelings about the incident and reassured him that his emotional reactions were normal. He also shared some of his critical incidents in which he had experienced similar reactions.

This supportive interaction, an illustration of positive peer support, greatly reduced the stress of the officer. One can imagine the damage that would have been caused if the officer involved in the traumatic incident had been ridiculed for showing his emotions. What was learned in a previous CISD enabled an officer to help his peer who had just experienced a traumatic incident.

7. THE CISD PROVIDES INFORMATION ON COPING WITH STRESS THAT HELPS AN OFFICER DEAL WITH THE PRESENT AND FUTURE SITUATIONS. The coping skills learned in a CISD not only help to reduce stress symptoms and pain stemming from the current situation, but also help officers cope with future critical incidents as well.

If an officer successfully resolves a critical incident, the next critical incident is easier to deal with. If the officer gets "stuck" dealing with issues of vulnerability and lack of control, not only is his present functioning impaired, but future critical incidents become even more difficult to resolve.

The positive coping promoted by a CISD can help prevent burnout and the effects of cumulative stress. Over time, attending CISDs after critical incidents builds healthy coping habits needed to deal successfully with future stressful events.

8. CISD ENABLES EARLY DETECTION OF INDIVIDUALS IN NEED OF PROFESSIONAL ASSISTANCE. People experiencing significant stress reactions can be identified during the debriefing and can be immediately referred for professional counseling. This early detection and referral prevents problems from getting worse.

All too often, stress reactions are hidden or denied by officers. Talking to a mental health professional, or seeking help, is perceived by many officers as a sign of weakness. Symptoms may not be detected by peers or supervisors until they have reached a severe level. Unfortunately peers or supervisors sometimes cover up for the officer rather than refer him to an appropriate resource for professional treatment. Debriefing aids in detection of significant problems and facilitates a quick, confidential referral.

A debriefing may identify officers who are experiencing post-traumatic stress symptoms from previous incidents that have never been addressed. The present critical incident often will trigger other unresolved situations.

For example, a debriefing was held for a multi-casualty automobile accident two days after the incident. One officer, experiencing significant distress, stated that the current accident did not bother him much. He added, however, that he had begun to experience vivid intrusive images of an accident that occurred two years previously in which he had been looking for victims and found himself standing on a person's brains.

He had never talked about this incident and had tried to forget about it. Now, emotions and images from the previous incident were flooding him. An immediate referral was made after the debriefing to help him resolve the buildup of traumatic incidents.

9. CISD PROMOTES INTERAGENCY COOPERATION. In a CISD, everybody at the scene comes together, including emergency personnel from other law enforcement agencies, ambulance crews, firefighters, and hospital staff. Coming together to deal with the emotional impact of a critical incident promotes good working relationships and mutual trust between other agencies. Moreover, it emphasizes that the reactions discussed are the result of a shared humanity, not simply the property of one's occupation.

10. CISD IS A COST EFFECTIVE PREVENTATIVE TOOL. Early intervention after a critical incident can prevent future emotional problems. Early identification of critical incident stress reactions and

prompt intervention can reduce claims for disability and early retirement and can decrease the costs of absenteeism, medical treatment, and litigation (Dunning, 1991). A CISD not only saves careers, marriages, and lives, it saves money.

Agencies that ignore the potential for mental injury following a critical incident risk expensive law suits claiming negligence in supervision, training, or retention if the mental injury contributes to work actions that harm a citizen (Dunning, 1991). Because of the known hazards of critical incident trauma, liability is reduced when agencies recognize the possibility of mental injuries and set up a critical incident program.

11. A CISM / CISD PROGRAM SHOWS THE DEPARTMENT CARES. It is important that law enforcement officers receive support from their departments. For many officers, the worst part of a critical incident may not be the incident itself, but what happens afterward (Horn, 1991). It is stressful to realize that a split-second decision made under life or death circumstances can be second guessed in court for years to come. Officers wonder if the department will stand behind them or will second guess them in a negative manner.

Quite often, there is an apparent lack of departmental concern following a critical incident. Impersonal treatment of one whose life has been put on the line may create a deep sense of abandonment, anger toward the department, alienation from the agency, and distrust of the administration.

A CISM program is a vital way for a department to demonstrate support for officers involved in a traumatic incident. Administrative backing of a CISD program sends out the message that the department is concerned about the well-being of its officers and recognizes them as human beings who have just undergone a traumatic experience.

CRITERIA FOR A CISD

Agencies should define the criteria for having a defusing or CISD according to their needs and experience. Some agencies allow affected officers the right to call for a debriefing (Flint, 1992, personal communication). Mitchell and Bray (1990) identify the following criteria to evaluate the need for a CISD:

1. the involved officers appear to be significantly distressed;
2. personnel demonstrate numerous behavior changes;
3. personnel make significant errors on calls occurring after the critical incident;
4. personnel request help;
5. the event is extraordinary;
6. personnel from various agencies involved in the situation are showing the same reactions; and
7. signals of distress continue beyond three weeks.

Examples of critical incidents where it may be beneficial to have a CISD include (Mitchell and Bray, 1990; Blak, 1991):

1. line-of-duty death of a fellow officer;
2. line-of-duty shooting involving injury or death;
3. situation where serious injury is inflicted on someone;
4. serious injury to a fellow worker;
5. suicide of a fellow worker;
6. serious multiple casualty incident;
7. traumatic death or serious injuries to children;
8. prolonged rescue operations in which victims expire;
9. hostage or barricaded suspect situation (especially if an officer is taken hostage);

10. events with excessive media interest;
11. special team (e.g., tactical units, bomb squad, canine unit, etc.) operation where unusual danger or circumstances are present;
12. observing an illegal activity (e.g., corruption, bribery) by a fellow worker;
13. sudden, unexpected removal of employee from work unit (e.g. fellow worker arrested);
14. any event that involves extreme vulnerability or has an unusually powerful impact on the personnel.

WHO SHOULD BE INCLUDED

All employees on-scene or involved in a meaningful way in the situation, including the dispatcher, should participate in the debriefing. Quite often, those who do not come to the debriefing develop the most significant problems. People reluctant to attend will sometimes respond well to the suggestion that other participants may benefit from their presence even if they themselves have no reason to attend.

Command staff or others not directly involved in the situation sometimes seek to be in the CISD to show support or to find out what happened. However, this may inhibit some participants from opening up. The rule of thumb for inclusion should be that a person may attend a CISD only if on-scene or directly involved. Trauma knows no rank!

For the more impactful incidents, peripheral and support personnel may need debriefing. Not uncommonly, officers on the periphery of a situation who can only guess what is going on or fear the worst have emotional reactions as serious as those officers in the middle of the incident (Blak, 1991). Some incidents, like a line-of-duty death or a serious injury to an officer, have no on-scene boundaries and impact many people. Though first attention should be focused at those most directly affected by the incident, debriefings should be made available to all affected personnel.

WHEN TO HAVE THE CISD

The ideal time for debriefing is between 24 and 72 hours following an acute traumatic incident. Quite often, the emotional numbness, shock, and/or fatigue immediately after the incident renders more immediate group debriefing ineffective.

If logistical and coordination problems create scheduling difficulties, it is certainly appropriate to have the debriefing later than 72 hours. Debriefings conducted after even several weeks can still be quite meaningful and helpful, especially in mass disaster situations.

SIZE OF GROUP FOR CISD AND OTHER LOGISTICS

The number of persons to be included in a debriefing depends on many factors. Some CISD personnel prefer to work with groups of twelve or fewer (Blak, 1991). Others may prefer smaller or larger groups. Breaking a large group into smaller groups may be helpful, depending on the number of CISD facilitators available. However, prior to getting into smaller groups, the incident commander can speed the process by going over details of what occurred and answering questions. It may also be constructive to have one of the CISD facilitators present information on critical incident stress. A didactic presentation can help introduce and structure the debriefing process (Dunning, 1988).

An effective method to sort participants into smaller groups is by matching people who share the same perspective. Those who share the same perspective have common reference points that make for easier understanding and empathy. For example, after a major operation involving thirty-four officers at three crime scenes, the officers and dispatchers who worked the same location were grouped together. Another debriefing was held later at the request of the command staff to help them deal with the emotional impact of overseeing a large scale operation.

INDIVIDUAL DEBRIEFING

Individual debriefings are conducted following critical incidents involving one officer and as a supplement to a group debriefing for officers directly involved in, or significantly affected by, high impact incidents. Individual debriefings should be conducted by a mental health professional.

In an individual debriefing, the emotional impact of the incident is assessed and explored as thoughts, feelings, and reactions are discussed. An effective format for individual sessions is to go over the incident "frame by frame," with the officer verbalizing the moment by moment thoughts, perceptions, sensory details, feelings, and actions that occurred during the incident. This format is healing because it helps the officer become aware, sort out, and understand what happened.

Getting in touch with the perceptions and frame of mind experienced during the incident helps a person understand why certain actions were taken or specific decisions were made. The "frame by frame" approach helps diffuse inappropriate self-blaming by helping a person differentiate what was under his control from what was not, and what was known at the time from what was impossible to know.

Solomon (1991) describes a "Dynamics of Fear" model based on experience with hundreds of officers who have survived deadly force encounters. This model describes how officers cope with fear and vulnerability during moments of peak stress, and can be a useful guide for a "frame by frame" intervention.

GROUP DEBRIEFING WITH ONE OFFICER

Many critical incidents involve only one officer. Along with an individual debriefing, an officer may benefit from meeting with fellow officers to talk about the incident, especially if they are peers who have been involved in similar critical incidents. One model to follow when one or two officers have been involved in a critical incident is to organize a group meeting with participants chosen by the officers from a list of the peer support team members. In this way, the officers choose only people with whom they feel comfortable.

The meeting begins with the team members giving a brief description of their incidents and their emotional reactions. This process provides education, normalizes reactions, and lets the involved officer know he/she is not alone or unique. When fellow officers are the first to reveal their experiences and reactions a recently involved officer shares experiences and feelings more easily. Experienced team members can be effective in helping the officer vent emotions by asking questions, validating reactions, and disclosing their own emotions. Team members follow-up informally with the officer. Individual counseling is scheduled as needed.

CAUTION WHEN THERE IS AN INVESTIGATION

For critical incidents involving a legal investigation, such as an officer involved shooting situation, it may be advisable not to have a group debriefing until the initial investigation has been completed and formal statements have been taken by investigators. Otherwise, debriefing participants may be viewed as "witnesses" who are subject to questioning about what was said. For particularly controversial situations or complicated investigations, it may be important not to have a group debriefing until the investigation has been legally resolved. Individual debriefings can be provided until it is appropriate to have a group debriefing.

In a line of duty shooting, the officers who fire their weapons may not want to participate in a group debriefing because the legal/investigative aftermath raises different issues. If this is the case, individual debriefings should be provided, with a group debriefing proceeding for other involved personnel. However, the officers who fire their weapons, quite often, want to participate in the group debriefing and benefit greatly from it.

CISD IN CONTEXT

A CISD is only one component of a comprehensive critical incident program. Because officers do not live in a vacuum, the availability of family intervention and support following a critical incident is also important. What affects one member of the family affects all members of the family (Wittrup, 1986). Family counseling and/or a debriefing for significant others can help them deal with their concerns and fears triggered by a critical incident. Since the issues confronting significant others differ markedly from the issues confronting the officers, debriefings should be separate (Hartsough, 1991; Mitchell, 1991).

Pre-incident education to prepare officers for traumatic incidents and educate them about both CISD and critical incident services available is also a vital component of a critical incident program. Similar training should also be made available for significant others.

On-scene support may be useful in incidents of long duration, e.g., disasters, prolonged investigations that are particularly gruesome, or prolonged tactical operations. Officers seriously affected by the incident can be assisted, command staff can be advised of personnel needs (e.g., who needs a break), and support can be provided to victims of the event or their family members (Mitchell, 1991). Obviously, it is important that support personnel not interfere with operations.

A complete program includes the availability of support from the moment a critical incident begins until emotional reactions are resolved. Immediate support, de-escalations, and follow-up services are vital services that can augment, supplement, or substitute for, a CISD.

IMMEDIATE SUPPORT

A critical incident, especially when there is significant distress, may call for immediate intervention for involved personnel individually or in small groups. Mitchell (1991) describes this process as a "defusing," when done in small groups. The SAFE-R model described in Chapter 12 of this volume may be used for one-on-one crisis intervention.

Mental health professionals or experienced peer support team members can provide this immediate support. However, for shooting situations or other situations where a legal investigation is involved, it is more advantageous to utilize a mental health professional who has privileged communication.

If a peer is providing the support, it is important not to talk about what happened until after the initial investigation and statements have been given (Solomon, 1988). This avoids having the peer support team member become a witness who can be interviewed by investigators at a later time.

Defusings are usually brief; about twenty to forty minutes in duration. It is not uncommon however for an officer to want to talk longer. Because of the confusion that takes place at the scene of a critical incident, contact with involved officers, unless otherwise authorized, should take place at a calmer location that affords privacy.

The following steps are effective when conducting an immediate intervention:

1. After a brief introduction, the support person makes a statement to the effect, "I am not part of the investigation or administrative proceedings. I am here for one reason and one reason only, I'm here for you." This supportive statement separates the intervention from the usual procedural and investigatory issues that commonly follow a critical incident. Confidentiality is also emphasized.

   The officer's level of involvement is accepted.

   Though talking is encouraged, it is not forced and the officer is free to refuse to talk or participate.

2. Ask the officer to describe what happened.

3. Inquire about the officer's reactions and feelings, e.g., the worst part of the incident, moments of vulnerability, and current concerns.

4. Give officers information on critical incident reactions they may experience and describe them as normal reactions to abnormal situations. Emphasize that they may not experience the reactions described, but if they do, they are normal. With such a caveat, one avoids suggesting that the officer is supposed to have symptoms. Also offer information on coping and stress reduction strategies.

5. Offer supportive, concrete services, e.g., talk to the family, get food or something to drink, provide information, make transportation arrangements, or offer other appropriate services.

6. Schedule a follow-up session and/or a group debriefing as appropriate.

DE-ESCALATIONS

De-escalation is a process that facilitates the transition from a major, prolonged event back to the usual routine (Mitchell, 1991). According to Mitchell (1991), de-escalations are reserved for large-scale incidents where a large percentage of available resources are committed to an incident for most of the shift or longer. After a prolonged situation, it is important to have a process to ease the "come-down" before officers go off duty or back to routine duties.

The de-escalation process begins with personnel reporting to a large meeting room upon leaving the scene of the incident, and staying with the team they were working with (e.g. tactical unit, outer perimeter team, surveillance team, etc.). A mental health professional or an experienced peer gives the officer a brief talk (e.g. ten minutes) and hand-outs on critical incident stress and coping strategies. Personnel are given the opportunity to make comments or ask questions, but there is no pressure to have group discussion. Further attention can be given if requested or if an officer is showing obvious signs of distress. After another twenty minutes or so to rest and have refreshments, personnel can be given instructions regarding returning to regular duties or can go off duty. This half hour process can help officers normalize and return to routine after a prolonged incident.

FOLLOW-UP SERVICES

A CISD does not take the place of individual counseling. When an incident has a significant impact, more therapeutic intervention than a CISD may be needed to work through the emotional aftermath. Individual sessions with a mental health professional should be available.

Even after initial acceptance and resolution of an incident, reactions can again surface. Going through a traumatic incident is like crossing a fence and losing one's naivete with no possibility of crossing back. Once officers confront their vulnerability and mortality, they have to learn to live with that reality. Situations similar to the critical incident may trigger the emotional reactions, as may involvement of a fellow officer in a similar incident. Anniversary reactions are also common. In addition, the ever frequent lawsuits can keep triggering the emotional impact as well as deepen the trauma. Follow-up counseling needs to be a part of a critical incident program to deal with issues and problems that arise down the road.

Critical Incident Peer Support Seminar: A useful follow-up is to provide a setting where officers can revisit their experience several months following a critical incident. The author has extensively utilized a seminar format where officers who have experienced a traumatic incident come together for two to three days. Mental health professionals, assisted by peer support officers, facilitate the seminar.

A multi-day format allows a more thorough presentation on critical incident stress and coping strategies than can be covered in a CISD, and provides sufficient time for participants to interact with each other. Further, the multi-day format allows time for participants to assess the impact of the incident on their lives. There is time to deal with unresolved emotions stemming from the incident, emotions that may have surfaced since the incident, or emotions that may arise during the seminar. Attending the seminar with other officers who have also experienced critical incidents allows participants the opportunity to receive peer support, and reinforces the realization that they are neither alone nor unique in their reactions. Learning more about trauma, spending time with fellow officers who have been involved in similar situations, and having several days to process their experience enables participants to achieve higher plateaus of understanding and integration of their incident.

With additional blocks of instruction, this seminar can also serve as peer support team training. Indeed, a vital part of peer support team preparation is being comfortable with one's own incident.

Preliminary observations by the author has found that such a seminar is highly therapeutic, particularly for the officer who is still experiencing problems as a result of the incident. Follow-up studies conducted two months and ten months following the seminar found that the emotional impact of the incident was significantly reduced, with the therapeutic gains stable over time.

The impact of a critical incident changes over time. Revisiting the experience several months down the road with fellow officers who have "been there," and are working through their own experience, is very healing.

CAVEAT

CISD and CISM programs are not panaceas. Even when a department does everything possible following a critical incident, an officer may still succumb to the traumatic experience and develop a post traumatic stress disorder.

There is no guarantee that emotional problems can be prevented, just as a bulletproof vest does not guarantee the officer will not be injured. A critical incident program, like the vest, most certainly decreases the risk.

There are positive aspects to critical incidents. After coming to grips with one's sense of vulnerability, one can emerge stronger and utilize this strength when facing life's other challenges.

SUMMARY

Critical incidents, situations in which people come face to face with their sense of vulnerability and/or the reality that they are often powerless to prevent tragedy, are an occupational hazard for law enforcement officers. The CISM program has many benefits for officers:

1. A CISM program speeds the healing process and prevents future emotional problems.
2. It counters the law enforcement culture's negative coping attitude that encourages hiding one's pain to portray a "macho" front.
3. A CISM program includes all involved personnel who potentially could have traumatic reactions.
4. It provides a setting where misconceptions and misunderstandings can be cleared up.
5. It promotes peer support and group cohesion.
6. It promotes a healthy, supportive work atmosphere.
7. It provides information on coping with stress that helps an officer deal with both present and future critical incidents.
8. It enables early detection of individuals in need of professional assistance.
9. It promotes interagency cooperation.
10. It is a cost effective, preventative tool.
11. It demonstrates the department cares.

In the past, law enforcement agencies provided critical incident services only to officers involved in line-of-duty shootings, as there was little or no awareness that all personnel at the scene were potentially affected adversely. Many agencies today acknowledge many other situations are traumatic and that all personnel at scene are potentially impacted.

Critical incident stress management services should be provided by mental health professionals knowledgeable about the law enforcement culture, critical incident trauma, and CISD. A peer support program is a valuable supplement to professional services. Peers validate and legitimize emotional reactions in a very credible manner, provide support immediately following a critical incident, assist in conducting a CISD, provide follow-up after a CISD, and refer officers for professional counseling. It is important that peer support team members carefully be selected, trained, and supervised by a mental health professional.

Management support is important for the successful implementation and utilization of a critical incident program. A policy should: 1) legitimize critical incident stress; 2) mandate critical incident aftercare to remove the negative stigma of seeking help; 3) provide administrative leave when appropriate; 4) emphasize the confidentiality of the program; and 5) detail the logistics of the program.

A CISD is the cornerstone of the CISM program but it is only one component of a comprehensive critical incident program. Immediate support, individual debriefings, and follow-up counseling augment and supplement group debriefings.

REFERENCES

Blak, R.A. (1990). Critical incident debriefing for law enforcement personnel: A model. In J.T. Reese, J. M. Horn, and C. Dunning (Eds.) *Critical Incidents in Policing* (pp. 39-51). Washington, DC: U.S. Government Printing Office.

Blak, R. A. (1991). Critical incident debriefing for law enforcementpersonnel: A model. In J.T. Reese, J. M. Horn, and C. Dunning (Eds.) *Critical Incidents in Policing, Revised* (pp. 23-30). Washington, DC: U.S. Government Printing Office.

Bohl, N. K. (1991). The effectiveness of brief psychological interventions in police officers after critical incidents. In J.T. Reese, J. M. Horn, and C. Dunning (Eds.) *Critical Incidents in Policing, Revised* (pp. 31-38). Washington, DC: U.S. Government Printing Office.

Britt, J. M. (1991). U.S. Secret Service critical incident peer support team. In J.T. Reese, J. M. Horn, and C. Dunning (Eds.) *Critical Incidents in Policing, Revised* (pp. 55-62). Washington, DC: U.S. Government Printing Office.

Dunning, C. (1988). Intervention strategies for emergency workers. In M. Lystad (Ed.) *Mental Health Response to Mass Emergencies: Theory and Practice*. New York: Brunner/Mazel Publications.

Dunning, C. (1991). Mitigating the Impact of work trauma: Administrative issues concerning intervention. In J.T. Reese, J. M. Horn, and C. Dunning (Eds.) *Critical Incidents in Policing, Revised* (pp. 73-82). Washington, DC: U.S. Government Printing Office.

Flint, R. (1992). Personal Conversation. Clinical Psychologist, Lafayette, California.

Fuller, R.A. (1991). An overview of the peer support team development. In J.T. Reese, J. M. Horn, and C. Dunning (Eds.) *Critical Incidents in Policing, Revised* (pp. 99-106). Washington, DC: U.S. Government Printing Office.

Hartsough, D. M. (1991). Stresses, spouses, and law enforcement: A step beyond. In J.T. Reese, J. M. Horn, and C. Dunning (Eds.) *Critical Incidents in Policing, Revised* (pp. 131-138). Washington, DC: U.S. Government Printing Office.

Havassey, V. J. (1991). Critical incident debriefing: Ritual for closure. In J.T. Reese, J. M. Horn, and C. Dunning (Eds.) *Critical Incidents in Policing, Revised* (pp. 139-142). Washington, DC: U.S. Government Printing Office.

Horn, J. M. (1991). Critical incidents for law enforcement officers. In J.T. Reese, J. M. Horn, and C. Dunning (Eds.) *Critical Incidents in Policing, Revised* (pp. 143-148). Washington, DC: U.S. Government Printing Office.

Horn, J. M. and Solomon, R. M.. (Spring, 1988). "Peer support: A key element for coping with trauma," *Police Stress*, (pp. 25-27).

Klein, R. (1991). The utilization of police peer counselors in critical incidents. In J.T. Reese, J. M. Horn, and C. Dunning (Eds.) *Critical Incidents in Policing, Revised* (pp. 159-168). Washington, DC: U.S. Government Printing Office.

Klyver, N. (1986). LAPD's peer counseling program after three years. In J. T. Reese and H. A. Goldstein (Eds.) *Psychological Services for Law Enforcement* (pp. 121-136), Washington, DC: U.S. Government Printing Office.

McMains, M. J. (1986). Post shooting trauma: Demographics of professional support. In J. T. Reese and H. A. Goldstein (Eds.) *Psychological Services for Law Enforcement* (pp. 361-364), Washington, DC: U.S. Government Printing Office.

McMains, M. J. (1991). The management and treatment of postshooting trauma. In J.T. Reese, J. M. Horn, and C. Dunning (Eds.) *Critical Incidents in Policing, Revised* (pp. 191-198). Washington, DC: U.S. Government Printing Office.

Mitchell, J. T. (1983). "When disaster strikes. . .the criticalincident stress debriefing process," *Journal of Emergency Medical Services (JEMS), 8* (1), 36-39.

Mitchell, J. T. (1991). Law enforcement applications for critical incident stress teams. In J.T. Reese, J. M. Horn, and C. Dunning (Eds.) *Critical Incidents in Policing, Revised* (pp. 201-212). Washington, DC: U.S. Government Printing Office.

Mitchell, J. T. and Bray, G. (1990), *Emergency Services Stress,* Prentice Hall, Inc.

Mitchell, J.T. and Everly, G.S. (1995). *Critical Incident Stress Management: An operations Manual.* Ellicott City, MD: Chevron Publishing.

Nielsen, E. (1991). Factors influencing the nature of posttraumatic stress disorders. In J.T. Reese, J. M. Horn, and C. Dunning (Eds.) *Critical Incidents in Policing, Revised* (pp. 213-220). Washington, DC: U.S. Government Printing Office.

Reese, J. T. (1991). Justifications for mandating critical incident aftercare. In J.T. Reese, J. M. Horn, and C. Dunning (Eds.) *Critical Incidents in Policing, Revised* (pp. 213-220). Washington, DC: U.S. Government Printing Office.

Reese, J. T. and Hodinko, B. M. (1991). Police psychological services: A history. In J.T. Reese, J. M. Horn, and C. Dunning (Eds.) *Critical Incidents in Policing, Revised* (pp. 213-220). Washington, DC: U.S. Government Printing Office.

Roberts, Michael (1976), Presentation to Law Enforcement Executive Development Seminar, FBI Academy, Quantico, Virginia.

Schmuckler, E. (1991). Peer support and traumatic incident teams: A state-wide multiagency program. In J.T. Reese, J. M. Horn, and C. Dunning (Eds.) *Critical Incidents in Policing, Revised* (pp. 315-318). Washington, DC: U.S. Government Printing Office.

Shaw, J. (June, 1981). "Post-Shooting Trauma," *Police Chief Magazine*.

Solomon, R. M. (October, 1988) "Post-shooting trauma," *Police Chief Magazine*, (pp. 40-44).

Solomon, R. M. (February, 1990) "Administrative guidelines for dealing with officers involved in on-duty shooting situations," *Police Chief Magazine*,(p. 40).

Solomon, R. M. (1991). The dynamics of fear in critical incidents: Implications for training and treatment. In J.T. Reese, J. M. Horn, and C. Dunning (Eds.) *Critical Incidents in Policing, Revised* (pp. 347-358). Washington, DC: U.S. Government Printing Office.

Solomon, R. M. and Horn, J. M. (1986). Post-shooting traumatic reactions: A pilot study. In J. T. Reese and H. A. Goldstein (Eds.) *Psychological Services for Law Enforcement* (pp. 383-394), Washington, DC: U.S. Government Printing Office.

Somodevilla, S. A. (1986). Post-shooting trauma: Reactive and proactive treatment. In J. T. Reese and H. A. Goldstein (Eds.) *Psychological Services for Law Enforcement* (pp. 395-398), Washington, DC: U.S. Government Printing Office.

Stratton, J. (1984). Post-traumatic stress: Study of Police Officers involved in shooting. *Psychological Reports*, 55, 127-131.

Vaughn, Jerry (November 18, 1987). "NRA Gives Distorted Message; Guns Will Not Make Us Safer," *The Omaha World Herald*, Washington Post Service.

van der Kolk, B. A. (1991). The psychological processing of traumatic events: The personal experience of posttraumatic stress disorder. In J.T. Reese, J. M. Horn, and C. Dunning (Eds.) *Critical Incidents in Policing, Revised* (pp. 359-364). Washington, DC: U.S. Government Printing Office.

Wagner, M. (1979). "Airline disaster: A stress debrief program for police," *Police Stress*, 2 (1), (16-20).

Wittrup, R. G. (1986). Posttraumatic stress disorders and the role of the family. In J.T. Reese, J. M. Horn, and C. Dunning (Eds.) *Critical Incidents in Policing, Revised* (pp. 387-389). Washington, DC: U.S. Government Printing Office.

Chapter 11

WORKER STRESS DURING LONGTERM DISASTER RECOVERY EFFORTS

WHO ARE THESE PEOPLE AND WHAT ARE THEY DOING HERE?

DIANE MYERS

About two months after the Midwest Flood of 1993, this author was co-directing a stress management program in a large Federal Emergency Management Agency (FEMA) office where about 500 local-hire and out-of-town FEMA personnel were processing applications for thousands of disaster victims from four states. Personnel put in grueling hours, feeling a great responsibility toward applicants who were depending on the workers to process their applications for assistance.

A male employee in his twenties came to the stress management office complaining of chest pain. Paramedics were called, and although the man's electrocardiogram showed no sign of irregularity, they decided to transport him to the emergency room for thorough assessment.

Diane Myers • Disaster Consultant, Monterey California.
In G.S. Everly, Jr. Innovations in Disaster and Trauma Psychology, Volume One: Applications in Emergency Services and Disaster Response. Baltimore: Chevron Publishing Corp, 1995.

Emergency room personnel should have been informed about the occupational stress the man was under, but unless they inquired, I doubted the young man would tell them. Disaster workers are tremendously committed to their work, often to the point of being "over-invested." They frequently deny fatigue, stress, and medical problems out of fear of being relieved of duty and "sent home."

I asked the paramedic to report to the emergency room personnel that this man had worked 12 hours a day, six days a week, for the past six weeks. He was diabetic and required insulin several times a day. He had not been eating well and frequently skipped breakfast (including the day of this incident), wreaking havoc with his blood sugar and general health. Ill with a cold for two weeks, he had developed a deep cough (an acute lung infection and pleurisy were later determined to be the cause of his chest pain). He had not gone to a doctor because he did not have medical benefits and did not want to take a day off from work. He was from out of state and had no local support system other than the people he saw each day at work.

After hearing these facts the paramedic for the first time took a good look at the workplace. Hundreds of workers in spaces separated only by partitions answered ringing phones, entered data into computers, and processed paper files. The noise level was high. There was no natural light, because the office was in the basement of the building. The place was a virtual beehive.

The medic looked at me and asked incredulously, "Who are these people, and what are they doing here?" I informed him that these people were FEMA workers from all over the country and personnel from all over the state working on flood recovery. Bewildered, he said "But ma'am, the water went down two months ago!"

His remark accurately reflects the general public's lack of knowledge about the efforts and responsibility of longterm recovery workers. When I briefly explained that these workers were processing applications from disaster victims, and that each case directly depended on the efforts of these workers, his reply was "This is totally awesome. I thought the disaster was over." This office was still in operation, although scaled-down, more than a year later.

ARE DISASTER WORKERS AFFECTED BY THEIR MISSION?

The research and literature addressing traumatic stress have increased considerably in the post-Vietnam era. A wide range of traumatic stressors and their sequelae has been studied, including war, child abuse, sexual abuse, domestic violence, violent crime, and disaster. A recent review of trauma-related abstracts published between 1970 and 1989 (Blake, Albano, and Keane, 1992) found that less than 7 percent of the citations were disaster related. With the advent of numerous major disasters in the United States since 1989, the research and findings about the psychological aftermath of disaster will undoubtedly increase (Hiley-Young, 1994). Nevertheless, research and literature on the traumatic effects of disaster is scant, and studies of the subpopulation of disaster workers are even more scarce.

Anecdotal and observational reports of emergency workers subsequent to disaster suggest that disaster deployment does have the potential to cause psychological, physical, and/or behavioral impacts on the workers involved (Armstrong, O'Callahan, & Marmar, 1991; Butcher & Hatcher, 1988; Conner, 1992; Dunning & Silva, 1980; Dunning, 1985; Dunning, 1988; Durham, McCammon, & Allison, 1985; Forstenzer, 1980; Hartsough & Myers, 1985; Jones, 1985; Mitchell, 1982; Mitchell, 1983; Mitchell & Bray, 1990; Mitchell & Everly, 1992; Mitchell & Everly, 1993; Moran, 1994; Myers, 1985a, 1985b, 1992, 1993, 1994a, 1994b; Myers & Zunin, 1993a, 1993b, 1994b; Wilkinson, 1983).

The limited empirical research about disaster worker trauma supports the anecdotal and observational findings (Keating, 1986; Mantell, 1986; Mitchell, 1985; Rosensweig & Vaslow, 1992; Sloan, Rozensky, Kaplan, & Saunders, 1994; Ursano & McCarroll, 1994). For example, in Mitchell's (1985) survey of 360 emergency services personnel, 86.9% reported that they had been emotionally and physically affected by their work. Ninety-three percent felt that psychological debriefings were necessary after a major emergency event such as a disaster.

DISASTER RESPONSE AND DISASTER RECOVERY: DIFFERENCES IN WORKER TASKS

Most of the references cited above examine the impact of disaster on emergency workers, or "first responders" such as police, fire, emergency medical personnel, and coroners and mortuary staff. Typically, first responder responsibilities in disaster include actions to save lives and property immediately before, during, and after impact. In the language of Comprehensive Emergency Management, these workers carry out disaster response functions. Examples of their work include evacuation, firefighting, search and rescue, first aid, body recovery and identification, and law enforcement.

The activities of disaster response are usually intense, focused, and relatively brief in duration (Conner, 1992), covering several hours to several days (longer in catastrophic disasters). These activities occur during what is commonly called the "heroic" phase of the disaster, when there is much altruism, courageous and valiant action, and positive media coverage of the response activities.

Following the response phase, disaster management moves into the tasks and responsibilities of the recovery phase. The recovery phase of disaster relief includes short and longterm activities. Short-term recovery activities attempt initially to compensate for damage to a community's infrastructure and quickly return its vital life-support systems to operation.

Longterm recovery activities are designed to return life to normal or improved levels. A wide array of human services, including crisis counseling, is available to disaster victims through government and private nonprofit agencies.

Disaster recovery personnel may be local or may come from out of town or out of state, staying in the impacted community for weeks or months at a time. Key FEMA and state personnel know that they will likely be involved in disaster recovery responsibilities for years following a major disaster. Following Hurricane Andrew in late

August 1994, more than five thousand federal workers were based at the Miami Disaster Field Office (DFO). Many of them knew they would be there for the "long haul." In early September, a mere two weeks into the disaster operation, a hand drawn picture of a Christmas tree appeared, prominently taped in a corner of one manager's office. The caption on the picture read "Christmas tree goes here." There would be little time at "home for the holidays" for many of the disaster workers involved.

ROLES AND TASKS OF LONGTERM RECOVERY WORKERS

In the United States, a large proportion of disaster assistance is government funded. Enormous sums of money are involved in both infrastructure support to local government and human services to individual survivors. Because public funds are expended, there must be a system of accountability. This requires activities such as application for funds, verification of damages, and processing of applications. The processing of disaster assistance applications provides many of the longterm recovery phase jobs for federal government personnel.

Both short and longterm mental health programs may be funded by a grant to the local or state mental health agency from FEMA in a presidentially declared disaster. Longterm mental health recovery activities under the FEMA Crisis Counseling Program typically include outreach, consultation and education, individual and group crisis counseling, support groups and information and referral services. Mental health staff involved in such Crisis Counseling programs typically provide services to disaster-affected communities up to or beyond the first anniversary of the disaster.

Another cadre of longterm recovery workers includes staff and volunteers from nonprofit disaster relief organizations. For example, the Red Cross provides casework services, financial assistance, building and repair of owner-occupied homes, medical and nursing care, and other forms of "additional assistance" to individuals and families for whom government programs are not available (American Red Cross, 1977).

Many other volunteer organizations are active in longterm disaster recovery, removing debris from private property, cleaning homes, and providing free labor to repair or rebuild homes (Bush, 1979). These workers spend long hours working side-by-side with victims for weeks on end.

The efforts of these longterm volunteer and paid staff are usually quiet and behind-the-scenes, and do not receive the media coverage of the heroic phase. Longterm recovery work is usually unknown and unseen by the public. Nonetheless, these disaster workers put in long hours for weeks, months, and sometimes years at a time, often on assignment away from home, in ongoing contact with victims and their suffering.

KEY ORGANIZATIONS IN LONGTERM RECOVERY

FEMA AND THE AMERICAN RED CROSS

While a wide range of organizations, both public and private, is involved in longterm disaster recovery, two organizations provide the largest cadre of workers: FEMA and the Red Cross. Each organization uses workers with a variety of job statuses. Workers may be paid professional staff with benefits, hourly staff with no job security or benefits, or volunteers. Their level of training varies from highly specialized disaster management training to brief on-the-job training. They may be local personnel, or may come from another part of the country. They may work on the disaster operation for a few days, a few months, or a few years. Disaster employment or deployment often occurs for a worker with little warning, and there is often little time to put one's "house in order" before reporting for duty. Job security may be nonexistent for the reservist or hourly local hire workers who can be released from work when they are no longer needed. Training may be excellent or may be scant, in which case workers often feel ill-prepared and unsure of themselves.

FEDERAL EMERGENCY MANAGEMENT AGENCY

The basic role of the federal government in emergency management is to protect life and property in a disaster and to help state and local governments in the recovery process. By executive order, the President has assigned emergency preparedness and operating responsibilities to certain federal agencies, with overall responsibility assigned to the Federal Emergency Management Agency (FEMA). In 1988, Public Law 93-288 was amended by Public Law 100-707 and retitled as the Robert T. Stafford Disaster Relief and Emergency Assistance Act.

The federal government recognizes local and state governments as being in charge of emergency response operations. Federal assistance under the provisions of the Stafford Act is supplemental to state efforts. The Stafford Act authorizes the President to declare a "major disaster" or "emergency" for an area affected by a disaster. This is done in response to a request by the governor of the affected state, when state and local resources are inadequate to respond effectively and to undertake recovery. Once a Presidential Declaration has been made, FEMA may direct any federal agency to help state and local governments directly.

Once a Presidential Declaration has been made, the FEMA director or designee appoints a federal coordinating officer (FCO) as the senior federal official who coordinates the administration of relief activities in the affected area. The governor appoints a state coordinating officer (SCO) to coordinate state and local response efforts with those of the federal government. The FCO and SCO work together in the disaster field office (DFO). The DFO is a temporary office established in or near the affected area for coordination and control of state and federal response and recovery operations. In large-scale disasters, the DFO may be in operation for years.

FEMA has several classifications of workers who may be active in disaster. *Permanent full-time* (PFT) employees are civil-service employees who regularly work in FEMA's ten regional offices and FEMA headquarters. In non-disaster time they may be involved in a variety of responsibilities, not always disaster-related. In time of disaster, these personnel are assigned to manage and staff the FEMA operations in the DFO for the impacted area. Their assignment is usually long in duration (weeks, months, sometimes years). Many PFTs managing the Northridge Earthquake in Los Angeles are from the San Francisco area, where they usually work in the Region IX office. They have virtually "moved in" to hotels and apartments in Los Angeles for their duration of their assignment. They get occasional weekend breaks to go home to their families.

Disaster Assistance Employees (DAEs) are of two types. *Reservists* are personnel who are prescreened and hired by FEMA, and are activated as needed. They are paid salary and overtime, travel and maintenance, and have no benefits. Their training, their role, and their length of deployment may vary from one disaster to another. They have no "job rights" or seniority, and can be let go whenever they are no longer needed, or if their performance is not adequate. In time of frequent disasters, they may work several disasters back-to-back, occasionally without the opportunity to go home between assignments.

The second group of DAEs are *local hire* employees who are recruited within the impacted community. They are paid an hourly wage (and overtime) based on the local economy. They are not reimbursed for travel or meals and do not receive benefits. Like reservists, they are hourly employees who are terminated when they are no longer needed or when their performance warrants. Many are themselves disaster victims who were unemployed before or because of the disaster. The indefinite length of their employment is a major source of stress for these workers. As downsizing and layoffs inevitably begin to occur as recovery operations scale back, anxiety escalates.

AMERICAN RED CROSS DISASTER STAFFING

The American Red Cross was mandated by Congressional charter in 1905 to help meet the human needs created by disaster. Thus, the Red Cross role in disaster is a legal mandate that Red Cross has neither the authority nor the right to surrender. Nonetheless, the Red Cross receives no government funding for its services, and relies solely upon voluntary contributions.

Several types of Red Cross personnel are used in disasters. *Professional staff* consists of paid personnel who work out of local chapters, regional offices, or national headquarters. Their regular roles entail a wide range of activities, not necessarily disaster related. After receiving the organization's disaster training, they may be assigned temporarily to a disaster operation anywhere in the country(Hartsough, 1985). For the local chapter in a disaster impacted community, staff may be involved in disaster-related activities and pressures for a year or more after a large-scale disaster.

The ***Disaster Services Human Resource Team*** (DSHR) consists of professional staff and volunteers who have received all of the basic Red Cross disaster-related courses, including CPR and First Aid. This cadre consists of about two thousand workers who are deployed for a minimum of three weeks' assignment, which can be extended at mutual agreement of the Red Cross and the worker. The professional staff are paid their usual salary, plus travel and maintenance. Volunteers on the team receive no salary, but are reimbursed for travel and maintenance.

The Red Cross also has a small cadre of experienced disaster workers on *reserve* status. When they are deployed to a disaster, they are paid for their work, travel, and maintenance. Unlike professional staff, reservists can choose whether to accept a particular assignment. They have received specialized training, and perform both frontline and supervisory duties (Hartsough, 1985).

Red Cross *volunteer* disaster workers may be ongoing volunteers with an impacted chapter, or may be brought in from other chapters. In every disaster, there are also a (sometimes large) number of "convergent" or "spontaneous" volunteers who report to Red Cross sites and offer to work for hours, days, or weeks. Volunteers vary in their training and experience, and for convergent volunteers, training is usually on-the-job. Mental health staff working for the Red Cross Disaster Mental Health program are volunteers, and receive travel and maintenance but no salary. They are required to take a special Red Cross class in Disaster Mental Health.

REVIEW OF THE LITERATURE ABOUT THESE WORKERS

The roles, responsibilities, stresses, and traumatic impact of longterm recovery activities on disaster workers have been scantily described in the literature, and have rarely been empirically studied. Hartsough (Hartsough and Myers, 1985) described the effects of flooding in Louisiana in 1983 on the Red Cross workers involved in recovery efforts in the first weeks following the disaster. In the same monograph, Myers described the typical phases involved in disaster work and the stressors inherent in each phase for the workers, including the "letdown" involved after longterm disaster assignments. She incorporated many of Hartsough's observations and concepts into a training manual for disaster worker stress management (Myers, 1985a).

Eby (1984) outlined some sources of stress for Red Cross workers involved in small, local disasters as well as those workers who responded to repeatedly to major disasters. Beginning with such observations of stressors for Red Cross workers early in the 1980s, the Red Cross began a collaboration with mental health professionals from the American Psychological Association (later expanded to include other professional groups) on mitigation of stress for Red Cross workers. In 1990, the Red Cross began development of a disaster mental health course to train mental health professionals to intervene with stress of both disaster survivors and disaster workers. The course is currently taught throughout the United States. With the course, the agency produced a series of brochures entitled *Coping with Disaster* that focuses on emotional health issues for disaster workers and their families.

The Center for Mental Health Services (CMHS, formerly the National Institute of Mental Health) and FEMA have a long history of collaborative efforts to reduce the stressful impact of disasters for workers as well as for victims. In the last decade and a half, FEMA and CMHS have developed many publications and training materials on management of disaster worker stress (Department of Health and Human Services [DHHS], 1988a; DHHS, 1988b; FEMA, 1987a; FEMA, 1987b).

Rosensweig & Vaslow (1992) conducted a study for FEMA and NIMH to identify sources of stress among FEMA Disaster Assistance Program employees. Five hundred FEMA employees were surveyed, and the resulting report made specific recommendations for stress reduction for FEMA workers. Myers (1992, 1993, 1994a, 1994b) and Myers and Zunin (1993a, 1993b, 1994b) incorporated many of Rosensweig and Vaslow's ideas into the stress management programs they developed and directed for FEMA workers in many disasters, including Hurricane Andrew, the Midwest Floods of 1993, and the Northridge Earthquake of 1994. Conner (1992) described some differences between first responders and longer-term disaster relief workers. Noting that already existent critical incident stress management (CISM) teams might be called upon for help in debriefing disaster workers, he made suggestions for how CISM teams could tailor their services to the different needs of these workers.

Armstrong et al. (1991) describe stressors experienced by Red Cross relief personnel working in the two-month period following the Loma Prieta Earthquake, and describe a multiple stressor debriefing model they developed for use in exit debriefings for personnel before they returned home. They also recommend an Entry Group for new workers coming into the disaster operation, using the debriefing model as a structured briefing on the many expected stressors for the specific disaster. In addition, they suggested a Mid-assignment Group to address current effects of the work on personnel and to focus on positive coping strategies.

Finally, a small number of studies have examined the impact of disaster recovery work upon mental health staff providing postdisaster counseling. These studies recommend that this specialized group of disaster recovery workers pay special attention to their vulnerability to stress and posttrauma sequelae, lest they become "victims-by-proxy" (Bartone, Ursano, Wright, & Ingraham, 1989; Berah, Jones, & Valent, 1984; Figley, 1994; Frederick, 1977; Hodgkinson & Shepherd, 1994; Raphael, Singh, Bradbury, & Lambert, 1984; Winget & Umabenhauser, 1982).

SOURCES OF STRESS FOR LONGTERM DISASTER WORKERS

Hartsough and Myers (1985) describe numerous stressors for disaster workers, of which two types are most prominent in the longterm recovery efforts: (a) event stressors, and (b) occupational stressors.

EVENT STRESSORS

Factors related to the disaster

The *type of disaster* will influence the postimpact recovery environment, and will have influence on worker stress during the longterm recovery phase. For example, technological disasters are often more stressful for workers than natural disasters because of the feeling that they could have been prevented. As workers are exposed to the longterm suffering of the victims, workers' anger and blame may increase rather than subside. Disasters involving human-to-human violence, such as riots and civil unrest, or disasters occurring in high crime areas challenge personnel with a work environment in which they may be continually anxious about personal safety. Disasters that involve hazardous materials contamination of a community may also leave workers anxious about health hazards in their work environment.

Continued threat of recurrence, or actual recurrence, such as repeated flooding in the Midwest in the months after the Great Flood of 1993 and aftershocks from most large earthquakes, subjects workers to prolonged, intermittent stress and fear. A strong aftershock rocked Los Angeles 11 months after the Northridge quake. One mental health nurse working in the disaster Crisis Counseling Program, who had suffered losses in the earthquake, said "This one felt worse than the original quake. I don't know if I can take this any more." Aftershocks are wearing on both the local workers who experienced the original quake as well as out-of-town workers who have no prior experience or training in earthquake safety and survival.

Personal loss or injury

When disaster workers are primary victims of the disaster, they themselves may have lost property, friends, or loved ones. Simultaneously struggling with personal recovery as well as holding a disaster recovery job may be a mixed blessing and burden for the worker. On the one hand, simply having a job will provide them with a necessary structure and financial stability. The ability to empathize with survivors may be enhanced by the worker's own losses. However, the worker must be able to maintain perspective and avoid the hazards of overidentification with survivors (Myers, 1994b). Many worker/victims have been known to immerse themselves in the disaster recovery work to the extent that they neglect their own needs. This may put the worker at real risk if personal, family, and financial needs are not being attended to in a timely manner and if the worker's own grieving for personal losses is postponed or ignored.

A worker may be injured by the aftermath of the event, e.g., aftershocks, unsafe conditions of roads and buildings, or unfamiliar commutes to work. Ten months after the Northridge earthquake, hospitals in Los Angeles reported a sharp rise in accidents and deaths among contractors working to rebuild and repair quake-damaged structures ("Worker Deaths Rise," 1994). Trauma was the result of falls from roofs, ladders, and scaffolding, as well as miscellaneous injuries such as self-inflicted wounds from nail guns. One building inspector died after falling 66 feet down a hole during reconstruction of a house.

Injury may occur because of crime in the community, especially in urban areas. Several months after Hurricane Andrew, one government worker was injured after leaving work late at night when her car was surrounded by a group of young men, the windows were smashed, and her purse was stolen. She was so traumatized that she returned home to the west coast the following day, never returning to work, and sought both medical and psychological care. In another incident several months after the Los Angeles Fires and civil unrest, a building inspector was robbed at gunpoint while doing a building inspection. He requested release from work and returned to his home in another state, never telling his supervisor what had occurred or how frightened he had been for his life. In both cases, the inability to continue the job was an additional painful loss on the heels of the original victimization.

Fatigue may also contribute to worker illness, accident-proneness, and injury. It is not uncommon for physicians and nurses caring for disaster workers to report a wide range of health problems that they believe to be related to the "wear and tear" of the longterm stress associated with the work. In addition, workers experience falls, sprains and strains, minor automobile accidents, and a host of other injuries that they quite candidly attribute to being exhausted and mentally overloaded.

Exposure to traumatic stimuli

Many of the traumatic stimuli to which disaster workers are exposed occurs during and immediately after impact, when workers are involved in search, rescue, and recovery of bodies. However, there continues to be traumatic exposure for workers in longterm recovery efforts.

One such source of trauma is continued sensory exposure to disaster damages. Sights, sounds, and smells continue to keep the disaster alive for many long months and, sometimes, years. One disaster mental health worker described her feelings every time she drove by the collapsed Northridge Meadows apartment complex (collapsed in the Northridge Quake, but not demolished for almost one year after the earthquake): "I thought my tears should be over by now, but I cry every time I go by it." The worker was affected by more than the sight itself. For months, she had been counseling victims who had survived the collapse, listening to their stories of helplessness and terror. Through the victims she counseled, she heard of the loss of their loved ones and friends who died in the building. "I now know some dead by name, and feel as though I know them personally. My clients' loss feels like my own loss and I cry for those people when I see this place." This candid remark was from an insightful, self-aware therapist who knew the dangers of "overidentification" with disaster victims' pain. Despite her efforts to protect herself through frequent debriefings, regular supervision, peer support, and a limited caseload of disaster clients, she had become a secondary victim.

Mission failure or human error

This stressor is most commonly found in immediate response, search, and rescue, when personnel are involved in life and death efforts that cannot always be successful. Such a losses often generates a strong sense of powerlessness, helplessness, frustration, and anger.

In longterm recovery, this stressor manifests itself in different situations. Workers often experience frustration at the length of time and perceived "redtape" involved in getting financial and material assistance to victims, and at the unexpected roadblocks to individual and community recovery. Most experienced disaster workers can tell at least one story of a time when they have overstepped the bounds of their formal role to provide a victim with financial or material assistance. Workers take this step because of their frustration at "the system" which does not seem to be helping in a timely manner. While such frustration is understandable, workers need to remain clear about legal and ethical role boundaries, and be alert to the problems of overidentification with the victim. Workers must do all they can responsibly do to assist and empower the survivor. Beyond that, they must be willing and able to "be with" and support survivors who may be suffering tragedy, enormous loss, and frustration without being compelled to "fix" every situation that needs fixing (Myers, 1994b).

OCCUPATIONAL STRESSORS

Many stressors impacting disaster workers have to do with the nature of disaster work itself. In longterm recovery, these may include the following:

Pressures

While the immediate pressure of saving lives and property is past, there remains a great deal of pressure on longterm recovery workers because of high public and self-expectations. As months pass, the sense of urgency to process applications, complete building inspections, and generally "fix things" often increases, especially for new workers who are not familiar with how long disaster recovery takes. Besides a sense of *time pressure*, workers feel tremendous *responsibility* pressure.

Pressures on workunits and individual workers will depend upon the tasks, responsibilities, and workload of the unit. As the work does get done and the pace of the work begins to wind down, personnel often experience a perceived "work underload" (Hartsough, 1985). They become bored by the slower, less "exciting" pace of the work, and tedium and symptoms of burnout may begin to creep in. Reservist and hourly employees are often reluctant to talk about these feelings, however, because they know they are vulnerable to layoff when they are no longer needed.

Perhaps the most commonly named pressure in disaster work, be it immediate response or longterm, is the pressure to *adapt to constant change*. As disaster recovery organizations seek to be as responsive as possible to the changing needs and political pressures of the recovering community, changes in procedure may be made. For workers, this requires a large dose of flexibility and adaptability, and can cause a great deal of aggravation and headache. Because of the unprecedented, catastrophic nature of Hurricane Andrew, there were many changes in usual response/recovery procedures for federal agencies. The constant change caused enormous pressure for personnel. It is not surprising that the most popular cartoon among disaster workers in Hurricane Andrew depicted a popular western film star with a handgun pointing at the viewer, with the caption "Go ahead, make one more change." The cartoon perfectly expressed the frustrations of the workers in that particular disaster operation, and illustrates how humor unique to the disaster worker culture is a stress mitigator for personnel.

Demands

In longterm recovery, work schedules tend to normalize for personnel, so they are working more reasonable hours, with regular days off, than during response and early recovery. However, many staff, especially management and supervisory personnel, continue to work long hours and long weeks. The *physical* demands of the work schedule require strength and stamina, and may affect health and family relationships. Similarly, *mental* demands on both workers and management include the need for good judgment, clarity of thinking, and the ability to make wise decisions and to set priorities under public scrutiny and public pressure. Hartsough (1985) illustrates the mental demands placed on Red Cross recovery workers having to make decisions on some unusual requests for assistance by victims of flooding in Louisiana. A new bathtub was requested by a man who woke up in his mobile home to find not only 3 inches of water covering his floor, but a cottonmouth moccasin in his tub. He shot the snake with a shotgun, also "killing" his bathtub! Claiming he lost his tub to the disaster, he requested that the Red Cross replace it for him. They did.

Workers are also subjected to a multitude of *emotional demands*. Hartsough and Myers (1985) emphasize that the emotional impact of disaster is especially strong for workers if contact with survivors is this prolonged. Workers identify with and sometimes take on the frustrations of the survivors who are struggling with setbacks and roadblocks in their rebuilding efforts. Continuous exposure to survivors' stories of loss and grief can be painful for workers and, if unrecognized, can play into an unconscious desire to avoid listening (Myers, 1994b). Conner also emphasizes this liability of longterm disaster work, pointing out that being on assignment for weeks or months at a time makes "professional detachment" a virtual impossibility for disaster recovery workers (1992). Figley (1994) has studied this phenomenon and refers to it as "compassion fatigue," or "secondary victimization." He notes that work which consists of relieving emotional suffering entails processing information about human suffering. It may also mean absorbing that suffering, as well.

It should also be recognized that recovery workers intervene at a different phase of the disaster than first responders. Immediate response occurs in what is called the "heroic" phase, in which victims and workers experience a high level of shock, disbelief, and gratitude to be alive. There is a great deal of heroism among both citizens and workers, and much altruism and appreciation of efforts. This emotional climate quiets down but continues with a general mood of optimism in the short-lived "honeymoon" phase. Hopes are high for quick recovery and expectations are high for assistance that is assumed will be forthcoming from the government and other agencies. Enter FEMA and the Red Cross, who provide a myriad of services and benefits, but whose resources were never intended by law or by charter to replace everything that was lost. The public's expectations for quick recovery and total replacement are dashed by reality. Simultaneously, the numbness and initial shock of the disaster are wearing off, and the implications of the financial and emotional losses are sinking in. Sadness, grief, tears, and later, depression, occur, and disappointment, frustration, and anger surface. This is the emotional climate of the "disillusionment" phase, which is the predominant phase over the first year postimpact. This is the phase in which longterm workers toil. They are vulnerable to strong identification with the feelings of the survivors. They are also often the target of displaced emotions of the victims, particularly anger.

Several months after a flood and mudslide disaster in northern California, survivors were angry at FEMA for what they perceived to be an inordinate delay in the processing of applications for assistance. In reality, the disaster was a very complicated one in terms of liabilities and benefits for victims, largely related to ambiguities about insurance coverage. Was the damage caused by earth movement, which might or might not be covered depending upon the wording of the homeowner's policy, or was it caused by flooding, which is definitely not covered by homeowner's insurance, unless the owner also has purchased a separate flood insurance policy? Until these questions were decided by the insurance companies, many FEMA programs were unavailable to survivors, as these programs are intended only to cover losses not covered by other sources. In one case, survivors banded together and took a wheelbarrow of mud from the flood into the FEMA office and dumped it on a worker's desk. While their frustration is understandable and their actions undoubtedly felt cathartic, the workers involved were themselves unwitting victims of displaced anger.

The anecdote illustrates an added stressor on workers: they are vulnerable to the community's perception of the agency by whom the workers are employed. The public is generally not knowledgeable of the complicated intricacies of the disaster recovery environment. Often, perceived slowness or unhelpfulness on the part of relief agencies can make a given agency extremely unpopular. Armstrong et al. (1991) note that victims' dissatisfaction with the relief efforts and victims' anger toward an "indifferent" bureaucracy represented by the Red Cross and FEMA was a significant source of stress for Red Cross workers in the Loma Prieta earthquake.

Work environment

Disaster recovery workers may be office-based personnel processing applications for assistance and performing other paperwork, computer, and phone functions. Because office space may be at a premium in a community impacted by a large disaster, conditions are often less than ideal. Offices may be in large warehouse-like facilities, with work units separated by moveable partitions. Noise, interruptions, poor lighting and air conditioning are frequent aspects of "less than ideal working conditions." As the workload and staffing needs change, work units frequently move from one location to another. Two months after the Northridge earthquake, federal and state workers were jokingly threatening to order some Northridge disaster worker t-shirts stating "My cubicle moved more times than your cubicle." For workers on field-based assignments, such as inspectors and outreach workers, their car may be their office, with the concomitant challenges of maintaining communication, completing paperwork, and the like. Field-based workers are additionally stressed by exposure to inclement weather; environmental hazards; travel challenges such as damaged roads, lack of road signs, destroyed street addresses on buildings, or complete lack of access (bridges out, etc.); continual sights of damages; and frequent interaction with victims.

Living conditions

There are two categories of workers to consider when examining living conditions: local workers and "out of towners."

Local workers may themselves be victims of the disaster, struggling to juggle the demands of damaged living quarters, temporary housing (or homelessness), family needs, and a stressful job with long hours and a long commute over damaged roads. Many locally hired disaster workers were unemployed before hire by the disaster agency, and need to hastily arrange childcare and other family support functions. In a stress management exercise with disaster personnel in the Northridge quake, the following were listed by workers as the stressors for local workers: being a new employee (many adjustments); arranging child care on short notice; concerns for family when away from home; being a victim of the disaster; damages to my house (buckets all over the place when it rains); personal losses; destroyed apartment and now living out of boxes and sleeping on a friend's couch; financial stresses; victim of the system (my own application, loan and insurance paperwork); too busy to apply for assistance for my own losses; long commute; long day at work; no time to do laundry, go to bank, post office, or doctor; too tired for sex and my spouse doesn't understand.

Out of town personnel list other stressors: packing and parting from home under pressure and with little notice; unfamiliarity with the community, the roads, the hotels, the culture, the resources for victims; finding resources for self (doctor, church, gym, dry cleaner, grocery stores, 12-step meetings, etc.); unknown environment and concern for personal safety; living in hotels with no refrigerator or cooking facilities; restaurant food and diet changes; worrying about and missing family and friends; obligations at home; unfamiliar climate/weather; no social life. Showing inimitable disaster worker humor, a flier appeared at the Disaster Field Office in the Northridge quake entitled "You Know It's Time To Go Home When:" you start referring to your hotel room as home; you start rearranging the furniture "at home;" you know trouble spots on the radio traffic report; the state you're working in tries to collect delinquent income tax from you; it is two seasons past whatever sport was in season when you left home.

Loss and letdown when the job is over

Disaster work is stressful, but it is also inherently rewarding. Workers experience excitement, intensity, stimulation, a sense of community, and feelings of helpfulness and accomplishment (Myers, 1985a). Strong bonds occur among disaster personnel and between workers and victims (Conner, 1992). One experienced disaster worker noted a common saying among disaster workers when it comes to go home and leave disaster worker friends: "It's time to leave our loved ones and go home to our families." The phrase captures two important aspects of the "letdown" phase for workers after an assignment.

First, leaving the operation is painful, and a grief response and some mild depression and mood swings for workers are common after going home (Conners, 1992). Workers often stay in touch via letters and phone calls, and sometimes wish or fantasize that they were back on the job. The second aspect of letdown has to do with the transition back into family and "life after disaster." It may be difficult for the worker to slow down and adjust to a normal pace and routine. While the worker craves sleep, the family may want and need attention, time, and energy. The worker may wish to talk about the experience, only to find that family want to talk about what happened to them in the worker's absence (FEMA, 1987b). Problems presented by the family may seem trivial compared to those encountered by the disaster worker on assignment (Conner, 1992). Recognizing, planning for, and coping with these reactions is an important aspect of coping with disaster worker stress.

Stress management programs for longterm disaster workers have found that a major source of anxiety for personnel occurs around the time of "downsizing" the disaster operation. While workers <u>know</u> cognitively that their jobs are temporary, at the time of release they often experience anger, frustration, and confusion about why certain workers were let go while others kept their jobs (Varblow, 1994). Exit groups (using modified debriefing techniques) can help personnel to express their feelings and deal with transition issues.

EFFECTS OF STRESS ON WORKERS

Symptoms of acute, delayed, and cumulative stress among emergency workers have been extensively covered in the literature (Hartsough & Myers, 1985; Mitchell & Bray, 1990; Mitchell and Everly, 1993; Myers and Zunin, 1994a). For the most part, stress reactions experienced by longterm disaster recovery workers fit those of the cumulative stress category. Commonly observed by stress management consultants and by crisis counseling staff working with disaster personnel are: fatigue and depression; concentration, memory, and cognitive problems; irritability and interpersonal conflicts; anxiety, especially related to job tenure and related to obligations at home that are "left undone"; feeling unappreciated; distancing from others and from the job; cynicism and negativity; use of derogatory labels; "sick" or gallows humor; blaming others; poor job performance; absences; physical complaints and illness; accident proneness; and alcohol and substance abuse.

Very little empirical research has been done on longterm disaster workers and the effects of their work-related stressors. The research that exists suggests that workers continue to experience significant levels of symptomatology during their entire tenure of disaster support work. Hodgkinson & Shepherd (1994), in their study of disaster crisis counselors, found significant levels of symptomatology twelve months into the disaster recovery work. Symptoms most frequently reported included cognitive difficulties, depression, and feelings of inadequacy and insecurity.

Following the Northridge Earthquake, a team of stress management consultants provided services to federal and state workers in the DFO and 42 other fixed and mobile sites for three months following the disaster (Myers & Zunin, 1994b). At the end of the three months, it was determined that stress management services were still needed, and should be continued under the direction of Project Rebound, the Los Angeles County FEMA Crisis Counseling Project. During the period seven to ten months after the earthquake, they provided services to 4,656 people (4134 received one-on-one services, while 522 participated in group services) (Varblow, 1994). This level of service delivery clearly indicates that workers both needed and sought out formal stress managment support for themselves.

STRESS MITIGATORS FOR WORKERS

Rosensweig & Vaslow (1992), in their survey of 500 FEMA personnel (permanent full-time and "reservists") ranked the top fourteen "stress reducers" listed by these experienced workers. They were:

1. Felt this was an opportunity rather than an imposition.
2. Shared and discussed pending deployment with family/ friends.
3. Had an action plan ready to go to take over current responsibilities (e.g., bill payment, childcare, household tasks/chores, list of all personal tasks to be completed prior to departure).
4. Kept in regular contact with friends and/or family.
5. Had "essentials" (e.g., toiletries, change of clothing, travelers' checks, alarm clock, telephone/address book, etc.) packed and ready to go.

6. Made sure there was quality time spent with family and/or friends.

7. Kept in mind the friends who might be on the assignment.

8. Received debriefing from family and/or friends regarding what had happened while away.

9. Made sure to get proper amount of rest/sleep.

10. Took time to reflect on all that had happened and how things could be done differently next time.

11. Used known techniques to alleviate stress (e.g., exercising, keeping a diary or journal, reading, sketching, etc.)

12. Paid strict attention to eating properly and/or regularly.

13. Reviewed briefing book on the roles and responsibilities of a disaster worker.

14. Allowed self to feel appreciated and honored for going beyond the call of duty, for being there for others in a time of need, for making a difference, etc.

Other coping mechanisms commonly described among longterm workers include: keeping and using their sense of humor; developing new friendships on the job; using peer support; using a buddy system; not taking victims' anger personally; keeping realistic expectations; using time management techniques to maximize "quality time" when off duty; playing tourist when off duty (out of towners); having family come to visit (out of towners); organizing sports events (softball and volleyball tournaments, etc.); potluck meals on and off-site; taking breaks between seeing victims; using religious/spiritual support; and utilizing stress management services and education.

A COMPREHENSIVE STRESS MANAGEMENT PROGRAM FOR WORKERS

In recent years, a variety of approaches and interventions have been used in helping disaster workers to cope with the demands and stresses of their work. With long-term recovery workers, there is no single intervention that will provide a panacea. A broad-based, comprehensive approach to disaster worker stress management is essential. For mental health personnel providing stress management services to disaster workers to rely on any single approach, such as debriefing, they are "functioning at less than a fraction of (their) capacity" (Mitchell & Everly, 1993).

An important first step in comprehensive stress management involves screening and selecting disaster personnel who have personal and professional qualifications that make them suited for the work (Myers, 1994b). Besides selecting staff with certain knowledge and competencies, it is recommended that specific training modules be included in the basic training of all disaster recovery personnel. These modules should include:

1) understanding the common reactions of disaster survivors;
2) understanding and applying culturally competent interventions as they apply to disaster response and recovery;
3) communication skills for dealing with survivors who may be bereaved, upset, confused, demanding, or angry;
4) disaster worker stress and stress management.

Beyond basic training in the above topics, the following range of services has been found to be effective in providing comprehensive stress management to state and federal workers in numerous, recent large-scale disasters (Myers, 1994a; Myers & Zunin, 1993a, 1993b, 1994b; Varblow, 1994):

A) NEEDS ASSESSMENT:

A needs assessment is the crucial first step in designing and implementing a stress management program for a given disaster. A needs assessment should be initiated by management staff in consultation with appropriately chosen stress managers. These consultants should have extensive experience in disaster mental health and stress management service delivery. Factors to be considered in assessing worker needs include size of disaster, intensity, degree of human and material losses, impact on the community, number of staff deployed, and other pertinent issues.

Stress management personnel must meet initially and regularly with top management staff in the disaster operation as an essential part of ongoing needs assessment. Direct observation of the work environments of personnel reveals both stressors and stress levels among workers. Interviewing line staff about sources of stress and how they observe stress reactions in their work unit and among coworkers is done as soon as possible. This process continues with regular, daily outreach in the work units.

B) CONSULTATION WITH MANAGEMENT:

Stress consultants need to meet regularly with management and key supervisory staff. This includes attending important staff meetings. These meetings provide a two-way exchange regarding work-related stressors, confidential issues concerning particular personnel situations, and anticipated changes that might affect workers. In addition, managers and supervisors can discuss confidentially any stress issues that are specifically affecting them.

C) OUTREACH:

Frequent rounds through the work units are an essential component of the stress management program. Outreach should occur in all sites where disaster personnel are working, including offices, community based centers, in the field, etc. Outreach involves circulating through work units and outdoor break areas and interacting with personnel. Brief suggestions, mild ventilation, ad-hoc stress management education and occasional suggestions for a brief individual consultation between consultant and worker can be made.

D) DEBRIEFING:

Modified debriefings with a significant educational emphasis may be held. A stress management consultant with specialized disaster CISD training leads the session. The specially modified CISD format assists workers in talking about the personal impact of job or disaster stress and helps them to identify, share, and reinforce healthy, adaptive coping techniques.

Debriefings can be held as periodic stress management groups for personnel in ongoing work assignments. They can also be held at the end of a tour of duty, as workers are demobilized and prepare to go home or to another work assignment.

E) EDUCATION AND TRAINING:

1) On-site stress management education:

   Brief "mini-classes" or stress-related discussions may be conducted with small groups in the work unit.

2) "Recharges":

Brief "defusing" sessions in the work units can allow personnel to discuss work-related stressors and effective coping approaches. Stress management tips may be taught and practiced, such as posture and ergonomics, deep breathing techniques, gentle stretching exercises for sore muscles, quick tips for stress breaks at the work site, techniques for handling distraught callers, tips for more effective communication with coworkers or supervisors, etc.

3) Seminars:

Seminars are held at regular times to help individuals understand the unique emotional aspects of disaster work and disaster worker stress management. Topics may vary depending upon the phase of the disaster and the needs, concerns, and interests of staff. Sessions typically include such topics as common emotional reactions of survivors and workers (both during and after disaster); practical suggestions for communicating by phone or in person with applicants; understanding and effectively communicating with specific cultural customs, values, styles, and protocols relevant to the region; dealing with anger; and conflict resolution. Stress management techniques are taught, with attention to developing effective coping tools. Preparations for "life after disaster" emotional reactions and coping strategies may be reviewed as demobilization of some staff or work units approaches.

4) Educational materials:

Workplace stress management handouts should be developed to fit the unique needs of disaster workers on the job and made widely available to workers.

F) INDIVIDUAL CONSULTATION:

Brief individual sessions can be made available to disaster worker staff both by appointment or drop-in basis to deal with work-related stress issues. The focus of the consultation is coping enhancement. It is not psychotherapy. When individual problems or needs are identified for which additional sessions are warranted, referral to a local mental health resource is indicated.

RECOMMENDATIONS FOR THE FUTURE

From observation and the limited research of the stressors impacting this population of workers, it would appear that there are at least two areas of risk resulting from the ongoing, unrelenting stresses of this occupational group.

First, it seems likely that this group is at risk for *health-related problems* resulting from several factors: exposure to hazards and toxins in the disaster environment; accidents as a result of poor concentration, fatigue, and excessive sensory stimuli; health influences from the culturally popular use of alcohol and stimulants such as caffeine and nicotine; ill-effects of poor diet; communicable diseases as a result of stress-induced immune system depression; increase in allergies and autoimmune diseases as a result of unmitigated stress; and target organ disease resulting from ongoing "wear and tear" on the body from unrelenting activation of the stress response.

A second area of likely vulnerability would be the arena of family relationships. The amount of time spent away from home (by both local and out-of-town staff) and the pressure of coping with relationship maintenance and activities of daily living in limited blocks of time can take a toll. In addition, the continual "good-byes and hellos" of disaster personnel who travel in their work, and the intensity of disaster worker relationships on the job cannot be without impact on the worker's family system. Just as CISM programs are increasingly recognizing the importance of family factors and support for emergency professionals' families, so too this area needs to be further studied and attended to for the disaster worker population.

Mental health and CISM personnel who seek to assist longterm recovery workers in managing their work-related stress could greatly benefit from empirical research further clarifying the stressors, stress impacts, and stress mitigators for this population. Outcome evaluation of stress management programs should be conducted to improve appropriateness and effectiveness. Such empirical research can help further fine-tune disaster worker selection procedures, training, and development of mental health education programs and stress management interventions to help this dedicated and at-risk group of personnel.

REFERENCES

American Red Cross. (1977). *Your Community Could Have a Disaster.* (ARC 1570).

Armstrong, K., O'Callahan, W., & Marmar, C. R. (1991). Debriefing Red Cross disaster personnel: The multiple stressor debriefing model. *Journal of Traumatic Stress, 4*, 581-593.

Bartone, P., Ursano, R., Wright, K., & Ingraham, L. (1989). Impact of a military air disaster. *Journal of Nervous and Mental Disease, 177*, 317-328.

Berah, E., Jones, H., & Valent, P. (1984). The experience of a mental health team involved in the early phase of a disaster. *Australia and New Zealand Journal of Psychiatry, 18*, 354-358.

Blake, D.D., Albano, A.M., & Keane, T.M. (1992). Twenty years of trauma: Psychology abstracts 1970 through 1989. *Journal of Traumatic Stress, 5*, 477-484.

Bush, J. C. (1979). *A handbook for church action*. Scottsdale, PA: Herald Press.

Butcher, J. M. & Hatcher, C. (1988). The neglected entity in air disaster planning. *American Psychologist, 43*, 724-729.

Conner, S. (1992). Debriefing disaster workers. *Life Net, 3*, 1-2.

Department of Health and Human Services. (1988a). *Prevention and control of stress among emergency workers: A pamphlet for team managers* (DHHS Publication No. ADM 88-1496). Washington, DC: U.S. Government Printing Office.

Department of Health and Human Services. (1988b). *Prevention and control of stress among emergency workers: A pamphlet for workers* (DHHS Publication No. ADM 88-1497). Washington, DC: U.S. Government Printing Office.

Dunning, C. (1985). Prevention of stress. In *Role stressors and supports for Emergency Workers*. (DHHS Publication No. ADM 85-1408). Rockville, MD: National Institute of Mental Health.

Dunning, C. (1988). Intervention strategies for emergency workers. In M. Lystad (Ed.), *Mental health response to mass emergencies: Theory and practice*. New York: Brunner/Mazel.

Dunning, C., & Silva, M. (1980). Disaster-induced trauma in rescue workers. *Victimology, 5*, 287-297.

Durham, T. W., McCammon, S. L., & Allison, E. J. (1985). The psychological impact of disaster on rescue personnel. *Annals of Emergency Medicine, 14*, 664-668.

Eby, D. L. (1984). A disaster worker's response. In *Role Stressors and Supports for Emergency Workers*. (DHHS Publication No. ADM 85-1408). Rockville, Maryland: National Institute of Mental Health.

Federal Emergency Management Agency. (1987a). *FEMA workers can be affected by disasters* (Brochure L-156). Washington, DC: Federal Emergency Management Agency and National Institute of Mental Health.

Federal Emergency Management Agency. (1987b). *Returning home after the disaster: An information pamphlet for FEMA disaster workers* (Brochure l-157). Washington, DC: Federal Emergency Management Agency and National Institute of Mental Health.

Figley, C.R. (1994, August). Compassion fatigue: A model and treatment implications of secondary PTSD. *Paper presented at the anual meeting of the American Psychological Association*, Los Angeles.

Forstenzer, A. (1980). Stress, the psychological scarring of air crash rescue personnel. *Firehouse, 7,* 50-62.

Frederick, C. J. (1977). Current thinking about crisis or psychological interventions in United States disasters. *Mass Emergencies, 2,* 43-49.

Hartsough, D. M. (1985). Stress and mental health interventions in three major disasters. In Hartsough, D. M. & Myers, D. G., *Disaster work and mental health: prevention and control of stress among workers*. (DHHS Publication No. ADM 85-1422). Rockville, MD: National Institute of Mental Health.

Hartsough, D. M., & Myers, D. G. (1985). *Disaster work and mental health: prevention and control of stress among workers*. (DHHS Publication No. ADM 85-1422). Rockville, MD: National Institute of Mental Health.

Hiley-Young, B. (in press). [Review of *Individual and community responses to trauma and disaster: The structure of human chaos]. Contemporary Psychology*.

Hodgkinson, P. E. & Shepherd, M. A. (1994). The impact of disaster support work. *Journal of Traumatic Stress, 7,* 587-600.

Jones, D. R. (1985). Secondary disaster victims: The emotional effects of recovering and identifying human remains. *American Journal of Psychiatry, 142,* 303-307.

Keating, J. (1986). *Psychological after effects of emergency workers at the Dallas/Fort Worth air crash.* Paper presented at the annual meeting of the Society for Traumatic Stress Studies.

Mantell, M. (1986). San Ysidro: When the badge turns blue. In J. Reese and H. Goldstein (Eds.), *Psychological services for law enforcement*. (U.S. Govt. Printing Office Publication No. 027-000-012-66-3). Washington, DC: U.S. Department of Justice, Federal Bureau of Investigation.

Mitchell, J. (1982). The psychological impact of the Air Florida 90 disaster on fire-rescue, paramedic, and police personnel. In R. A. Crowley (Ed.), *Mass casualties: A learned lesson approach*. Washington, D.C.: U.S. Department of Transportation.

Mitchell, J. (1983). When disaster strikes... the critical incident stress debriefing process. *Journal of Emergency Medical Services, 8*, 36-39.

Mitchell, J. (1985). Healing the helper. In *Role stressors and supports for emergency workers*. (DHHS Publication No. ADM 85-1408). Rockville, MD: National Institute of Mental Health.

Mitchell, J., & Bray, G. (1990). *Emergency services stress: Guidelines for preserving the health and careers of emergency services personnel*. Englewood Cliffs, NJ: Prentice-Hall.

Mitchell, J., & Everly, G. S. (1992, November). *The prevention of work-related post-traumatic stress: The critical incident stress debriefing process (CISD)*. Paper presented at the second APA/NIOSH Conference on Occupational Stress, Washington, D.C.

Mitchell, J., & Everly, G. S. (1993). *Critical incident stress debriefing: An operations manual for the prevention of traumatic stress among emergency services and disaster workers*. Ellicott City, MD: Chevron Publishing Company.

Myers, D. (1985a). Helping the helpers: A training manual. In Hartsough, D. M. & Myers, D. G. *Disaster work and mental health: prevention and control of stress among workers*. (DHHS Publication No. ADM 85-1422). Rockville, MD: National Institute of Mental Health.

Myers, D. (1985b). Role simplification in disaster: A response. In *Role Stressors and Supports for Emergency Workers*. (DHHS Publication No. ADM 85-1408). Rockville, Maryland: National Institute of Mental Health.

Myers, D. (1992). *Hurricane Andrew Disaster Field Office Stress Management Program After Action Report*. Washington, DC: Federal Emergency Management Agency.

Myers, D. (1993). *After Action Report, 1993 California Winter Storms*. Washington, DC: Federal Emergency Management Agency.

Myers, D. (1994a). *A stress management program for FEMA disaster workers* (Contract No. 93MF06480701D). Washington, DC: Federal Emergency Management Agency.

Myers, D. (1994b). *Disaster response and recovery: A handbook for mental health professionals.* (DHHS Publication No. SMA 94-3010). Rockville, MD: Public Health Service, Substance Abuse and Mental Health Services Administration, Center for Mental Health Services.

Myers, D. & Zunin, L.M. (1993a). *After Action Report: 1993 Florida Winter Storms Disaster Field Office Stress Management Program.* Washington, DC: Federal Emergency Management Agency.

Myers, D. & Zunin, L. M. (1993b) *After Action Report: 1993 Midwest Floods Central Processing Unit Stress Management Program.* Washington, DC: Federal Emergency Management Agency.

Myers, D. & Zunin, L. (1994a). *Cumulative stress reactions.* Unpublished training materials.

Myers, D. & Zunin, L. (1994b). *Stress Management Program After-Action Report: 1994 Northridge Earthquake.* Washington, DC: Federal Emergency Management Agency and California Governor's Office of Emergency Services.

Raphael, B., Singh, B., Bradbury, B., & Lambert, F. (1984). Who helps the helpers? The effects of a disaster on the rescue workers. *Omega, 14,* 9-20.

Rosensweig, M. A., & Vaslow, P. K. (1992). *Recommendations for Reduction of Stress Among FEMA Disaster Workers.* Washington, DC: National Institute of Mental Health.

Sloan, I. H., Rozensky, R. H., Kaplan, L., & Saunders, S. M. (1994). A shooting incident in an elementary school: Effects of worker stress on public safety, mental health, and medical personnel. *Journal of Traumatic Stress, 7,* 565-574.

Ursano, R. J., McCaughey, B. G., & Fullerton, C. S. (Eds.). (1994). *Individual and community responses to trauma and disaster: The structure of human chaos.* Cambridge, England: Cambridge University Press.

Varblow, P. (1994). Stress Management. In Los Angeles County Department of Mental Health, *Project Rebound, 2nd Quarterly Report* (FEMA DR-1008-CA: Northridge Earthquake). Los Angeles, CA.

Wilkinson, C. (1983). Aftermath of disaster: Collapse of the Hyatt Regency Hotel skywalks. *American Journal of Psychiatry, 140,* 1134-1139.

Winget, C. N., & Umbenhauer, S. L. (1982). Disaster planning: The mental health worker as "victim-by-proxy." *Journal of Health and Human Resources Administration, 4,* 363-373.

Worker deaths rise in quake's aftermath (1994, November 21). *The Monterey County Herald*, p. 5A.

PART III

INNOVATIONS IN INTERVENTION

PART III

INNOVATIONS IN INTERVENTION

Part III represents the final section of this volume. Contained within this section, the reader will find discussed various innovations in intervention strategies and technologies.

Chapter 12 provides the reader with a description and implementation protocol for a one-on-one crisis intervention technique that may be used "in the field" by mental health professionals as well as by specifically trained peer support counselors. The SAFE-R model of crisis intervention was developed specifically for use in the emergency and disaster related professions. It is also applicable for use by military personnel during combat.

Chapter 13 reviews "neurocognitive strategic therapy" for the treatment of post-traumatic stress. This therapy is not a specific therapeutic technology but rather represents a means of conceptualizing both post-traumatic stress as well as the specific tactical interventions ultimately employed for therapy.

As a natural corollary to Chapter 13, Chapter 14 introduces that which may be the most exciting technologic breakthrough in the field of traumatic stress ... Eye Movement Desensitization and Reprocessing (EMDR). Chapter 14 not only introduces the EMDR technology, but examines it by virtue of the neurocognitive model introduced in Chapter 13.

Finally, Chapter 15 describes a unique CISM intervention with a community volunteer fire service three and one half years after a tornado struck an elementary school. This intervention may be the first one of its kind ever attempted.

Chapter 12

CRISIS INTERVENTION: THE SAFE-R MODEL FOR EMERGENCY SERVICE, DISASTER RESPONSE, AND MILITARY PERSONNEL

GEORGE S. EVERLY, JR.

Critical incident stress management (CISM) programs have evolved far beyond their origins, having been spawned largely from the pre-incident stress education and Critical Incident Stress Debriefing (CISD) protocol developed by Jeffrey Mitchell (1976, 1981, 1983). Clearly then, CISM is more than the ability to implement the CISD protocol as noted in Chaper 7. It may be argued that no CISM program is truely complete unless it contains the ability to provide crisis intervention services on an individual basis at the scene, or venue, of any given critical incident, crisis situation, or disaster.

It is the premise of this chapter that effective one-on-one crisis intervention is an essential element of any CISM program, and further that such one-on-one interventions can be implemented by either licensed mental health practitioners or by specially trained

---

George S. Everly, Jr. • International Critical Incident Stress Foundation, Ellicott City, Maryland.
In G.S. Everly, Jr. Innovations in Disaster and Trauma Psychology, Volume One: Applications in Emergency Services and Disaster Response. Baltimore: Chevron Publishing Corp, 1995.

paraprofessional emergency service "peer support" personnel. In the present context, the term peer support personnel refers to individuals who have been operationally trained in one of the emergency services, disaster response, public safety, military, or humanitarian aid professions. In addition, however, the individuals have received further specialized training in the provision of psychological support services and crisis intervention. Such training might include courses in CISD applications, paraprofessional counseling techniques, crisis intervention, suicide intervention, stress management, and family support techniques.

The purpose of this chapter is to present the SAFE-R model for crisis intervention. This model was developed by the author expressly for use with emergency service, disaster response, and military personnel at the actual crisis, disaster, or combat venues, ie, "on-scene."

THE NATURE OF CRISIS

The essence of crisis from a psychological perspective is an individual finding him/herself unable to cope with a challenging, threatening, or otherwise aversive situation. Caplan (1961) defines a crisis as a situation in which an individual is confronted by a challenge or obstacle which proves insurmountable through the use of customary coping strategies. Under such conditions, the individual may be at a loss to resolve the crisis independently.

CRISIS REACTIONS

Although it is clear that individuals respond to crisis in very personal and idiosyncratic ways, it may be suggested that an overview of the crisis process may be constructed by way of a generic algorithm. See Figure 12.1.

Figure 12.1 delineates a generic alogorithm that may be applicable in understanding an individual's response to a crisis situation.

FIGURE 12.1
A CRISIS ALGORITHM

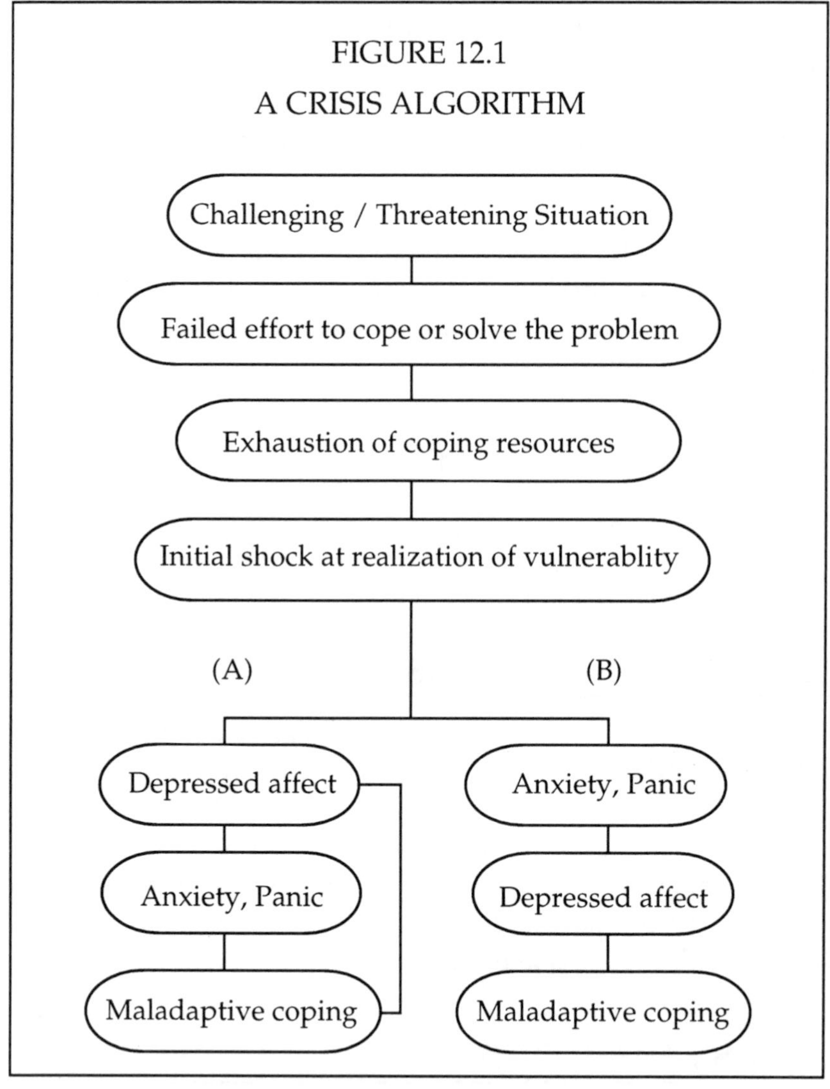

To begin, an individual finds him/herself in a challenging or threatening situation. The situation does not need to be physically threatening, it could be intellecually, emotionally, or professionally challenging.

In response, the individual typically employs coping strategies or problem-solving techniques that have proven historically successful. However, the crisis situation unfolds as the individual witnesses the failure of these usually successful behaviors.

At some point, as the crisis situation grows in intensity, the individual exhausts his/her compensatory resources.

For many individuals, there will be an initial "shock" at the realization that traditional coping resources have been exhaused. The intensity of the shock and the intensity of the subsequent decompensation process will be highly correlated with the degree of personal vulnerability that is perceived by the person in crisis.

From this point in the model, there exists a conceptual bifurcation. Some individuals will become increasingly depressed at their inability to resolve the crisis (A). This growing depression may lead to states of anxiety or panic, while later engendering maladaptive behavior patterns. Or, other individuals see their growing depression as leading directly to maladaptive coping behavior.

On the other hand, some individuals will become increasingly anxious exhibiting paroxysmal panic attacks (B). As the anxiety intensifies a prevailing sense of depression may prevail, then leading to maladaptive coping. Or, other individuals may attempt to deal with their anxiety through various maladaptive coping behaviors more immediately.

An individual may progress through the algorithm in Figure 12.1 in minutes, hours, days, or weeks. The most common type of crisis situation encountered by emergency response personnel requires a relatively short period of time for progressive deterioration through the algorithm.

Common signs and symptoms of crisis include cognitive slippage, decreased decision-making ability, panic, anxiety, depression, irritability, anger, hostility, interpersonal withdrawal, self-medication (eg, alchol, nicotine, caffeine, antihistamines, and various illicit drugs) and possibly acute psychophysiologic complaints.

GOALS OF CRISIS INTERVENTION

Most simply, crisis intervention is the provision of "emotional first aid." Crisis intervention is an exercise in psychological "damage control." Whether a mild crisis or an acute trauma situation, the concept of emotional first aid remains applicable.

Specific goals of crisis intervention may be thought of a follows:

1) Stopping the acute process of psychological deterioration/ decompensation that typifies a crisis condition.

2) Stabilization of cognitive and affective processes.

3) Management of acute symptoms of psychological distress/ dysfunction.

4) Restoration of independent adaptive functioning, or providing assistance in receiving continued acute care.

Crisis intervention is NOT psychotherapy, therefore, the use of traditional psychotherapy techniques designed to promote abreaction, the uncovering of repressed information, and the explicit discouragement of transference reactions are usually contraindicated.

HISTORICAL PERSPECTIVES

The concept of crisis intervention is by no means a new concept. According to Greenstone (1993) crisis intervention centers first emerged in the U.S. within the first decade of the 20th century and were seen primarily as suicide prevention centers. Greenstone goes on to note that crisis intervention, as we know today, emerged largely from the work of two individuals Gerald Caplan and Erich Lindemann, as discussed by Mitchell in Chapter 7.

Lindemann (1944) studied grief reations among those who lost loved ones in the Coconut Grove Club fire in Boston in 1942. Lindemann was joined by Gerald Caplan in the creation of a community mental health program affiliated with Harvard University where they refined their approach to patients in crisis.

The field of crisis intervention grew dramatically during the late 1960's and through the 1970's. Crisis intervention centers and telephone hotlines could be found in virtually every major urban setting. Law enforcement agencies began developing special crisis units (Greenstone, 1993). The crisis intervention movement grew largely because of the influx of paraprofessional and non-professional volunteer workers in response to the economic, political, and cultural turmoil that characterized the 1960's and 1970's.

The use of "peer support" personnel in the provision of crisis intervention services to emergency response and military personnel is not without controversy. There are some that believe that crisis intervention should be the sole domain of the licensed mental health professional. Yet the historical support for the use of "peer counselors" is extremely significant ranging from the Alcoholics Anonymous and similiar 12-step programs, through the youth services bureaus of the 1970's, up to the utilization of peer support personnel and CISM teams in police departments, fire services, and hospitals throughout the U.S. The U.S. Army and Marine Corps. also successfully utilize peer support models. Catherall and Lane (1992) powerfully argue the pros and cons of peer support model as it pertains to Vietnam veterans. Their comments provide insight for peer support programs wherever they are applied, however. Peer counselors possess the value of instant credibility, operational expertice, and unparalleled empathic ability. The peer counselor possesses unique disadvantages in the form of potentially contaminating countertransference reactions and the potential inability to recognize subtle but significant states of psychopathology. To reiterate, however, this chapter supports the view that peer counselors can be uniquely effective in providing support and crisis intervention services to emergency response and military personnel.

Having mentioned the suitability of peer support personnel, it seems appropriate to briefly mention the mental health practitioner and crisis intervention. Not all mental health practioners receive formal coursework nor receive supervised training in crisis intervention. Such experiences may often be "electives" in their training programs. Therefore, it seems important in the creation a crisis intervention component for any given CISM effort to select mental health practitioners carefully. Some criteria to consider might be:

1) formal supervised training in crisis intervention

2) experience in working with a) emergency response or military personnel, and b)the unique challenges that these personnel face

3) a personal tolerance for ambiguity

4) a personal tolerance for acute high pressure situations

5) formal supervised training in post-traumatic stress

While most mental health practitioners will possess the ability to rapidly and accurately assesss psychopathology while maintaining an appropriate objective distance, they may lack the operational understanding or familiarity with the emergency response "culture" to be initially effective. Thus the mental health practitioner may need to supplement his/her original training to be maximally effective in crisis situations.

Let us now examine the actual processes of crisis intervention themselves.

THE SAFE-R MODEL OF CRISIS INTERVENTION

As noted earlier, the concept of crisis intervention is not new, however, experience in working with emergency services and disaster response professional has taught that some alterations in otherwise accepted notions and mental health protocols may be of value when dealing with these task-directed, action-oriented individuals. The SAFE-R model represents a model of crisis intervention developed over a five year period which is directed specifically for use with emergency response and military personnel. The model may be employed by peer counselors as well as mental health practitioners. This model is summarized in Table 12.1 provided below. Let us take a closer look at this crisis intervention protocol.

TABLE 12.1	
THE SAFE-R MODEL:	
Crisis Intervention with Emergency Services, Disaster Response and Military Personnel	
Step One -	**S**timulation reduction
Step Two -	**A**cknowledgment of the crisis 1. "What happened?" 2. "How are you doing?"
Step Three -	**F**acilitation of understanding and normalization of symptoms / reactions
Step Four -	**E**xplanation of basic concepts of crisis, stress, and stress management; create coping plan
Step Five -	**R**estoration of independent functioning promoted *or* provision of assistance in obtaining acute care.

STIMULATION REDUCTION

The first step in crisis intervention must always be some form of introduction as the crisis interventionist approaches the person in crisis. This introduction should consist of a personal identification as well as some statement of one's intent/reason for approaching the person in crisis. Having achieved this goal, the next step in the SAFE-R model urges the crisis interventionist to reduce the level of stimulation affecting the person in crisis. Most commonly, this involves removing the individual in crisis from the acute crisis situation. This may be achieved by "taking a walk", "getting a cup of coffee", or any other diversionary process that provides the individual withsome "psychological distance" away from the source of the acute crisis or any other cues that appear to fuel the crisis situation.

ACKNOWLEDGMENT OF THE CRISIS

The second stage in the SAFE-R model is the acknowledgement of the crisis itself. This stage is actually a two-step process and is fostered by a skillful use of basic therapeutic communication techniques. The first step within this step of the model typically begins with the crisis interventionist asking the person in crisis to describe "what happened." This question is designed to stimulate cognitive processes within the person in crisis who is most likely affectively oriented at this point in time. Focusing upon cognitive processes serves to break any escalating emotional spirals and superimposes a structure upon the prevailing sense of chaos. Once havingallowed the individual to describe the crisis situation cognitively, the second step of this stage is approached so as not to deny the person in crisis the experience of affectively oriented cathartic ventilation, the crisis interventionist asks "How are you reacting to all of this now?"; or "How is all of this making you feel now?" Thus, the crisis interventionist allows the person to revisit the emotions associated with the crisis but in a more controlled manner and within a safe psychological climate.

FACILITATION OF UNDERSTANDING

The third stage in the present model involves a transition back to the cognitive psychological domain for the person in crisis. In this third stage, the crisis interventionist begins to actively respond to the information revealed by the person in crisis during the previous stage. Here, the person in crisis is encouraged to view his/her reactions to the crisis as generally "normal", expected reactions being experienced by a "normal" individual, in response to a abnormally challenging situation, ie., a crisis situation. The primary goals of this stage of the SAFE-R model are: 1) to assist the person in crisis in returning to the cognitive domain of psychological processing, and 2) to encourage the person in crisis to see his/her symptoms as basically "normal" reactions to an extraordinarily stressful event. It is important to note that when the crisis intervention process fails, the roots of the failure are most often within this stage. More specifically,

TABLE 12.2

A SUMMARY OF THE SAFE-R MODEL

Stage	***Content***	***Process***	***Action***	***Goal***
One	Stimulation reduction (and Introduction)	Behavioral	To remove the person in crisis from provocative cues.	To mitigate affective escalation. Allows mental status assessment.
Two	Acknowledgement of crisis	Cognitive - Affective	To have the person in crisis describe "what happened" and current emotional reactions.	To encourage cathartic ventilation to reduce arousal and rumination. Establish rapport and sense of safety. Allows mental status assessment.
Three	Facilitation of Understanding	Affective - Cognitive	To explain symptoms and nature of normal crisis reactions.	To have the person in crisis view symptoms as "normal" reactions albeit potentially problematic.
Four	Explanations of basic concepts of crisis and stress mamagement	Cognitive	To teach basic stress management and develop a plan for coping.	To improve immediate and short term coping.
Five	Restoration of Functioning	Behavioral	Assessment of mental status and current adaptive functioning as adequate or seek further assistance.	Re-establishment of psychological homeostasis or provision of continued acute care.

the failure is rooted in the crisis interventionist's inability to assist the person in returning to the cognitive domain after experiencing the affective domain at the end of the previous stage.

EXPLANATIONS OF BASIC CONCEPTS OF CRISIS AND STRESS MANAGEMENT

The fourth stage of the model represents what is usually the most overtly active stage with regard to the behavior of the crisis interventionist. Here the interventionist engages in teaching of basic concepts in 1) crisis, 2) stress, and 3) stress management. As with the previous stage, it takes place within the cognitive domain of psychological processing. Basic stress management techniques (Everly, 1989; Mitchell and Bray, 1990) may be discussed and a plan for coping with the acute crisis situation is conjointly developed by the crisis interventionist and the person in crisis. Once again, it is imperative that this stage not be attempted until some cognitive orientation has been achieved by the person in crisis. Any attempts to cognitively construct a plan for coping will obviously fail unless the person in need of the plan is receptive to cognitive input.

RESTORATION OF INDEPENDENT FUNCTIONING

The goal of the previous four stages is always to assist the person in reestablishing independent psychological and behavioral functioning. In the vast majority of cases, this will have been achieved by this point in the process. In some instances, however, it will be evident that the person in crisis remains in a highly unstable condition. If such is the case, the crisis interventionist's goal becomes that of providing assistance in obtaining continued acute care. Resources for such continued care might be family members, other departmental resources, or in extreme cases where no other resources seem suitable, an emergency room at a local hospital, or psychiatric triage venue.

To review, the SAFE-R model is designed for use by either emergency services peer counselors or by mental health trained professionals working with emergency services disaster response, and military personnel who are in crisis. The model consists of four basic stages with a final resolution stage or determination stage. The model possesses several key elements within each stage: 1) a content structure, 2) a process domain, 3) an action, and 4) a goal. These are presented in Table 12.2.

It should be noted that within Stage One and Stage Two of the SAFE-R model, mental status assesment is performed. Rather than employing a laborious challenging mental status exam, as is the typical intake practice within most psychiatric venues, the crisis interventionist is encouraged to employ their basic communication and listening skills to perform a "passive" mental status assessments. This mental status assessment goes on throughout the entire SAFE-R process, but especially in the first two stages.

CONCLUSION

This chapter has presented the notion that no CISM program is complete without the inclusion of the programmatic ability to offer on-scene, one-on-one crisis intervention support. The bias of this current perspective is that basic crisis intervention services may be provided by either licensed mental health practitioners or by specially - trained "peer support" personnel.

Having expressed the necessity of possessing capabilities for on-scene crisis intervention support services, this chapter has gone on to offer the SAFE-R model of crisis intervention as a potential operational template. The SAFE-R model was developed expressly for use with emergency services, disaster response, and military personnel.

REFERENCES

Captan, G. (1961). *An Approach to Community Mental Health.* NY: Grune and Stratton.

Catherall, D. and Lane, C. (1992). Warrior therapist. Vets treating ets. *Journal of Traumatic Stress*, 5, 19-36.

Greenstone, J.L. (1993). *Critical Incident Stress Debriefing and Crisis Management*. Austin, TX: Texas Dept of Health.

Lindemann, E. (1944). Symptomatology and management of acute grief. *American Journal of Psychiatry*, 101, 101 - 148.

Mitchell, J.T. (1976). Rescue Crisis Intervention. *EMS News*. 4,4.

Mitchell, J.T. (1983). When disaster strikes...The critical incident stress debriefing process. *Journal of Emergency Medical Services*, 8,36-39.

Mitchell, J. and Bray, G. (1990) *Emergency Services Stress*. Englewood Cliffs, NJ: Brady Co.

Mitchell, J.T. and Resnik, H.L.P. (1981). *Crisis Intervention*. Bowie, MD: R.J. Brady.

Chapter 13

A NEUROCOGNITIVE STRATEGIC THERAPY (NST) FOR THE TREATMENT OF POST-TRAUMATIC STRESS

GEORGE S. EVERLY, JR.

"Any new formula which suddenly emerges ... has its roots in long trains of thought;"
Oliver Wendell Holmes

The previous chapter addressed a model of crisis intervention, this chapter shall address a model of psychotherapy. It is important to keep in mind a cautionary note, offered not only in this volume, but elsewhere (Mitchell and Everly, 1995). The goal of crisis intervention is acute stabilization and restoration of functioning, while the goal of therapy is resolution and resumption of long-term growth and adaptation. Given that the goals of crisis intervention vis-à-vis psychotherapy are indeed different, so too will be their basic strategic and tactical processes. This chapter introduces "neurocognitive strategic therapy" (NST) as a metatherapeutic approach to the treatment of post-traumatic stress. Not only may this construction be used as a template for the development of specific interventions, but it may be used as a means of assessing extant therapeutic techniques as well as analyzing and reformulating treatment resistant cases.

George S. Everly, Jr. • International Critical Incident Stress Foundation, Ellicott City, Maryland.
In G.S. Everly, Jr. Innovations in Disaster and Trauma Psychology, Volume One: Applications in Emergency Services and Disaster Response. Baltimore: Chevron Publishing Corp, 1995.

NEUROCOGNITIVE THERAPY AS A STRATEGIC PROCESS

Therapy may be conceived of as possessing a two—fold constituency: 1) strategic processes (plans), and 2) tactical methods (techniques).

Neurocognitive Strategic Therapy (NST) represents a strategic therapeutic formulation, not a tactical one. That is to say, NST represents an overarching strategic plan for therapeutic intervention rather than a specific therapeutic technique. Consistent with the words of da Vinci, "First study the science, then practice the art," NST may be used by clinicians to identify the most appropriate targets for therapeutic intervention. NST does not dictate a specific therapeutic intervention, but rather allows the clinician to utilize existing therapeutic skills and methods within a focused therapeutic plan for the treatment of post-traumatic stress.

A TWO-FACTOR FORMULATION

In Chapter Two, post-traumatic stress was portrayed as possessing a two-factor pathognomonic nature. Let us briefly review each factor.

The first pathognomonic factor within post-traumatic stress may be described as a functional neurologic hypersensitivity existing within the potentially volatile neural substrates of the limbic system. Amygdaloid and hippocampal cells seem to be especially implicated. The aforementioned neural hypersensitivity may be conceived of as a functionally lower depolarization threshold for the affected cells (Everly, 1990). Resultant behavioral symptoms are likely to include, but not be limited to: irritability, impulsivity, episodic anger, aggressive inclinations, hyperstartle, anxiety punctuated with panic and/or a myriad of sympathetically mediated physical complaints, and in some cases a general hypomania.

The biology of such neural hypersensitivity has been postulated to be: 1) an augmentation of excitatory neurotransmitters, 2) a functional decrease in inhibitory neurotransmitters, and/or 3) changes in the micromorphology of the synapse (Everly, 1993). Neural hypersensitivity as described above may possess a self-sustaining property. Thus post-traumatic stress may be viewed as a "disorder of arousal" wherein a key feature is its propensity for, or status of, limbic over-excitation (Everly, 1990; Everly and Benson, 1989).

The second pathognomonic factor within the present formulation of post-traumatic stress has been postulated to be a violation of the victim's worldview, or Weltanschauung, specifically as it pertains to safety and security (Everly, 1993).

According to Maslow (1970) except for physical survival itself, the need for safety and security is the most important and basic of all human motives.

So strong is the need for safety and security that one will search a lifetime until it is met, putting all else beneath it in terms of importance.

So strong is the need for safety and security that one will even go so far as to create "delusions of safety" that permit one to live and/or work in otherwise objectively "unsafe" or "high risk" conditions.

In most instances, however, safety and security are derived from "meaning" or understanding of oneself and the world within which one lives. Thus humanity may be perceived of as engaging in an ever-expanding search for meaning, understanding, and relevance (Frankl, 1959).

Psychological trauma, by definition, represents a violation, contradiction, or destruction of some core belief about oneself or the world within which one lives. This core belief had previously provided meaning and therefore safety and security (see Janoff-Bulman, 1992; Everly and Lating, 1995). Psychological trauma represents a piece of the puzzle of life that does not seem to fit historical precedents. The legacy of psychological trauma may then be a life-long search to, once again, make sense of the world so as to, once again, see the world as a safe and secure place.

In sum, post-traumatic stress may be thought of as possessing two pathognomonic factors: 1) neurologic hypersensitivity existing within the subcortical limbic substrates, and 2) a psychological hypersensitivity existing as a violation or contradiction to some core aspect of the victim's worldview as it pertains to the safety and security; perhaps, as it pertains to the essence of oneself, or the essence of the world itself (Everly and Lating, 1995).

Analytic postulations such as these may ultimately serve to enhance therapeutic formulations by serving to enhance strategic planning and, therefore, tactical focus.

THE THERAPEUTIC STRATEGIES OF NST

It would be an obvious deduction that if, indeed, post-traumatic stress represents a two-factor pathognomonic consistency, then the therapy of post-traumatic stress needs to be directed toward those two "lesions" in order to maximize recovery. Using the formulations above, a "neurocognitive strategic construction emerges. That is, a neurocognitive strategic construction for therapy argues that recovery from post-traumatic stress is maximized when: 1) the neurologic hypersensitivity is reduced, and 2) the violated worldview is attended to in such a manner as to restore a sense of safety in the world and/or confidence on oneself.

If one of the strategic goals of therapy is to reduce neurologic hypersensitivity, it seems prudent to employ therapeutic tactics which may achieve that end, i.e., neurologic desensitization as an endpoint.

Four primary therapeutic tactics may be used to achieve neurologic desensitization:

1) ***Catharsis*** (Pennebaker and Susman, 1988). Evidence suggests that either the verbal or written expression of stressful events serves to reduce arousal.

2) ***Relaxation Response*** (Benson, 1974; Everly and Benson, 1989; Everly, 1989). The relaxation Response may be viewed as a

hypometabolic physiologic response characterized by a decrease in sympathetic nervous system activity. It may be engendered by a myriad of technologies including, but not limited to, mantra meditation, the pre-suggestion phase of hypnosis, repetitive breathing practices, progressive neuromuscular relaxation, biofeedback, etc.

3) ***Psychotropic medications*** (Friedman, 1990). Psychotropic medications such as benzodiazapines and selective serotonergic reuptake inhibitors may be of special value.

4) ***Aerobic Exercise*** (see Everly, 1989 for a review). Aerobic exercise may serve to ventilate both the psychological and physiological components of human stress arousal.

Mending the contradicted assumptions, or violated core beliefs, about the world which lie in the wake of psychological traumatization may be approached by way of several routes (Everly, 1994).

1) Integrating the traumatic event into the patient's existing belief structure about the world, i.e., worldview.

2) Allowing the trauma to be understood as a parallel aspect of the existing worldview, i.e., an "exception to the rule."

3) Using the traumatic event to demonstrate the invalidity of the present worldview, and therefore validating the need to create a new, more healthful worldview wherein the trauma more readily fits.

Since the above mentioned means of coping with traumas are general strategies, the clinician is left with a wide range of specific therapeutic tactics that may be employed to achieve the aforementioned strategic goals. No specific therapeutic tactic seems universally superior.

THE THERAPEUTIC PROCESSES OF NST

Previous pages in this chapter have described NST as a strategic therapy, not a tactical one. Specific strategic suggestions have similarly been made, yet the chapter has stopped short of recommending specific tactical interventions, per se. In this section, a brief discussion of the therapeutic processes of NST will be provided.

Almost regardless of the specific therapeutic tactics employed, NST may be used as an overarching strategic template upon which the tactical formulations may be applied. The structural processes of NST may be described in the following 5-step TEACH model:

1) *Telling the trauma story.* Once sufficient rapport has been achieved, the patient is encouraged to tell his/her story as it relates to the traumatic event. This disclosure involves not only describing the details of the traumatic event, but involves describing any symptom patterns that have emerged as a result of the trauma.

2) *Educating the patient.* This phase consists of explaining: a) the nature and adaptive value of some traumatic stress symptoms, and b) the nature of psychological trauma itself, conceptually.

3) *Arousal reduction.* In this phase of the model, the patient is taught to practice the relaxation response as a means of neurologic desensitization. Psychotropic medications may be prescribed, as well.

4) *Contradiction to the patient's worldview as represented by the traumatic event is assessed and analyzed.* The goal of this process is to reveal the psychologic "lesion" which will ultimately serve as the target for the therapeutic tactics.

5) *Helping the patient mend the violated assumptions about his/her world,* via:
   a. integrating the traumatic event;
   b. creating an "exception to the rule" condition;
   c. developing a new worldview to take the place of the old worldview.

The therapeutic processes underlying the TEACH model may exist as the following:

1) *T*elling the "trauma story," serves to allow the patient to engage in the cathartic ventilation while at the same time receiving interpersonal acceptance from the clinician. Telling the story also allows the patient to psychologically re-examine the traumatic event in a safe environment.

2) *E*ducating the patient, serves to demystify traumatic stress, dispel delusions of unique "weakness" on the part of the patient and serves to normalize symptoms. This exercise in patient education serves to reassure the patient that psychological trauma and traumatic stress are ***normal*** reactions experienced by ***normal*** individuals as a result of an exposure to an ***abnormal*** event. Finally this phase serves to contradict the sense of a "loss of control" that is experienced by many victims of trauma.

3) *A*rousal reduction serves to initiate the neurologic desensitization process and also serves to mitigate panic episodes, if present.

4) Assessing the Contradiction to the patient's worldview which is represented by the traumatic event serves to identify the "traumatic core", or target, for therapy.

5) The final steps in the TEACH model entail actually neutralizing the toxic nature of traumatic event. This phase usually entails the most time, energy, and effort. It is here that the clinician employs the tactical therapeutic arsenal that he/she is most experienced and skillful using whether it be a cognitive therapy, an affective therapy, hypnotic restructuring, family therapy, or some form of integrative psychotherapy.

SUMMARY: GUIDING PRINCIPLES OF NST

Listed below are several basic principles of NST that may serve as a useful summary:

1. NST is a strategic therapy, not a tactical one. That is to say, NST represents a plan for intervention as opposed to a specific intervention technique.
2. NST is built around a postulated two-factor pathophenomenology of post-traumatic stress.
3. NST is suited for individual or group format implementation.
4. NST does not require the clinician to learn nor employ new specialized therapeutic techniques, but rather offers a strategic formulation within which to apply therapeutic techniques with which the clinician may already be familiar.

Thus, in this chapter, NST as a strategic plan for the treatment of post-traumatic stress has been introduced. In the subsequent chapter, a most exciting and innovative therapeutic tactic will be discussed. While the focus of the next chapter, Eye Movement Desensitization and Reprocessing (EMDR) does indeed represent a tactical therapeutic intervention, it is the therapeutic technique that most closely embodies the tenets of NST within one intervention. The following chapter explores EMDR.

REFERENCES

Benson, H. (1974). *The Relaxation Responce.* NY: Marrow.

Everly, G.S. (1989). *A Clinical Guide to the Treatment of the Human Stress Responce.* NY: Plenum.

Everly, G.S. (1990). Post-traumatic stres disorder as a "disorder of arousal". *Psychology and Health,* 4, 135-145.

Everly, G.S. (1993). Psychotraumatology: A two-factor formulation of post-truamatic stress. *Integrative Physiology and Behavioral Science,* 28, 270-278.

Everly, G.S. (1994). Short-term psychotherapy of acute adult onsetpost-traumatic stress. *Stress Medicine,* 10, 191-196.

Everly, G.S. and Benson, H. (1989). Disorders of arousal. *International Journal of Phychosomatics,* 36, 15-22.

Everly, G.S. and Lating, J.M. (1995). *Psychotraumatology,* NY: Plenum

Frankl, V. (1059). *Mans Search for Meaning.* Boston: Beacon.

Friedman, M. (1990). Interrelationships between biological mechanisms and pharmacotherapy of post taumatic stress disorder. In M. Wolf and A. Mosnaim (eds). *Post-traumatic Stress Disorder* (pp. 204-225). Wash. D.C.: APA Press.

Janoff-Bulman, R. (1992). *Shattered Assumptions.* NY: Free Press

Maslow, A. (1970). *Motivation and Personality, 2nd Ed.* NY: Harper and Row.

Mitchell, J.T. and Everly, G.S. (1995) *Critical incident stress debriefing: An operations manual.* 2nd Edition. Ellicott City, MD: Chevron Publishing.

Pennebaker, J. and Susman, J. (1988). Disclosure of traumas and psychosomatic processes. *Social Science and Medicine,* 26, 327-332.

Chapter 14

EYE MOVEMENT DESENSITIZATION AND REPROCESSING: NEUROCOGNITIVE INFORMATION PROCESSING

FRANCINE SHAPIRO
ROGER SOLOMON

The Neurocognitive Strategic Therapy model (Everly, 1993; Everly and Lating, 1995), which is based on a two-factor analysis of post-traumatic stress disorder (PTSD) (described in the previous chapter), appears extremely pertinent to the specific therapeutic method known as Eye Movement Desensitization and Reprocessing (EMDR). Both of these approaches stress the importance of addressing neurological and cognitive processes in the treatment of PTSD and both are representative of the relatively recent move toward integrative therapeutic approaches (Goldfried, 1980; Goldfried & Padawer, 1982; Norcross, 1986). Clearly, the reports that approximately one half of the Vietnam combat veterans originally diagnosed with PTSD are still considered to be suffering from chronic psychological effects (National Center for PTSD, 1993) indicate the need for a new paradigm and associated therapeutic procedures.

Francince Shapiro • Mental research Institute, Palo Alto California
Roger Solomon • On Site Academy, Gardner, Massachussets.
In G.S. Everly, Jr. Innovations in Disaster and Trauma Psychology: Applications in Emergency Services and Disaster Response. Baltimore: Chevron Publishing Corp, 1995.

BACKGROUND

The EMDR method was originated by the first author in 1987 when she noted that disturbing thoughts suddenly and permanently disappeared whenever she engaged in saccadic eye movements. Furthermore, if these thoughts were deliberately retrieved, they were no longer experienced as upsetting. The apparent effect of the eye movements motivated the development of the interactive, multi-faceted methodology that came to be known as EMDR and which has proven quite successful in a variety of therapeutic contexts. For example, the results of a survey funded by the Veterans Administration indicated that 74% of trained clinicians who have treated over 10,000 clients obtained more beneficial treatment effects with EMDR than with other methods, while only 4% had fewer successes (Lipke, 1992). In addition, since the initial efficacy study (Shapiro, 1989a,b), positive therapeutic results with EMDR have been reported with a wide number of populations, including: (1) combat veterans (Boudewyns, et al., 1993; Lipke & Botkin, 1992; Daniels, Lipke, Richardson & Silver, 1992); (2) phobics (Kleinknecht, in press; (3) victims of panic disorder (Goldstein, 1992 and in press); (4) crime victims (Baker & McBride, 1991; Klienknecht, 1992; Page & Crino, 1993; (5) victims of loss and grief (Puk, 1991; Solomon & Shapiro, in press); (6) traumatized children (Shapiro, 1991; Pellicer, 1993); (7) sexual assault victims (Puk, 1991; Rothbaum, 1992; Shapiro, 1991; Wolpe & Abrams, 1991; Spector & Huthwaite, 1993); (8) burn victims (McCann, 1993); and (9) victims of sexual dysfunction (Levin, 1993; Wernick, 1993); as well as as a wide variety of diagnoses (Marquis, 1991).

A NEUROCOGNITIVE PERSPECTIVE

While there are a variety of components to EMDR treatment that appear essential for its therapeutic effectiveness, a consistent element is a sequential pairing of the content of the target event (e.g., picture, cognition, somatic response) with repeated sets of eye movement (SEM). Apparently congruent with the formulation suggested in the Neurocognitive Therapy model, the initial phase of treatment is termed desensitization, while the final stage includes an installation and enhancement of a positive cognition. The success of the cognitive restructuring aspect of EMDR appears to be due to the fact that the directed eye movements diffuse and weaken negative imagery and self-statements while simultaneously vivifying and self-validating the client's positive imagery and beliefs (Shapiro, 1989a, 1991a).

As with Everly's formulation (1993; Everly and Lating, 1995), EMDR was viewed initially as a means of desensitizing the over-arousal elicited by traumatic memories (Shapiro, 1989a/b). Thus, it was proposed that the directed eye movements in EMDR serve to inhibit the disturbing memory by eliciting a reflexive relaxation response. Initial support for this hypothesis was provided by a controlled study (Shapiro, 1989a, b) which demonstrated the effectiveness of EMDR in reducing traumatic memory-induced distress as measured by the Subjective Units of Disturbance scale (SUDs; Wolpe, 1982), as well as the associated symptomatology (e.g., nightmares, flashbacks). The use of the SUD scale in the experiment indicated a decrease in physiological arousal, since it had been shown to be correlated with a number of standard physiological measures (Thyer et al., 1984). More evidence that EMDR reduces the physiological hyperarousal associated with targeted traumatic memories was provided by Wilson et al. (1993) who found that EMDR eliminated intrusive symptomatology while simultaneously reducing SUDs levels and the cardiac and galvanic responses evoked by the memories.

The second factor of the Neurocognitive Therapy model is the pathogenic cognitive distortion found in many victims of PTSD (DeFazio, Rustin, & Diamond, 1975; Keane, Fairbank, Caddell, Zimering, & Bender, 1985). In the EMDR method, this element and its therapeutic modification are assessed by means of the Validity of Cognition (VOC) scale (Shapiro, 1989) which is a simple semantic differential scale ranging from 1 (completely false) to 7 (completely true). In the pre-treatment application of this scale clients are requested to hold the target memory in mind and verbalize the negative self-statement(s) that best describe their view of themselves in relation to the traumatic event. Generally, these statements reveal low self-worth and self-efficacy and a perceived lack of safety. For instance, the rape or molestation victim may make statements such as, "I am worthless," "I am not in control," or "I should have done something." Clients are then requested to identify the cognition(s) they would prefer to believe. Generally, these statements are polar opposites such as "I am worthwhile", "I now have choices," or "I did the best I could." The client is then asked to rate the positive statement on the VOC scale according to its perceived or "gut level" validity. The post-treatment effects are judged by another rating on the VOC scale. The treatment is not considered satisfactorily completed until the client is able to give a VOC rating of 6 or 7 which indicates that the positive self-statement is fully believed on an emotive level. In sum, the EMDR treatment is considered successful when the client responds to the targeted traumatic memory with very low distress and an adaptive interpretation of his/er role with respect to it.

Like the Neurocognitive model, EMDR considers both the obvious physiological reactivity of the PTSD victim and his/er negative cognitions to be clear evidence that the traumatic event remains a powerful psychological experience that has not yet been adequately assimilated into the individual's schemata. Thus, traumas that have not been satisfactorily resolved are associated with negative perspectives on issues of self-control and empowerment which, along with inappropriate affect, manifest themselves in many forms throughout one's life. In contrast, traumatic events that have been fully processed are typified by an adaptive perspective, together with positive cognitions and appropriate affect. According to the EMDR model, the successful treatment of PTSD, entails a clinician-assisted "self-healing" process by which the trauma-induced dysfunctional information which is stored in the nervous system is reprocessed. Clinical experience has demonstrated that, when addressing a single traumatic experience, only 1-4 sessions with EMDR are generally necessary to eliminate the anxiety, pronounced symptomatology, and negative self-assessments associated with this isolated event. It appears that EMDR accelerates the information processing necessary to allow an assimilation of the trauma into previously established positive frameworks, or shift cognitive perspectives to accommodate the new material. However, EMDR must be used as part of a full treatment plan that addresses all areas of potential resistance, including issues of secondary gains, dual diagnoses, and deficits of early life experiences. As with any therapeutic approach, full resolution cannot be expected without a clear definition of the entire clinical picture. Thus, it is important to remember that EMDR should not be considered "one-shot therapy." Rather, treating a trauma with this method is often compared to removing a "quilt from the mattress," to uncover other problem areas beneath. For instance, successfully treating the intrusive symptomatology of a rape victim may reveal the existence of a dysfunctional marriage or employment problem that must be addressed. Because of this fact, EMDR clients are requested to maintain an on-going log of current disturbing experiences the targeting of which, along with modeling and rehearsal of appropriate future action, is as much part of the EMDR methodology as the reprocessing of the traumatic memories.

ACCELERATED INFORMATION PROCESSING

The theoretical framework within which EMDR may be placed is referred to as the Accelerated Information Processing (AIP) model (Shapiro, 1991a, 1993b, in press). According to this model, there exists an innate information-processing system that facilitates mental health in much the same way as the body tends to heal itself when physically injured. When operating appropriately this system responds to a traumatic event by bringing it to an adaptive resolution. That is, useful information and the appropriate affect are stored and accessible for future use. Thus, when the information-processing mechanism is working properly we will think, talk, read, and/or dream about a disturbing event until we have learned what we can from it. The end results is a a memory without associated pathological emotional distress. In terms of Everly's Neurocognitive conceptualization, the cognitive restructuring of EMDR takes one of these forms: (1) the information becomes integrated into the client's functional worldview, (2) it is viewed as an acceptable exception to the rule, or (3) the individual's dysfunctional extant worldschemata is changed in order to accommodate the new information.

One characteristic of the presenting pathology, according to the AIP model is that the information-processing mechanism is not functioning appropriately because of the stress engendered by the traumatic event. Therefore, the information perceived at the time of the trauma is maintained in state-dependent form. The blocked information-processing mechanism prevents the disturbing pictures, thoughts, sensations, beliefs, etc., from progressing through the normal steps of adaptive integration. The nightmares, flashbacks and intrusive thoughts associated with PTSD are thus explained in terms of the continued activation of this information, by external or internal stimuli, or perhaps because of repeated unsuccessful attempts of the mechanism to complete its own processing. Since the non-adaptively stored trauma is functionally compartmentalized from the appropriate information, the perceived event cannot be integrated into the existing world-view. The dysfunctional state also prevents the learning necessary to inaugurate an adaptive shifting of inappropriate extant beliefs.

EMDR appears to stimulate the processing system so that it can metabolize and integrate the dysfunctional information stored in the memory networks. Thus, the client can progress spontaneously and rapidly through the adaptive stages of affect and insights regarding such issues of (1) appropriate levels of responsibility, (2) present safety, and (3) availability of future choices (Shapiro, 1991c; Solomon and Shapiro, in press). These processing effects also include a remission of pronounced symptomatology, and often the spontaneous emergence of new, more appropriate behaviors. It should be emphasized, however, that the reduction of physiological arousal, the progression through the appropriate levels of insight, and the consequent cognitive restructuring apparent in EMDR treatments are considered to be the spontaneous effects of the client's own successful information processing. Therefore the degree of disturbance or the content of the material that the client may experience during the processing cannot be adequately predicted before initiating treatment. For instance, although the targeted trauma may be a Vietnam combat experience, the veteran may quickly shift to a childhood experience of a molestation that is stored associatively because of the feelings of helplessness and despair common to both traumatic events. In such instances, the earlier memory must be appropriately processed in order to achieve a therapeutic resolution. For clients who remain within the context of a single memory, the elicited sensory experience can either be quite intense or merely a shadow of its initial level. It is clear, then, that strategies for facilitating the individualized processing will be dictated by the needs of the client, underscoring the view that EMDR is a complex and interactive method.

Congruent with the concept of spontaneous, accelerated information processing is the fact that clients treated with EMDR frequently report that previously traumatic visualizations become progressively blurred, smaller or perhaps even impossible to retrieve. Sometimes it is the content that changes. For instance, as the client reports increased feelings of self-efficacy a threatening, scowling face may become a harmless, smiling one. Likewise, when clients are asked to "think of the incident" after treatment, they report spontaneously visualizing the resolution of the incident, together with a sense of safety. Thus, their responses generally indicate that the traumatic material is being processed rapidly and ultimately integrated into their schemata (Shapiro, 1989a, b, 1991, in press). Also frequently observed is a generalization of adaptive responses to other, related memories. For example, when a specific traumatic memory of a sexual molestation victim is treated by EMDR, other memories of molestation when subsequently accessed appear to be less anxiety-provoking and to have undergone a similar cognitive restructuring. Thus, the adaptive information-processing mechanism appears to weaken the negative associations while strengthening the positive and self-enhancing ones.

As will be seen below, somatic response and cognitive restructuring are key elements in the spontaneous reprocessing of the traumatic experiences during the EMDR treatment. In addition, aspects of (1) responsibility, (2) safety, and (3) choices mentioned previously (Shapiro, 1991; Solomon and Shapiro, in press; Shapiro, in press) are especially salient factors in the recovery from trauma. These factors will be discussed in the following case examples that illustrate the global treatment strategies outlined in the Neurocognitive Therapy model. These strategies are derived from the observation that the recovery from trauma involves integrating and assimilating the traumatic event into one's worldview, and/or rebuilding one's assumptive world in a way that accommodates the event (Everly, 1993, Janoff-Bulman, 1992; Horowitz, 1986). Each case will be preceded by one of the three global strategies outlined by Everly in this volume and elsewhere (Everly and Lating, 1995).

CASE EXAMPLE 1: REINTEGRATING THE TRAUMA INTO CLIENT'S EXISTING WORLDVIEW

Resolution of a traumatic incident can occur if the event can be reinterpreted in a manner consistent with the client's existing worldview. According to Everly (1993) integration of the event can take place by reinterpreting the trauma along several dimensions such as the event's outcome (e.g. success vs. failure); valence (e.g. something positive was learned); the role the person played in the event (e.g. dispute the overtaking of responsibility); or the overall importance of the trauma (e.g. event less important than originally assumed). The following example illustrates how EMDR can result in a different, adaptive perspective of the trauma that is compatable with the client's current worldview.

A truck driver was driving along a residential street when an eleven year old boy on a bicycle slammed into the side of the truck and landed on the street in front of the driver. The driver tried to stop the truck as fast as possible, but the front wheels ran over the child, killing the child.

The driver's worldview involved the importance of being a responsible adult. This worldview became pivotal in his taking an inappropriate level of responsibility for the accident, and blaming himself for the death of the child.

For the next three months the truck driver had severe intrusive imagery, anxiety, guilt and sleep disorder. He found it difficult to work, being overly cautious while driving, and experienced moderate panic attacks when he saw children playing in the street. His physician referred him for psychological treatment.

EMDR was utilized to deal with the traumatic incident. The image that arose when he thought of the event was the child lying underneath the truck, bleeding. The negative cognition associated with the image was, "I killed that child....I'm horrible". The feelings associated with the image and negative belief were guilt and anxiety. The positive cognition was, "It was beyond my control....I did the best I could". Initially, these positive cognitions had little validity as he believed he should have been able to do something to prevent the accident.

After several sets of eye movements (SEM), he reported his anxiety was subsiding and the image was fading. He realized he had done everything possible to stop the truck as fast as he could, and had done so competently. After several more SEM he realized he had no control over the child's actions. Having the client focus on this thought for the next SEM led to the client realizing that the child had caused the accident. All he could do was react to the best of his ability. After having the client focus on these thoughts during the next SEM, the image was more distant, the SUDs was low, and the incident felt like a past event.

The positive cognition, "It was not my fault and I did the best I could", was congruent with how he perceived the event. Another SEM reinforced the validity of this belief. Now, when he thought about driving his truck and seeing children, he reported that he no longer felt the anxiety. He realized he was a safe, responsible driver. When he thought about driving in the future he said that all he could do was control his actions although he was going to be extra alert around children.

A follow up three days later and two weeks later by his physician showed that he was driving comfortably and his post-traumatic symptoms had stopped. He still felt sad about the tragedy, but no longer blamed himself. Treatment results have remained stable for three and one-half years.

In this example, resolving the issue of responsibility allowed the incident to integrate into the client's worldview that he was a safe, responsible driver. When he finally differentiated what was under his control from what was not, he realized he was not responsible for the child's actions and that he had done the best he could. Consequently, his worldview regarding the importance of being a responsible driver remained intact, and encompassed the appropriate level of responsibility in regard to this incident.

It should be noted that he still was going through a grieving process over the death of the child. He felt quite sad about the death of the child. EMDR, however, had removed a major obstacle to his emotional recovery.

CASE EXAMPLE 2: REINTERPRETING THE EVENT AS AN "EXCEPTION TO THE RULE"

A traumatic event, in violating core assumptions, may not invalidate them. The victim can integrate the trauma by understanding that his or her worldview is generally correct, but that exceptions sometimes occur. The next example illustrates how such a perspective was facilitated by EMDR, enabling integration of the event.

A police officer was making an emergency run with his overhead lights and siren on. As he was going through an intersection he noticed headlights coming at him from his left. He attempted to swerve away, but was hit by the car. The officer was seriously injured.

The officer's foremost focus during his recuperation period was getting better and returning to work. He experienced few post-traumatic symptoms during his recuperation. He reported for duty eight months after the accident. His first order of business was to go to the driving track and get reacquainted with his new car and practice his driving skills. Upon attempting to drive he experienced intense feelings of anxiety and fear, and intrusive images of the car's headlights coming at him. After several attempts at driving his squad car, he referred himself for treatment.

The officer's basic assumption was that, "I'm safe when I am driving my squad car". Because the accident contradicted this worldview, he no longer felt safe or in control when driving, and experienced intense anxiety at the driving track.

EMDR was used to deal with his trauma. The initial focal point was the image of the car's headlights coming at him. The negative cognition associated with the image was, "I am vulnerable and powerless". Intense feelings of fear accompanied this cognition and the image. His positive cognition was, "I survived and can exercise control". This statement recognizes his attempt to swerve as exerting control.

After several SEM, the image of the headlights became dimmer and smaller. He verbalized that he suddenly realized the accident was not his fault. He said he had always known this, but now he believed it at a deeper level. He admitted that in the back of his mind he had been second guessing himself for not being able to do something to avoid impact. He then verbalized that he might get hit again by a motorist and not be able to avoid it. This thought was associated with feelings of fear. The therapist asked the client to stay with the thought and feeling for the next SEM. The client then said that although a similar accident was possible, it was not probable. After having the client focus on this thought for the next SEM, he reported the accident was "just one of those things", meaning that a similar was unlikely to occur, e.g. the event was an exception to the rule. After another SEM where he focused on these thoughts, the image became more faint and distant. He said his feelings of vulnerability were also greatly diminished. He realized he had done something effective; he had swerved and avoided worse injuries or even losing his life. Staying with these thoughts for the next SEM, led to the client reporting that the image was gone, the incident felt "over" (e.g. like a past event), and he felt more in control.

His recent anxiety-provoking experience at the drive track was then targeted. Now when he thought of the incident, there was much less anxiety. The effects of the EMDR on the original accident appeared to have generalized to the more recent event. Several SEM were done while he was thinking of the recent event to further lower his anxiety and reinforce his feelings of being able to be comfortably in control. Next, he imagined going back to the driving track. Several SEM were done with him imaging driving his car at a progressively higher rates of speed and feeling in control.

The following day he went back to the drive track and successfully completed the driving course. In a therapy session the next day he reported that he now knew he "still had it". EMDR was used to enhance this feeling by doing SEM as he imagined driving feeling in control. He reported for full duty the next day. Treatment effects have remained stable for three years.

In this example, the client's assumption that he was safe while driving was violated by the accident. As a result, he experienced significant vulnerability when he attempted to drive his car. After concluding that the accident was not his fault, he had to address the issue of whether such an event could happen in the future. With further processing, the officer then was able to understand the event as "just one of those things". Just because the accident had happened did not necessarily mean he was unsafe. Hence, he was able to integrate the event by viewing it as a parallel aspect of his existing worldview - an exception to the rule. This enabled him to experience a sense of control and confidence in his ability to drive.

CASE EXAMPLE 3: UNREALISTIC CORE ASSUMPTION IS VIOLATED

Sometimes an unrealistic core assumption is contradicted by a traumatic event, leaving the victim with no system within which to integrate the experience. The therapeutic task is then to help the client create a new, more adaptive worldview that can assimilate the event. The next example illustrates how EMDR can facilitate the creation of a more adaptive assumptive world.

An officer, engaged in an undercover surveillance, was sitting in a car, watching a residence. All of a sudden, a car with three people in it pulled up along side him. The passenger pulled out a gun and aimed it at the officer. The officer ducked just as the suspect started shooting. The officer managed to draw his gun, return fire, start his car, and drive away. The suspects started chasing him and continued shooting at him. The officer, after calling for help, then thought to himself, "This is bull-shit, I've got to put a stop to this". He then turned his car around and started to return fire. A shot hit one of the suspects, and the car drove away. He continued to chase the suspects, but they escaped. They were captured a few days later.

The shooting situation severely impacted the officer. He had never felt so helpless as when the suspects pulled up in their car and started firing at him. He had believed he was going to be killed and, for the first time in his life, he faced his mortality. A big, strong man who had played football in college, he had known his job was dangerous and that he could get hurt, but he had never emotionally faced his own mortality. Further, he always felt he was in control. After this incident a basic assumption about life, "I'm always supposed to be in control", was violated. He no longer felt safe.

He had vivid flashbacks, nightmares, and a heightened sense of danger. He experienced suicidal ideation and other depressive symptoms. He started emotionally withdrawing from his wife and was divorced within a year. He also alienated himself from his friends and co-workers. His paperwork became slipshod and was often turned in late, behaviors that were not present prior to the shooting incident. At work he experienced a significant degree of hypervigilance and began to overreact to perceived danger. He got a different assignment, working in a different part of the city, but found it difficult to deal with potentially dangerous situations. He seriously started thinking about leaving his career in law enforcement. Six months after the incident, he felt so out of control he gave his gun to his supervisor. He then started psychological treatment. He began seeing one psychologist in his local area and was referred to the second author, some distance away, for EMDR. EMDR was given in the context of an overall treatment plan that included psychotherapy, stress reduction strategies, peer support, and time off.

EMDR started with the officer focusing on his worst intrusive image; the suspect pointing the gun at him. The thoughts associated with the image was, "I'm going to die, I am powerless". The positive cognition was, "I survived". During EMDR he relived the incident and experienced a significant degree of emotion. One hour later, he could think of the incident with much less affect. His thoughts about the incident were, "I survived, and I fought back". These thoughts were reinforced through subsequent sets of eye movements.

The next EMDR session was two months later. He had continued treatment sessions with his regular therapist, taken time off, and had started exercising regularly. He reported that the intrusive imagery and anxiety were still present, but to a lesser degree. What was bothering him was that the incident could happen. Because he believed that he was always supposed to be in control he had not thought somebody could ever get the "drop" on him and surprise him. The situation had shown him that he was not always in control, but his worldview led him to feel shame and guilt. He believed there was something wrong with him if someone could put him in mortal danger without his knowing about it.

EMDR initially focused on the negative intrusive image of the gun being pointed at him. The negative cognition was, "I'm a failure" and was associated with feelings of helplessness and inadequacy. The positive cognition , "I did alright", still had an undertone of feelings of inadequacy. However, this was the best he could come up with at that time. Despite discussion with his therapists and fellow officers, he found it difficult to acknowledge that he had handled the situation competently, had done nothing wrong, and did exercise appropriate control.

During EMDR, intense feelings of fear arose as he relived his moments of terror and not being in control. He reported, "They just came up out of nowhere and started shooting....it was beyond my control." After a few minutes of eye movement while staying with his thoughts and emotions, the emotional intensity subsided. He experienced the realization that it was not his fault, "It could have happened to any police officer doing such an undercover assignment." The level of tension had significantly reduced, but he was still uncomfortable when he thought of the situation. Further sets of eye movement did not lower the tension any further.

When asked what was preventing the tension from lowering, he replied that knowing the situation was not his fault also meant that danger beyond his control could again confront him. He realized he again might be confronted with an unpreventable life and death situation. This cognition was associated with feelings of powerlessness. When asked to go over the part of the incident when he began to respond to the danger, he recalled the moment he decided to fight back. He was asked to concentrate on this moment for the next SEM. He relived the moment and decided to take action ("This is bullshit..."), and began thinking of the decisions and actions (the control) he initiated. He focused on his ability to respond to the danger, how he had kept an optimal frame of mind during the life and death encounter, and regained control over the situation.

Several minutes later, he reported that he had done pretty well. The suspects had tried to kill him, but instead he shot one of them. After further SEM while he focused on these thoughts, he said, "I resolved it". Now when he thought of the incident, the thought was, "I was not helpless;I was able to do something....I can respond to danger." He finally could accept that he might not be able to control potential future dangers, but that he could control his response to the situation. After installing these positive beliefs, further SEM was used to assist his mental rehearsal of responding to dangerous situations.

Two weeks later he reported his tension level had significantly decreased and the intrusive imagery had stopped. He felt better about work and life, and had received comments from co-workers that he seemed back to his old self. At a follow-up session eight months later, he reported that he had been in another undercover situation that had started to escalate. As he attempted to calm the situation verbally, he became aware of a part of him saying he was in control and could shoot if he had to. He also experienced a congruent, strong feeling. He comfortably continued to talk to the suspect, feeling in control of his options should the danger escalate. His verbal strategy worked and the situation resolved peaceably. After this encounter, he knew he could respond confidently to unexpected danger. However, he said he really knew his past shooting was resolved when he drove past the location where the incident had occurred, and did not realize it until three blocks later.

In the above example, an unrealistic core belief ("I'm always supposed to be in control") was contradicted by the shooting situation, creating a high level of traumatic stress. The initial EMDR session had a limited effect because this belief had not been addressed. He felt highly vulnerable and thought he was a failure for not being in control. After he realized the situation could happen to anyone, and he was not a failure, the event partially integrated in his existing worldview that he was competent. However, tension still existed because he was equating not being in control with powerlessness. He did not have the cognitive framework necessary for assimilating or accommodating not being in control of a dangerous situation. The officer needed a new, more adaptive, worldview in order to face future dangerous situations where he was not in control. With the clinician's guidance, he was able to perceive his thoughts and actions following the worst moments of vulnerability as instances of strength and control. Now he could interpret the incident as an example of being able to respond competently to a dangerous situation beyond his control. A more adaptive worldview ("I can respond to danger") took the place of the unrealistic, shattered assumption, enabling the officer to go on with his career.

The above example only describes the EMDR aspect of treatment. The officer also received psychotherapy and peer support. The positive treatment outcomes are viewed as the result of the combination of treatment methods and approaches.

It should be noted that the conceptualization of EMDR as a facilitated "self-healing" process is underscored by the spontaneous transmutation of cognitive interpretation illustrated in the case examples. Although all three suggested strategies delineated in the Neurocognitive Therapy model are addressed, the process is distinctive to each client. Although the selection of negative and positive cognition assisted by the therapist is an important element in proper case formulation, the form, content, and sequence of the appropriate insights is generated spontaneously by the client. Since the primary factor of EMDR treatment is an attempt to catalyze internal processing, the clinician maintains a stance of minimal intrusion while facilitating the client by offering appropriate support during high levels of disturbance and making the appropriate interventions if the processing becomes blocked during the session.

It should be emphasized that although only the SEM are mentioned in the examples given above, the clinical choice points and variations of the EMDR method that were used were not discussed. In addition, besides eye movements, other rhythmic motor responses such as hand-taps and auditory tones have proven effective and are presently being used in therapy (Shapiro, 1991, 1993). The fact that a variety of other stimuli have proven useful indicates that some beneficial aspects of the eye movements may be duplicated and suggests that the salient elements of effect may include dual-attention and simultaneous processing. The latter elements may also be found in the use of forced-focus eye-fixation. However, clinically, eye-movement appear highly effective for eliciting certain therapeutic intangibles such as a sense of co-participation between client and therapist, along with the ability to monitor potential dissociation effects when disturbed clients stop tracking.

The utility of directed eye movements in EMDR may be related to the positive effects of REM sleep (Nielson, 1991; Shapiro, 1989a, b). That other stimuli besides eye movements may catalyze the information-processing mechanism does not, however, detract from the REM hypothesis. Clinically, there are certainly more choices available in the waking state than in the sleeping state. In addition, a number of experimental observations in the field of sleep studies appear to support the REM-EMDR connection. For example, while earlier research suggested that REM patterns might be associated with scanning the dream environment, a recent study (Hong et al., 1992) indicates that the density of REM is correlated to the intensity of the emotional state. In addition, in support of an association between REM and cognitive processing, Karni, et al. (1992) found that the ability to learn new material is reduced when REM sleep is interrupted. Finally, suggestions (Shapiro, 1989a/b) that directed eye movements may have an inhibiting effect on stress, while excessive stress may reciprocally inhibit the eye movements, appears supported by the conclusions of other investigators that disrupted REM sleep is a marker for PTSD (Ross, et al., 1990).

CONCLUSION

There is, of course, a great deal more to EMDR that the eye movements or other motoric responses. Thus, until controlled studies have examined each of the various aspects of EMDR (cf. Shapiro, 1991, in press), it can only be claimed that the entire procedure has the ability to catalyze the information processing system and allow traumatic memories and their associated negative cognitions to be resolved. Further, the fact that EMDR is a complex interactive method demands that clinicians be trained in its use in order to ensure client safety, as well as the highest likelihood of therapeutic success (Shapiro, 1991b). Finally, it is vital that EMDR be used within an treatment plan that deals with the complex configuration of client symptoms, along with pertinent issues of potential resistance. However, the utility of the method for the treatment of isolated trauma supports the Neurocognitive Therapy model as a welcome addition to integrative paradigms for the treatment of PTSD.

REFERENCES

Baker, N. & McBride, B. (August, 1991) Clinical Applications of EMDR in a Law Enforcement Environment: Observations of the Psychological Service Unit of the L.A. County Sheriff's Department. *Paper presented at the Police Psychology (Division 18, Police & Public Safety Sub-section) Mini-Convention at the APA annual convention*, San Francisco, CA.

Boudewyns, P.A., Stwertka, S.A., Hyer, L.A., Albrecht, J.W. and Sperr, E.V. (1993). Eye movement desensitization and reprocessing: A pilot study. *Behavior Therapy*, 16, 30-33

Daniels, N., Lipke, H., Richardson, R. & Silver, S. (1992, October) Vietnam Veterans' Treatment Programs Using Eye Movement Desensitization and Reprocessing. *Symposium presented at the International Society for Traumatic Stress Studies annual convention*, Los Angeles, CA.

DeFazio, V., Rustin, S., & Diamond, A. (1975). Symptom development in Vietnam veterans. *American Journal of Orthopsychiatry*, 43, 640-653.

Everly, G.S. (1993). Neurophysiological considerations in the treatment of post-traumatic stress disorder: A neurocognitive perspective. In J. Wilson and B. Raphael (Eds.) *International handbook of traumatic stress syndromes*. New York: Plenum.

Everly, G.S. and Lating, J. (1995). Psychotraumatology. NY: Plenum.

Goldfried, M.R. (1980) Toward the delineation of therapeutic change principles. *American Psychologist*, 35, 991-999.

Goldfried, M.R., & Pawdawer, W. (1982). Current status and future directions in psychotherapy. In M.R. Goldfried (Ed.), *Converging themes in psychotherapy: Trends in psychodynamic, humanistic, and behavioral practice*. New York: Springer.

Goldstein, A. (August,1992) Treatment of panic and agoraphobia with EMDR: Preliminary Data of the Agoraphobia and Anxiety Treatment Center, Temple University. *Paper presented at the Fourth World Congress on Behavior Therapy,* Queensland, Australia.

Goldstein, A. (in press). Eye movement desensitization and reprocessing for panic disorder: A case series. *Journal of Anxiety Disorders.*

Hong, C., Gillin, C., Callaghan, G.A., and Potkin, S. Correlation of rapid eye movement density with dream report length and not with movements in the dream: Evidence against the scanning hypothesis. *1992 Annual Meeting Abstracts, Association of Professional Sleep Societies,* 6th Annual Meeting, Phoenix, Arizona. Poster #12.

Horowitz, J.L. (1992). *Stress response syndrome (2nd ed.).* New Jersey: Jason Aronson Inc.

Janoff-Bulman, R. (1992). *Shattered assumptions.* New York: Free Press.

Karni, A., Tanne, D., Rubenstein, B.S., Askenasi, J.J.N., Sagi, D. (1992). No dreams, no memory: The effect of REM sleep deprivation on learning a new perceptual skill. *Society for Neuroscience Abstracts,* 18, 387.

Keane, T.M., Fairbank, J.A., Caddell, J.M., Zimering, R.T. & Bender, M.A. (1985). A behavioral approach to assessing and treating post-traumatic stress disorder in Vietnam veterans. In C.R. Figley (Ed.), *Trauma and its wake.* New York: Brunner/Mazel.

Klienknecht, R. (1992). Treatment of post-traumatic stress disorder with eye movement desensitization and reprocessing. *Journal of Behavior Therapy and Experimental Psychiatry, 23,* 43-50.

Klienknecht, R. (in press). Rapid treatment of blood and injection phobias with eye movement desensitization. *Journal of Behavior Therapy and Experimental Psychiatry.*

Levin, C. (July/Aug 1993). The enigma of EMDR. *Family Therapy Networker,* 75-83.

Lipke, H. (1992, October). A survey of EMDR-trained practitioners. *Paper presented at the International Society for Traumatic Stress Studies Annual Conference,* Los Angeles, CA.

Lipke, H. & Botkin, A. (1992). Brief case studies of eye movement desensitization and reprocessing with chronic post-traumatic stress disorder. *Psychotherapy,29,* 591-595.

Marquis, J. (1991). A report on seventy-eight cases treated by eye movement desensitization. *Journal of Behavior Therapy and Experimental Psychiatry,* 22, 187-192.

McCann, D.L. (1992). Post-traumatic stress disorder due to devastating burns overcome by a single session of eye movement desensitization. *Journal of Behavior Therapy and Experimental Psychiatry,* 23, 319-323.

National Center for Post-traumatic Stress Disorder (1993). *Post-traumatic stress syndrome and disorder information packet.* Menlo Park: Department of Veteran Affairs.

Nielson, T. (1991). Affect desensitization: A possible function of REMs in both waking and sleeping states. *Sleep Research,* 20.

Norcross, J.C. (1986) (ed.) *Handbook of eclectic psychotherapy.* New York: Brunner Mazel.

Page, A.C. & Crino, R.D. (1993). Eye-movement desensitisation: A simple treatment for post-traumatic stress disorder? *Australian and New Zealand Journal of Psychiatry,* 27, 288 - 293.

Pellicer, X. (1993). Eye movement desensitization treatment of a child's nightmares: A case report. *Journal of Behavior Therapy and Experimental Psychiatry,* 24 73-75.

Puk, G. (1991). Treating traumatic memories: A case report on the eye movement desensitization procedure. *Journal of Behavior Therapy and Experimental Psychiatry,* 22, 149-151.

Ross, R.J., Ball, W.A., Dinges, D.F., Kribbs, N.B., Morrison, A.R., and Silver, S.M. (1990). REM Sleep Disturbance as the Hallmark of PTSD. *Paper presented at the Conference of the American Psychiatric Association,* New York.

Rothbaum, B.O. (1992). How does EMDR work? *Behavior Therapist,* 15, 34.

Shapiro, F. (1989a). Efficacy of the eye movement desensitization procedure in the treatment of traumatic memories. *Journal of Traumatic Stress Studies,* 2, 199-223.

Shapiro, F. (1989b). Eye movement desensitization: A new treatment for post-traumatic stress disorder. *Journal of Behavior Therapy and Experimental Psychiatry,* 20, 211-217.

Shapiro, F. (1991a) Eye movement desensitization & reprocessing procedure: From EMD to EMDR--a new treatment model for anxiety and related traumata. *Behavior Therapist*, 14, 133 - 135.

Shapiro, F. (1991b) Eye movement desensitization and reprocessing: A cautionary note. *Behavior Therapist*, 14, 188.

Shapiro, F. (1991c). Stray Thoughts. *EMDR Network Newsletter*, 1, 1-3.

Shapiro, F. (1993a). The status of EMDR in 1992. *Journal of Traumatic Stress*, 6, 413-421.

Shapiro, F. (1993b). Whence EMDR?--Commentary. *EMDR Network Newsletter*, 3, 18-19.

Shapiro, F. (in press). EMDR: In the eye of the paradigm shift. *The Behavior Therapist*.

Shapiro,F. (in press) *Eye movement desensitization and reprocessing: Principles, protocols and procedures*. New York: Guilford.

Solomon, R. & Shapiro, F. (in press). Eye movement desensitization and reprocessing: An effective therapeutic tool for trauma and grief. In C. Figley (Ed.) *Death and trauma.* New York: Brunner Mazel.

Spector, J. & Huthwaite, M. (1993) Eye-movement desensitisation to overcome post-traumatic stress disorder. *British Journal of Psychiatry*, 106-108.

Thyer, B.A., Papsdorf, J.D., Davis, R., and Vallecorsa, S. (1984), Autonomic correlates of the subective anxiety scale, *Journal of Behavior Therapy and Experimental Psychiatry*, 15, 3-7.

Wernik, U. (1993). The role of the traumatic component in the etiology of sexual dysfunctions and its treatment with eye movement desensitization procedure. *Journal of Sex Education and Therapy*, 19, 212-222.

Wilson, D., Covi, W., Foster, S. & Silver, S.M. (1993, April). Eye movement desensitization and reprocessing and ANS correlates in the treatment of PTSD. *Paper presented at the California Psychological Association Annual Convention, San Francisco. Paper submitted for publication.*

Wolpe, J. (1982). *The Practice of Behavior Therapy*. Pergamon Press, New York.

Wolpe, J. & Abrams, J. (1991) Post-traumatic stress disorder overcome by eye movement desensitization: A case report. *Journal of Behavior Therapy and Experimental Psychiatry* 22, 39-43.

Chapter 15

COLDENHAM: TRAUMATIC STRESS INTERVENTION IN A COMMUNITY FIRE SERVICE

GEORGE S. EVERLY, JR., JEFFREY T. MITCHELL, GUY SCHILLER

So far in this text, the evolution of the field of disaster and trauma psychology as it applies to emergency services and disaster response personnel has been chronicled. The specific application of the principles of trauma psychology to the emergency and disaster response professions has been referred to by some as "critical incident stress management" (CISM) as noted earlier. Clearly, however, critical incident stress management typically denotes interventions which target acute rapid-onset traumatic events and their acute post-traumatic sequelae (see Mitchell and Everly, 1994, 1995). These interventions have seldom been applied to chronic post-traumatic situations. This chapter briefly describes a totally unique application of CISM principles to a community fire service three and one-half years after a disaster shook, not only the community fire service, but the community at large. We know of no other such application having ever been made.

George S. Everly, Jr. • International Critical Incident Stress Foundation, Ellicott City, Maryland.

Jeffrey T. Mitchell • University of Maryland Caltimore County, Catonsville, Maryland.

Guy Schiller, •Family Counseling Services, Cheshire, Connecticut.

In G.S. Everly, Jr. Innovations in Disaster and Trauma Psychology: Applications in Emergency Services and Disaster Response. Baltimore: Chevron Publishing Corp, 1995.

THE COLDENHAM TORNADO

Coldenham is a small community of nestled in the middle eastern portion of New York state.

In mid November, 1989 tragedy struck this quite community. At 12:26 PM on November 16, 1989, what is believed to be a tornado struck the elementary school. The point of impact was the outside wall of the lunch room. The brick wall of the lunch room collapsed as just over one hundred children, ranging from eight to ten years of age, were eating their lunches.

Over 300 emergency personnel from 27 ambulance companies, 10 fire departments, 6 police agencies and several state agencies, as well as several private organizations, responded to the scene. Eighty emergency personnel were said to be directly involved in the extrication of the victims as well as the management of the dead and wounded children. Subsequent retrospectives on the operational aspects of the emergency response effort concluded that the emergency responders at Coldenham had performed heroically. Working under adverse weather-induced conditions, rescuers had been able to extricate and initiate transportation of all wounded children within minutes. An almost miraculous achievement given the operational conditions.

Despite the aforementioned heroic efforts of the Coldenham rescuers, seven children were reported to be immediately killed while 21 were injured. Of those 21, 7 children sustained serious injuries while 14 sustained moderate injuries. Two of the wounded children later died.

The tragedy grew when another child from the same school was killed in an automobile accident in front of the elementary school only a few days later. This child was killed while her family was assisting another family with the funeral preparations for their child who had been killed earlier when the tornado struck the school.

This last child was considered by the community as if she were among the dead from the actual tornado. Obviously, her loss sent another shock wave of grief through the already traumatized community.

THE DISASTER'S WAKE

Newspaper, television, radio, as well as personal accounts of the disaster documented the shock and profound grief that had descended upon Coldenham. Personal friendships were tested, families were torn with grief, lawsuits emerged, and discord within the volunteer community fire service arose, by many reports.

Of those most intimately involved with the dead and injured children, 18 firefighters and emergency medical personnel reported significant post-traumatic stress reactions which were identified as interfering with personal and work-related activities (Mitchell, Everly, Schiller, 1994). It was later reported that the maximum firefighting capability had decreased substantially in the wake of the Coldenham elementary school disaster.

Although law enforcement officers from various agencies were intimately involved in the disaster, the adverse impact upon them seemed to be less severe. These law enforcement officers were provided with various support services and critical incident stress debriefings (CISD) within two weeks of the disaster by members of the Employee Assistance Program of the New York State Police. None of these law enforcement agencies nor individuals contacted in June of 1993 reported continued psychological discord nor performance disruptions to their work or personal lives; although the memories of the disaster were still somewhat vivid.

THE INTERVENTION PROGRAM

In Spring of 1993, fire service officials and interested parties in Coldenham contacted the International Critical Incident Stress Foundation, a nonprofit organization that assists emergency service and disaster response personnel in the prevention and mitigation of post-traumatic stress reactions associated with the performance of their high-risk job functions. The officials from Coldenham were seeking assistance in mitigating the adverse post disaster reactions that had now become systemically debilitating some three and one-half years subsequent to the actual elementary school disaster itself. Initial reviews of newspaper reports and personal accounts of the November, 1989 disaster were begun.

In June of 1993, a critical incident response team (CIRT) was assembled to go to Coldenham, despite the fact that no precedent existed for the application of CISM interventions so many years after such a disaster.

The response team consisted of two doctoral psychologists, a mental health counselor, and 5 emergency service professionals. The 5 emergency service personnel were all fire service professionals who were formally trained in CISD and emergency services peer support crisis intervention and counseling techniques as described by Mitchell and Everly (1994, 1995). The emergency service "peers" were all drawn from other parts of New York State as well as neighboring states.

Prior to the actual intervention, CIRT members began an intensive review of newspaper accounts and personal accounts of the disaster. The Coldenham intervention as carried out by the CIRT is overviewed in Table 15.1.

On June 16, 1993, the CIRT arrived in Coldenham. The first order of business was to meet with the fire chaplain and fire department administrators to receive updated information on the status of the community fire service as well as the community at large. The disaster site was visited by the CIRT. Although completely rebuilt, the site visit was helpful in putting operational details into perspective. Also visited was a memorial stone erected in memory of the children who had lost their lives. Finally, the evening of the first day was spent continuing to review videos and other sources of information which chronicled the disaster on November 16, 1989.

The second day began as the CIRT was divided into operational subteams consisting of one mental health member and typically one

TABE 15.1
THE COLDENHAM INTERVENTION

Spring, 1993	Meetings with Coldenham fire service and community leaders.
June, 1993	1. Critical Incident Response Team (CIRT) formed: 3 mental health professionals 5 fire service 2. CIRT reviews records of disaster.
June 16, 1993 *(Day One)*	1. CIRT arrives in Coldenham. 2. CIRT meets with fire service chaplin and administrators to receive updated information. 3. CIRT visits elementary school and memorial. 4. Videos, newspaper accounts, official reports, personal accounts reviewed.
June 17, 1993 *(Day 2)*	1. Mental health and peer subteams initiate interviews with 30 fire service personnel and 11 spouses in a series of individual sessions. 2. CIRT meets with current fire service command staff. 3. CIRT holds community education and outreach sessions, open to entire community; local TV, Radio, and newspaper coverage obtained to broaden community outreach. 4. CIRT meets in evening to review progress and formulate plans.
June 18, 1993 *(Day 3)*	1. Individual interviews continue. 2. CIRT holds luncheon with community leaders including community mental health, Red Cross, psychologists in order to establish "after intervention" resource pool to assure continued follow-up.
June 19, 1993 *(Day 4)*	1. Peer counsellor initiated outreach to fire service per sonnel who have not yet responded. 2. Interviews continued by subteams.
June 20, 1993 *(Day 5)*	1. CIRT holds CISD in morning. 2. CIRT holds open community education session to summarize progress and future plans. 3. Final meeting with current fire service command staff and fire board members. 4. CIRT departs from Coldenham.
Follow-up	For a 4 month period, a CIRT subteam made visits to Coldenham to coordinate follow-up activities.

fire service peer counselor. These subteams began a process of confidential interviews and assessments wherein 30 community fire service personnel and 11 spouses were seen. These were in no way perceived of as psychotherapeutic encounters, but rather were carried out as information gathering and crisis intervention tactics.

CIRT leaders met with current Coldenham fire service commanders to review plans. The current command staff was made up of individuals different from those who were in command in November 1989.

A major community education and outreach session was held in the evening. Aided by TV, radio, and newspaper coverage, information concerning the nature of trauma, in general, and as it pertained to the elementary school disaster was reviewed. The purpose of the CIRT intervention was reviewed and expectations set.

On the third day of the intervention, interview sessions continued in the morning. The CIRT co-sponsored a luncheon wherein community leaders including Red Cross, community mental health officers, and local psychologists were brought together to review expectations for the CIRT intervention and begin to establish a resource pool to guarantee that "after intervention" support would be available to the community of Coldenham. Finally, an important meeting with the individuals who represented the fire service command staff on November 16, 1989 was held.

June 19th was the fourth day of intervention. Subteam intervention continued. Peer counselor initiated outreach to Coldenham fire service personnel was begun.

June 20th was the fifth and final day of the formal CIRT intervention. The CIRT conducted a critical incident stress debriefing (CISD) in the morning. Later in the day, the CIRT held an "open door" community education meeting to summarize activities and teach basic trauma and stress management concepts as detailed in Everly (1989) and Mitchell and Everly (1995). A final meeting with current Coldenham fire service command staff was held. The CIRT departed Coldenham on this day.

The CIRT realized the importance of follow-up services to Coldenham. Therefore, in addition to having initiated efforts to utilize local community resources, CIRT subteam follow-up was provided. For a 4 month period, a CIRT subteam returned to Coldenham, initially at bi-weekly intervals, to provide whatever coordination services were needed.

At the end of the four month follow-up period significant individual improvement was noted among many of the Coldenham rescuers most intimately involved in the November 16, 1989 disaster (Mitchell, Everly, Schiller, 1994). Also important to note was that information obtained from fire service personnel indicated that community firefighting capabilities had significantly improved over pre-intervention levels.

CONCLUSION

The CIRT intervention at Coldenham, NY represents the only known effort of its kind. It represents an endeavor where in the boundaries of critical incident stress management, which is usually confined to acute situations, were pushed beyond recognized limits to provide support to a disaster venue 3.5 years post disaster.

It is important to note that the Coldenham intervention was planned meticulously, if not reluctantly at times. Intervention activities were cautiously implemented receiving feedback from relevant sources continually.

As the field of disaster and trauma psychology extends itself continuous application of extant principles is highly recommended, but clearly the field is in its infancy and will expand as the need for disaster support services is recognized and tested.

REFERENCES

Everly, G.S. (1989). *A Clinical Guide to the Treatment of the Human Stress Response.* NY: Plenum Publishing Corp.

Mitchell, J.T. and Everly, G.S. (1994). *Human Elements Training for Emergency Services and Disaster Response Personnel.* Ellicott City, MD: Chevron Publishing Corp.

Mitchell, J.T. and Everly, G.S. (1995). *Critical Incident Stress Debriefing: An Operations Manual, 2nd Ed.* Ellicott City, MD: Chevron Publishing Corp.

Mitchell, J.T, Everly, G.S., Schiller, G. (1994, Feb). Coldenham community in crisis: Posttraumatic stress intervention in a community fire service. *Paper presented to the Sixth Montreux Congress on Stress*, Montreux, Switzerland.

Chapter 16

SUMMATION

GEORGE S. EVERLY, JR.

This volume has endeavored to present important innovations in disaster and trauma psychology as they are most relevant to emergency services personnel, disaster and humanitarian aid workers, as well as, public safety personnel.

This volume reflects the bias of its primary author that operational proficiency is deeply rooted in phenomenological sophistication; hence, Part I examined the nature and impact of traumatic stress upon the aforementioned specialized populations. From that point onward, the remainder of the volume reviewed important contributions to the field of critical incident stress management (CISM). These contributions ranged from specific intervention technologies, through comprehensive CISM programs from various aspects of the world, to far-reaching strategic formulations which may be used to guide the development of future programs and intervention technologies.

In the beginning of this volume, it was mentioned that the emergency services professions represent "the lost generation" of psychotraumatology. Historically, they have been the last to be considered as vulnerable to traumatic stress. This may be because of the "macho image" that is often projected by these professionals, it may be because these individuals willingly enter these professions and are merely expected to be able to handle traumatic stress as a normal occupational hazard, or it may be because of a false belief that to recognize traumatic stress as a valid occupational risk factor may open a plethora of legal, ethical, and emotional issues that would threaten the foundations of the professions themselves.

The experiences and expert opinions amassed within this volume cogently argue that, not only is it valid to recognize emergency service professionals as being at extraordinary risk for disabling traumatic stress, not only is it humane, but it is good business. The observations of this author have been that when CISM programs are initiated and promoted by emergency services organizations, it serves to strengthen organizational commitment, organizational climate, loyalty, and overall dedication to the quest for "a job well done." Even if such observations are somewhat limited, it seems logical that any workforce that is maintained at an optimum level of psychological and physical functioning will ultimately perform their occupational functions in a more technically proficient and cost effective manner. Such is clearly the goal of any workforce, but in the emergency services it means greater proficiency at saving human lives. What goal could be more important?

Finally, perhaps the best way to conceptualize CISM programs is as highly advanced, "high tech" programs designed to make strong people stronger, and proficient people more proficient. Emergency services professionals fight a never ending war against human suffering, crime, destruction, and mass disaster. CISM provides these professionals with a whole new armamentarium to take into battle. CISM benefits everyone involved in a critical incident.

INDEX

A

B

C

H

I

J

L

M

N

O

P

R

S

T

V

W